Learn to Code

with Games

Learn to Code with Games

John M. Quick

Digipen Institute of Technology, Singapore

CRC Press
Taylor & Francis Group
Boca Raton London New York

CRC Press is an imprint of the
Taylor & Francis Group, an **informa** business

AN A K PETERS BOOK

CRC Press
Taylor & Francis Group
6000 Broken Sound Parkway NW, Suite 300
Boca Raton, FL 33487-2742

Printed on acid-free paper
Version Date: 20150813

International Standard Book Number-13: 978-1-4987-0468-7 (Paperback)

Visit the Taylor & Francis Web site at
http://www.taylorandfrancis.com

and the CRC Press Web site at
http://www.crcpress.com

This book is dedicated to the students who experienced this educational approach without the support of a textbook, as well as the future coders of the world who will benefit from this book.

Contents

2. Characters and Characteristics   17

3. The Bounds of the World   39

4. Sprinting and Sneaking   59

5. Collectables   89

6. Spawning Objects   103

Preface

World leaders, governments, and organizations around the world are calling for citizens to *learn to code*. They have identified coding as an essential 21st-century skill for all people. Have you ever wanted to learn to code, but were turned off by the technical jargon? Are you an ambitious young coder or forging a new career path later in life? Have you ever dreamed of making your own games and software? Now is your time to shine. This book makes coding accessible to a broad audience of aspiring coders, including you.

Learn to Code with Games presents a novel approach to coding for the complete beginner. With this book, you will come to see coding as a way of thinking and problem solving, rather than a domain of obscure languages and syntaxes. If you're looking to explore coding through a practical, hands-on approach, this is the book for you. This book will challenge you to code real game components and provide you with guidance along the way. With a little effort, you will come to think and act like the code hero that you truly are. Your quest begins today.

Challenges

This book is structured as a series of challenges that help you learn to code by creating a video game. In each chapter, you will expand your coding knowledge by defining and implementing your own solutions to game development challenges. Guidelines and hints are provided along the way to help you put your ideas into code. Ultimately, your success as a coder is determined by you. This book puts you into the position to succeed today and in the future.

Goals

Every challenge is accompanied by a set of goals. These are the coding techniques that you will be able to implement by the time you finish each challenge. They can be found in the *Goals* section at the beginning of each chapter.

Required Files

Files have been provided for every challenge. You can find these in the *Software* folder for each chapter available at http://crcpress.com/product/isbn/ 9781498704687. The *Challenge* folder contains everything you need to code your own solution. The *Solution* folder contains a completed example project, which you can compare against your own solution. The *Demo* folder contains a playable version of the completed example project, which you can use to guide the development of your own solution. At the start of each challenge, the *Required Files* section describes exactly which files you will need to use.

Demo

A demo is included for each challenge you will face in this book. It is a good idea to test the demo before attempting to code your own solution to each challenge. The demo will help you visualize what you are working toward. Both Mac and PC versions of each demo are provided.

Unity Game Engine

The Unity game engine is used throughout the challenges in this book. The primary focus of this book is helping you learn to code by applying a variety of game development techniques. While the focus is not on learning Unity itself, you will become familiar with some of the basic features of Unity. This is because Unity is your gateway to rapidly coding and creating games. To complete the challenges in this book, you need to download and install Unity on your computer. Unity is free to use and available on both Mac and PC. You can download the Unity installer from http://unity3d.com. Once downloaded, open the installer on your computer and follow the step-by-step instructions. In no time at all, you'll be ready to start making games.

Code Editor

By default, Unity includes a code editor named MonoDevelop. Whenever you double-click to open a script file in Unity, it will open in MonoDevelop. However, you may use any code editor that you wish throughout this book, including a basic text editor. The choice of a code editor is a matter of personal preference and makes no difference in your ability to successfully complete the challenges in this book. If you work on Mac, you might consider alternatives like Xamarin, TextWrangler, or Sublime Text. If you work on PC, you might consider alternatives like Notepad++ or Visual Studio.

Additional material is available from the CRC Website: http://www.crcpress.com/product/isbn/9781498704687.

Acknowledgment

Thanks to Carrie Heeter, PhD, Professor of Media and Information at Michigan State University, whose advice transformed the course of this book for the better.

Author

John M. Quick is an expert in the strategic enhancement of motivation, learning, and performance. He collaborates with industry and university clients to strategically solve the greatest challenges in motivation, learning, and performance.

John earned a PhD in educational technology at Arizona State University, where he researched enjoyment and individual differences in games. He created the Gameplay Enjoyment Model (GEM) and Gaming Goal Orientations (GGO) model to guide the design of effective game-based solutions.

John has released more than 15 digital games. His games focus on innovative topics, such as learner engagement, employee performance improvement, and cutting-edge interfaces.

John has over 5 years of classroom experience at the higher education level. He has instructed courses on computer literacy, game design, and programming at Michigan State University, Arizona State University, and DigiPen Institute of Technology Singapore.

1 Our Hero Is Stuck!

Luna (Figure 1.1) has ventured into the wilderness for the first time. She has spent her entire life underground in the Dark Elf capital city of Clandis. By sneaking out of the underground to explore the surface world, she has broken a sacred bond that will prohibit her from ever returning to her homeland. Yet, Luna is a brave and curious person. She excitedly begins her new adventure among the people and places of the surface world.

Upon reaching the surface, Luna sees sunlight for the first time. She feels the soft grass under her feet and breathes fresh air. Luna also realizes that there is a bit of a problem. She cannot move! She twists left, right, up, and down, but it seems her feet are firmly planted into the ground. If only someone with knowledge of how the surface world works could help, Luna could continue on her quest.

▌ Goals

By the end of this chapter, you will be able to apply these coding techniques:

- Make a character move inside the game world

- Draw process maps to visualize solutions to coding problems

- Write pseudocode to create logical solutions to coding problems

I

Figure 1.1 This is Luna. She is embarking on an adventure that you will help to code.

- Modify variable values in a code editor

- Position objects in the game world using a two-dimensional (2D) coordinate system

- Determine the position of an object using Unity's `Transform` and `Vector3` properties

- Handle user key presses using Unity's `Input.GetKey()` functions

▮▮ Required Files

In this chapter, you will need to use the following files from the *Chapter_01 > Software* folder:

- *Challenge > Assets > Scenes > Map.unity* to run, modify, and test your solution

- *Challenge > Assets > Scripts > UserMove.cs* to code your solution to the challenge

- *Demo > Mac/PC > PlayerMove* to demonstrate how your completed solution should work

- *Solution > UserMove.cs* to compare your solution to the provided example solution

▮▮ Demo

Double-click on the *PlayerMove* demo to run the working version of the game. Notice how you can use the arrow keys to move Luna around the screen. This is the way your version of the game should work once you have completed this challenge.

Unity Game Engine

If you have not already installed Unity on your computer, you can download the Unity installer from http://unity3d.com. Once downloaded, open the installer on your computer and follow the step-by-step instructions. In no time at all, you'll be ready to start making games.

Challenge: Make Luna Move

Go to the *Chapter_01 > Software > Challenge > Assets > Scenes* folder and double-click on the *Map.unity* scene to open it in Unity. Then, press the *play* button (Figure 1.2) near the top-center area of the Unity interface. This will launch the current version of your game in the Game window.

Try to use your keyboard's arrow keys to move Luna around the screen. As you can see, Luna is stuck in place and needs someone to help her move. This is where you come in. Using your coding skills, you will help create Luna's world and determine the outcomes of her quest. Your first challenge is to help Luna move.

In Unity, find the Project window. Inside, open the *Assets > Scripts* folder. There, you will find a file named *UserMove*. Double-click to open this file in your code editor. By default, Unity uses a code editor named *MonoDevelop*. You may use any code editor you wish throughout this book, including a basic text editor. The choice of a code editor is a matter of personal preference and makes no difference in your ability to successfully complete the challenges in this book.

Whenever the player presses the arrow keys (up, down, left, or right), the UserMove script updates Luna's position in the game world. Inside *UserMove*, find (Ctrl + F on Windows, Command + F on Mac) the `CheckUserInput()` function. For this challenge, you should modify the code inside this function to get it working properly. Currently, the arrow keys are being recognized, but Luna's movement direction is not being updated. You need to modify the `newDirX` (new X direction) and `newDirY` (new Y direction) variables so Luna moves in the indicated direction. Right now, these variables are set to 0, regardless of which key is pressed.

```
//excerpt from CheckUserInput() function
//notice that the newDirX and newDirY values are all set to 0

//if player holds up arrow
if (Input.GetKey(KeyCode.UpArrow)) {

    //move up along the Y axis
    newDirY = 0;

} //end if

//move down
//if player holds down arrow
if (Input.GetKey(KeyCode.DownArrow)) {
```

Figure 1.2 The *play* button is located near the top center of the Unity editor. When pressed, your game will be launched in the Game window. Press the *play* button again to stop the game.

```
    //move down along the Y axis
    newDirY = 0;

} //end if
//move left
//if player holds left arrow
if (Input.GetKey(KeyCode.LeftArrow)) {

    //move left along the X axis
    newDirX = 0;

} //end if

//move right
//if player holds right arrow
if (Input.GetKey(KeyCode.RightArrow)) {

    //move right along the X axis
    newDirX = 0;

} //end if
```

To make Luna move, the values of newDirX and newDirY must be modified based on which key is pressed. Therefore, you must think of which values are related to which directions that Luna can move in.

Before proceeding, take a moment to think through a possible solution to this problem. You should write out your thoughts on a piece of paper. Use drawings and diagrams to help visualize your solution and think of ways that you can solve the problem. Luna's quest depends upon it.

▌ Hint: Visualizing the Game World

If you are having trouble jumping right into the problem, it may be helpful to visualize the game world. To do this, you could simply use a piece of paper and a pencil to draw a picture of the situation (Figure 1.3).

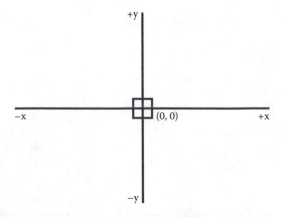

Figure 1.3 The game world can be represented as a 2D coordinate plane. Drawing is an effective way to help you sort out a solution to many coding problems.

1. Our Hero Is Stuck!

1. Draw a rectangle to represent your screen.

2. Place a square in the center to represent Luna.

3. Draw a horizontal line through the center of your screen and label it *x*. This represents your x axis.

4. Draw a vertical line through the center of your screen and label it *y*. This represents your y axis.

You have created a 2D coordinate plane and placed Luna at the position of (0, 0). Reconsider the challenge at hand using your visualization of the situation. You know that pressing the up, down, left, and right arrow keys should update the direction in which Luna moves. Ask yourself these questions: How will I know if she is moving right (or left or up or down)? What will happen to the value of her x and y coordinates as she moves? See if you can come up with a solution based on this information.

Hint: Visualization and Code

To further aid yourself in finding a solution, compare your drawing to the code in the `CheckUserInput()` function. Recall that you placed Luna at the (0, 0) position in your drawing. In the code, `newDirX` and `newDirY` are currently set to 0 when a player presses any arrow key. This means Luna's direction is not being updated, no matter what key the player presses. That is why she is always stuck in the same place! What other values might you give to `newDirX` and `newDirY` to ensure that Luna moves when an arrow key is pressed?

Hint: Position

In our 2D game world, the location of all visible objects is represented by an X and Y position in the coordinate system. In the case of Unity, every object has a `Transform` component. Within each `Transform`, a `Vector3` variable stores X, Y, and Z values to represent the position of the object in the world. Since we are working in 2D and Z represents three-dimensional (3D) depth, we are only concerned with the X and Y values at this time.

Return to the Unity editor. In the Hierarchy window, click on the Player object. Then, turn your attention to the Inspector window. Here, you will see that our Player object has a number of subcomponents. The first one is its `Transform`. Within the `Transform`, you will find the mentioned `Position` variable with its X and Y values (Figure 1.4). Since Luna is currently at position (0, 0) in our game world, her X and Y values are set to 0.

Transform			
Position	X 0	Y 0	Z 0
Rotation	X 0	Y 0	Z 0
Scale	X 1	Y 1	Z 1

Figure 1.4 Every Unity object has a `Transform` component. The `Position` variable stores the coordinates of the object in the game world.

Go to the Scene window in the Unity editor. Zoom in until you can see Luna. Click and drag her to a different place in the window. Afterwards, look back at her position in the Inspector window. It will have changed from (0, 0) to something different, like (1.31609, 0.62832). What this demonstrates is that movement is equal to changing Luna's position in the game world. Think back to your code. If a player presses an arrow key, you want to change Luna's position, rather than keeping it stuck at (0, 0). Thus, you need to change the values of newDirX and newDirY to ensure Luna's position updates correctly. You may need to use negative values to represent some directions. Try dragging Luna up, down, left, and right. Take note of how her position values change in the Inspector window. Equipped with this information, see if you can solve the problem in your code by changing the values of newDirX and newDirY to match the arrow key directions.

By the way, if you want to reset Luna's position back to (0, 0), click on her and look to the Inspector window. Go to Luna's Transform > Position variable, place your mouse cursor inside the X box and type 0. Do the same for Y. Luna will return to her original position in the center of the screen.

▐ Problem-Solving Techniques

At this point, you should have a pretty good idea of how to get Luna moving again. Perhaps you even have the game working in your own version of the project. If so, congratulations on completing your first challenge. If not, there is no reason to worry. Before sharing an example solution to this challenge, we will explore some problem-solving techniques. These will help you solve coding problems efficiently and effectively in the future.

Pseudocode

Pseudocode is a problem-solving technique that involves writing logical solutions to coding problems in human-readable language that can easily be converted into computer language. The value of pseudocode is that it helps us solve the logic behind our solution before we try to code it. Jumping straight into the code without logically solving a problem is a certain way to waste time, get confused, and become frustrated. However, if you clearly identify the logic of your solution first, and only then begin to code it, you will be much more effective at solving computer problems.

To examine an example of pseudocode, imagine that Luna has just encountered a locked door. How might we write out the logic of whether Luna can open the door? Perhaps we could say something like this:

```
The door IS locked
IF Luna HAS key, THEN open door.
```

Our pseudocode suggests that we need to know whether Luna has the key to the door. If she has the key, then the door will open. If she doesn't have it, then the door will remain locked.

Notice that keywords like *is*, *if*, *has*, and *then* appear in our pseudocode. These types of words translate well into code because computers are good at interpreting raw logical conditions. The more straightforward and unambiguously a given state can be expressed, the better a computer will understand it. Unlike humans, computers are not capable of daydreaming about what color to make a character's clothes or critically analyzing how enjoyable a game is to play. In contrast, computers only understand the literal instructions that are provided to them and execute those instructions to the best of their ability. Thus, our goal when pseudocoding is to use familiar language to write a logical set of instructions similar to what a computer understands. If we succeed at this task, then it is relatively simple to convert our pseudocode into computer code. For instance, if we convert our locked-door pseudocode to computer code, it looks like this:

```
door.isLocked = true;

if (Luna.hasKey == true) {

    door.isLocked = false;

}
```

The main difference between this code and our pseudocode is the inclusion of computer language syntax, such as brackets, parentheses, periods, and semicolons. Meanwhile, the logic of the code is identical to our pseudocode. Again, this demonstrates the value of pseudocoding. We understand our own language better than code, whereas computers understand their own language better than ours. Pseudocoding allows us to separate the logic of a problem from computer code. As a result, we can solve the logic portion of a problem in human language. Afterwards, we can convert the logical solution into computer language. This separation of tasks relieves us of having to simultaneously write code in a language very different from our own, while also trying to derive a logical solution to a problem. By solving the logic first and then converting the solution into code, our problem-solving process is more efficient and effective.

Note that there are no strict guidelines for pseudocoding. The purpose is to help you understand the situation at hand and sort out a logical solution to any problem. You may choose to use language that appears more human or more computer-like. In terms of our locked-door example, you might use the phrase "unlock the door." This is well suited to human understanding of the logic. However, you might instead write something like "set door locked is false," which is closer to what a computer would understand. Both describe the same logic. One is more like what one person might say to another, whereas the other is closer to what a person might tell a computer to do through code. Regardless of your approach, the important thing is that you are conceptualizing the logic of your solution and preparing yourself to succeed at subsequently implementing the code. You might even translate your ideas through a series of pseudocode steps. You can begin with a clear interpretation that you understand well and then work to gradually convert it into computer language.

A brief summary of the commonly used pseudocode keywords is provided here. For a complete listing of many useful pseudocode keywords and examples of how they can be used, see the pseudocode reference in Appendix A of this book.

- Status: destroy, has, is, in, load, lose, new, on, reload, reset, set, update, win

- Conditional: but, else, for, if, instead, otherwise, so, then, therefore, whether

- Boolean: and, false, not, or, true

- Math: add, divide, equal, greater than, less than, modulus, multiply, subtract

- Process: begin, check, continue, do, end, finish, loop, pause, start, stop, try, while

- Timing: after, again, before, except, first, last, next, until, when

- Permission: allow, can, cannot, only, must, prohibit, should

Process Mapping

Process mapping is a problem-solving technique that involves creating a visual diagram to demonstrate how a system functions. This technique is used in a variety of fields, including business, engineering, manufacturing, and computer programming. Process maps, also known as *flowcharts*, are useful for depicting how information flows through a computer program and describing how states change as a result of different events. Fortunately, process mapping has a fairly standardized set of symbols that can be used. Nevertheless, styles and practices will differ between people, so feel free to do what suits your needs and helps you solve problems. The most fundamental process mapping symbols are described in Table 1.1. By putting these symbols together in a variety of different orientations, you can visualize a virtually unlimited number of processes.

Table 1.1 Common Process Mapping Symbols

Symbol	Shape	Description
(rectangle)	Rectangle	Defines a single state, action, activity, or step in the overall process
(arrow)	Arrow	Connects one object to another, indicating the direction of information flow
(diamond)	Diamond	Indicates a decision point at which the process can branch into multiple paths (from the different edges of the shape)
(rounded rectangle)	Rounded rectangle or oval	Designates a start or end point for the process
(parallelogram)	Parallelogram	Represents information entering or exiting the process (e.g., user input, a call to an external process, or data passed to another process)
(circle)	Circle	Used to connect different sections of a process map together (e.g., when a diagram spans across multiple pages)

To demonstrate process mapping, let's reconsider our example whereby Luna encountered a locked door. How might we map the logic of whether Luna can open the door? Perhaps we could draw something like the map shown in Figure 1.5.

This diagram represents the locked door as a starting point using an oval shape. The process then comes to a decision diamond that asks whether Luna has the key. If yes, the process reaches its terminal point with an unlocked door. If no, the door remains locked and the process repeats. Ultimately, this leads us to identical computer code as our pseudocode example did, but with an emphasis on visuals and information flow, rather than sequenced instructions.

```
door.isLocked = true;

if (Luna.hasKey == true) {

    door.isLocked = false;

}
```

For additional information and examples, see the process mapping reference in Appendix B of this book.

Pseudocode versus Process Mapping

Both pseudocode and process mapping offer valuable insights for solving computer problems. It is possible to use them interchangeably, as personal preference dictates. For instance, you may prefer the literal step-by-step instructions that pseudocode provides, or you might like the visual nature of a process map. However, these techniques can also be used in tandem to provide a more complete picture of a solution that both is visual and offers codelike instructions. Pseudocode emphasizes the detailed instructions that will ultimately be given to the computer through code, whereas process mapping emphasizes the overall state and information flow of the program. Together, these techniques can help us determine a logical solution to any problem before trying to code it. It is recommended that you try using each technique for yourself to discover what works best for you. Whether you ultimately end up using pseudocode, process mapping, or a combination of both, you will be well on your way to solving problems more efficiently and effectively.

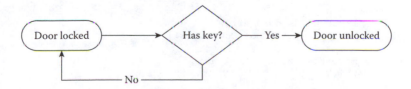

Figure 1.5 A process map illustrates the logic behind a locked-door scenario.

A Note about Example Solutions

The following section describes how the problem of getting Luna to move can be solved. This is not the only possible solution. As you face increasingly complex challenges throughout your coding journey, it is important to remember that many potential solutions to any problem exist. In fact, even in seemingly trivial cases, different people will come up with different solutions to the same problem. They will use different numbers, variables, functions, and arithmetic. They will use different code formatting that contains unique names, spacing, and outlining. As you become more proficient at coding, you will develop your own personal style that is different from everybody else's. Thus, solving problems with computers is not about finding the right answer. It is about finding ways to create what you want to in a way that suits the requirements of your project. Therefore, the provided examples demonstrate just one way of successfully solving the challenges in this book. Your solutions may or may not be similar. What matters most is that the solutions work and that you can apply what you have learned in these challenges to solve the future challenges that you face.

Example Solution: Make Luna Move

Your challenge was to modify the `newDirX` and `newDirY` variables in the UserMove script's `CheckUserInput()` function, such that Luna's direction is updated when the player presses the arrow keys. The relevant code for this challenge is provided:

```
//check user input
private void CheckUserInput() {

    //store the new movement direction based on user input
    int newDirX = 0;
    int newDirY = 0;

    //check for movement input
    //move up
    //if player holds up arrow
    if (Input.GetKey(KeyCode.UpArrow)) {

        //move up along the Y axis
        newDirY = 0;

    } //end if

    //move down
    //if player holds down arrow
    if (Input.GetKey(KeyCode.DownArrow)) {

        //move down along the Y axis
        newDirY = 0;

    } //end if
```

```
//move left
//if player holds left arrow
if (Input.GetKey(KeyCode.LeftArrow)) {

    //move left along the X axis
    newDirX = 0;

} //end if

//move right
//if player holds right arrow
if (Input.GetKey(KeyCode.RightArrow)) {

    //move right along the X axis
    newDirX = 0;

} //end if

    //update current direction attempted
    _newDir = new Vector2(newDirX, newDirY);

} //end function
```

In the challenge code, note that newDirX and newDirY are set to 0, meaning that Luna's direction never gets updated when keys are pressed. On the contrary, we know that we want to update Luna's movement direction whenever the player presses an arrow key. Hence, instead of using zero values, we need to represent direction through different values. Consider how pseudocode can help us to conceptualize the solution for moving in the upward and downward directions:

```
IF player presses up arrow, THEN character moves in positive y
    direction
IF player presses down arrow, THEN character moves in negative y
    direction
```

Our pseudocode identifies upward movement as positive along the y axis and downward movement as negative along the y axis. But, how do we know this? Recall that our game world exists in a 2D coordinate space. Think back to the diagram in Figure 1.3 that we used to conceptualize our problem. As you can see, in our game world, upward movement relates to positive y values, whereas downward movement relates to negative y values for Luna's position. Accordingly, when the player presses the up arrow, we can indicate the change in direction by setting our newDirY value to 1. Similarly, when the player presses the down arrow, we should set our newDirY value to –1. The values of 1 and –1 represent positive (upward) and negative (downward) movement along the y axis.

To complete our solution, let's consider how process mapping can be used to determine the newDirX values for left and right movement (Figure 1.6).

Again, our problem-solving technique assists us in understanding the situation. When dealing with the x axis in our game world, we can see that leftward movement is negative and rightward movement is positive.

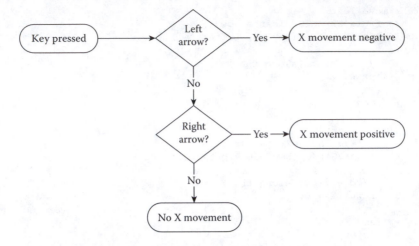

Figure 1.6 A process map illustrates Luna's left and right movement through the game world.

Therefore, when the player presses the left arrow key, we set `newDirX` to –1. Meanwhile, when the player presses the right arrow key, we set `newDirX` to 1. The final, working code for the challenge follows. All modified lines are shown in bold:

```
//check user input
private void CheckUserInput() {

    //store the new movement direction based on user input
    int newDirX = 0;
    int newDirY = 0;

    //check for movement input
    //move up
    //if player holds up arrow
    if (Input.GetKey(KeyCode.UpArrow)) {

        //move up along the Y axis
        newDirY = 1;

    } //end if

    //move down
    //if player holds down arrow
    if (Input.GetKey(KeyCode.DownArrow)) {

        //move down along the Y axis
        newDirY = -1;

    } //end if

    //move left
    //if player holds left arrow
    if (Input.GetKey(KeyCode.LeftArrow)) {
```

```
        //move left along the X axis
        newDirX = -1;

    } //end if

    //move right
    //if player holds right arrow
    if (Input.GetKey(KeyCode.RightArrow)) {

        //move right along the X axis
        newDirX = 1;

    } //end if

    //update current direction attempted
    _newDir = new Vector2(newDirX, newDirY);

} //end function
```

Let's walk through our functioning code to be sure we know exactly how it works. This section of our UserMove script checks for user input in the form of arrow key presses. If a key press is found, it updates the associated x or y direction variable. Take the first segment as an example:

```
//move up
//if player holds up arrow
if (Input.GetKey(KeyCode.UpArrow)) {

    //move up along the y axis
    newDirY = 1;

} //end if
```

This code checks for an up arrow key press. If pressed, the y axis movement direction variable is updated to 1. Recall that a positive value of 1 in our game world represents upward movement along the y axis in the 2D coordinate system. The if keyword and associated opening and closing brackets, { and }, ensure that the enclosed direction variable does not get updated unless the key is pressed. The if statement gets told whether or not the key press occurred by the code within the opening and closing parentheses, (and). Inside the parentheses lies Unity's function for checking key presses, Input.GetKey(). This function checks for a given key and returns a true value if the key is held down. Otherwise, it returns false. Since we need to know whether the up arrow key is pressed, we tell the Input.GetKey() function to listen for KeyCode.UpArrow. Whenever the player holds down the up arrow key, the if statement is true and the newDirY variable is updated. If the key is not pressed, the if statement is false and the newDirY variable is not changed.

A nearly identical process is used to handle down, left, and right movement. Each direction has its own if statement that checks for a specific key press using the Input.GetKey() function. The given key values for each direction are

KeyCode.DownArrow (down), KeyCode.LeftArrow (left), and KeyCode.RightArrow (right). As with upward movement, when a related key is pressed, the newDirX or newDirY variable is updated to 1 or –1. The direction values are used to represent how Luna should move within the 2D coordinate system of the game world.

Perhaps you are wondering why we only used 1 and –1 values to indicate direction. Indeed, we could have put any number of similar values, such as 2, –4, or 38, into our code and it would still function. However, 1 and –1 are the ideal values to use in this case. This is because we are only defining the direction of Luna's movement, not her speed. From physics, you may be familiar with the definition of velocity as speed times direction. Our UserMove script applies this formula to determine Luna's movement. Thus, for movement to occur in our script, we need both direction and speed. Toward the end of the UserMove script, you will find the following lines of code:

```
//excerpt from MoveObject() function

//change in movement based on user input and speed
float deltaMoveX = _newDir.x * _speed; //the x-axis change
float deltaMoveY = _newDir.y * _speed; //the y-axis change
```

Here, the x and y directions that we set earlier are multiplied by Luna's speed to calculate an overall change in movement. If we were to use values other than 1 and –1 to represent direction, we would be throwing off this calculation. Instead, our UserMove script handles speed and direction separately. Only the _speed variable is responsible for determining how fast Luna will move, while only our direction variables are responsible for determining where Luna will move. For the complete example solution code and Unity project, see the files in the *Chapter_01 > Software > Solution* folder.

▐ Bonus Challenge: Make Luna Move Faster (or Slower)

Search through the UserMove script and find where the _speed variable's value is set to 0.05. Change this value and run your project in Unity to test the outcome. Note whether Luna moved faster or slower. Experiment with changing the _speed value to adjust how quickly Luna moves in the game world.

▐ Bonus Hint: User Input in Unity

In this challenge, we used Unity's Input.GetKey() function to determine whether a key was being held. This method is useful for handling character movement, since players typically hold the direction key down for as long as they want a character to move and release the key when they want the movement to stop.

However, Unity has other functions for checking user input as well. For instance, `Input.GetKeyDown()` only checks for the first time that a button is pressed. This method is useful for certain applications, like a pause feature. If the player holds the *pause* button, we wouldn't want the game to erratically flicker in and out of the pause state. Instead, we want to pause the game the instant the button is pressed once. Later, when the player presses the button again, the game continues.

In contrast to `Input.GetKeyDown()`, `Input.GetKeyUp()` only checks for the moment that a button is released. That is, a player can press a key without any action occurring until the key is later released. Again, this function is useful to implement in certain circumstances. For example, user interface buttons that start or quit a game may use this method. We wouldn't want a player to instantly quit out of a game by accident, as might happen with `Input.GetKeyDown()`. Instead, we can use `Input.GetKeyUp()` to allow the player an extra moment to decide (and possibly cancel) before committing to the action. If, and only if, the key is released over the interface button will the command be executed. This gives the player a chance to rethink an important decision before committing to it.

Another set of functions in Unity involve button input rather than keyboard input. These are `Input.GetButton()`, `Input.GetButtonDown()`, and `Input.GetButtonUp()`. They operate in a fashion similar to that of the keyboard functions, but handle buttons like those found on a mouse or handheld game controller. There are other types of input functions as well. See the Input section of the Unity scripting reference documentation to explore more options for handling user input (Unity Technologies n.d.).

Summary

You have risen to the challenge and solved your first coding problem. Before proceeding to the next challenge, make sure you are comfortable with the following coding techniques. Revisit the activities of this chapter and make sure you are confident applying these methods before moving on.

- Make a character move inside the game world

- Draw process maps to visualize solutions to coding problems

- Write pseudocode to create logical solutions to coding problems

- Modify variable values in a code editor

- Position objects in the game world using a 2D coordinate system

- Determine the position of an object using Unity's `Transform` and `Vector3` properties

- Handle user key presses using Unity's `Input.GetKey()` functions

Luna thanks you for allowing her journey on the surface world to continue. Now that she can move, there are many new places that she is excited to explore. There are also many more challenges to face as you learn to code.

Reference

Unity Technologies. n.d. Input. http://docs.unity3d.com/ScriptReference/Input.html (accessed January 28, 2015).

2 Characters and Characteristics

Before Luna continues on her journey, let's take some time to consider what characteristics she has as an adventurer. When coding, we can represent different attributes using variables and data types. In addition, we will use these coding techniques to design additional characters for our game world.

▐ Goals

By the end of this challenge, you will be able to apply these coding techniques:

- Design stats for game characters

- Define variables to represent different characteristics

- Choose valid and meaningful variable names

- Select the appropriate data types for variables

- Set the appropriate access levels for variables

- Initialize variable values

- Use Unity's `Start()` function

- Write meaningful single-line and multiline comments to identify the purpose of code

▌ Required Files

In this chapter, you will need to use the following files from the *Chapter_02 > Software* folder.

- *Challenge > LunaStats.cs, LilyStats.cs, LargStats.cs*, and *PinkBeardStats.cs* to code your solution to the challenges

- *Solution > LunaStats.cs, LilyStats.cs, LargStats.cs*, and *PinkBeardStats.cs* to compare your solution to the provided example solutions

▌ Challenge: Data Types

Your first challenge is to help define the characteristics for Luna by coding variables. *Variables* are used to store information in a computer that can be called upon at a later time. Open the LunaStats script in your code editor. You will see that a number of different characteristic variables have been outlined for Luna, such as `_firstName`, `energy`, and `groupExpBonus`. However, these variables are incomplete. For valid code, each variable must be assigned a data type. A *data type* represents the kind of information that is stored in a variable. It is your responsibility to complete this code by providing an appropriate data type to each variable. You should choose from the most common data types available, which include Boolean (`bool`), integer (`int`), floating point (`float`), double precision (`double`), and character string (`string`). Use the descriptive comments above each variable to help guide your decision about which data type is most suitable.

To begin, find the `_firstName` variable near the top of the LunaStats script. To give a data type to a variable, replace the entire `/*REPLACE THIS COMMENT WITH THE DATA TYPE*/` comment (including the asterisks and slashes) with one of `bool`, `int`, `float`, `double`, or `string`. Provide a data type for each variable in this manner. To assist yourself with choosing appropriate data types, think about the kind of information that should be stored in each variable.

▌ Hint: Data Type Descriptions

The following data types are the most common ones you will encounter when coding games. They will be suitable for most software applications. However, note that there are many data types to choose from, as well as some slight differences between computer languages. For the purposes of our work in this book,

2. Characters and Characteristics

the data types provided here will be more than enough. Nevertheless, you may encounter future situations in your coding career that require additional data types that are not covered in this section.

Boolean (`bool`)

A Boolean value can only take one of two forms, either `true` or `false`. To assign a Boolean data type to a variable in C#, use the `bool` keyword (Microsoft Corporation 2015a). Boolean variables are useful when you need to represent something that has only two possible states. For example, to indicate whether or not Luna currently has a ring, we might make a Boolean variable called `ring`. If Luna does have the ring, we set the variable equal to `true`. If she does not have the ring, we set it to `false`. Furthermore, it is common to append Boolean variable names with an action word like *is*, *can*, or *has* to help identify it as something that can only be true or false at a given time. Take, for instance, the variable `hasRing`, which gives a clearer indication that the variable stores information about whether Luna has a ring. Alternatively, you might prefix Boolean variables with the letter *b*, as in `bRing`, to designate the data type. Using such techniques is a matter of personal preference and up to the individual coder to decide. However, adding brief appendages like these to your variable names helps make your code easier to read and remember, thereby making your work more efficient in the long run.

Integer (`int`)

The integer data type represents values as whole numbers. For example, the numbers 0, 1, and 138 can all be represented as integers. In fact, a C# integer can be any whole number between –2,147,483,648 and 2,147,483,648. Meanwhile, fractions or partial values, such as 0.5 and 82.49, cannot be represented using the integer data type. In C#, an integer data type can be assigned to a variable using the `int` keyword (Microsoft Corporation 2015e). Integers are useful for data that require more than two options (hence, Boolean is not suitable), but whose values can be represented using whole numbers, without the need for decimals. For instance, you might represent Luna's health points (HP) using an integer, such as 10. If she were injured, you could subtract a whole number value from the total HP. Conversely, if healed, you could add an integer value back to her HP.

Another useful way to apply integers is as a coding scheme for more complex information. As an example, suppose Luna has magical abilities that are associated with nature, like sun, moon, or stars. You could develop an integer coding scheme like 0 = sun, 1 = moon, 2 = stars. Then, using an integer variable like `magicType`, you could assign Luna a magical type, such as 1, to represent that she commands the power of the moon. A coding scheme like this can be more efficient for the computer to process, since computers tend to prefer simple numbers over words. It can also make your code easier to update if you change plans later and help to keep your code cleaner as you perform more complicated operations using these values.

Similar to Booleans, it can be useful to append your integer variables to make them easy to identify. Two possible choices are num, as in numHealthPoints, and i, as in iMagicType. Both help to clarify that the data are represented using whole numbers and the integer data type.

Floating Point (float)

A floating-point value, designated in C# by the float keyword, is used to represent nearly any number, whole or partial, up to seven digits long. This roughly equates to a range of values from -3.4×10^{38} to 3.4×10^{38} (Microsoft Corporation 2015d). Example floats include 3.0 and 1.234567. Whereas Booleans are the go-to choice for binary situations and integers are best for whole numbers, floating points should be used in cases where partial, fraction, or decimal values are required. For instance, in the previous chapter's challenge, Luna's speed was represented with a floating-point value of 0.05. Naturally, a Boolean value would not make sense here, because speed is not something that can be true or false. If we were to use integers, we would be greatly restricted in what our options would be. Since our actual value was 0.05, an integer would only allow 0, which would create no movement, or 1, which would be far too fast to be playable. Therefore, a floating-point value is the better choice. It gives us a range of possible values that we can use to adjust Luna's speed to a level that is suitable for players. We could easily change the speed to something like 0.02 to make her slower or 0.09 to make her faster. When deciding whether to use a floating-point or integer value, think about whether you require the precision offered by a floating-point value. If whole numbers are sufficient, just use an integer. If you need partial values or greater precision in your calculations, a floating-point value would be necessary.

As with other data types, you may choose to prefix your floating-point variables with the letter *f*, as in fSpeed. This identifies the variable as using a float data type. In addition, when setting values for floating points, it is important to include a lowercase *f* or uppercase *F* suffix to the actual value. That is, you should set your fSpeed variable to a value of 0.05f or 0.05F. The purpose behind this suffix is that computer languages have many ways in which they can represent decimal values. By including the suffix, you are explicitly telling the computer that you want it to treat this value as a float data type. Otherwise, the computer may default to handling the value in a different way. In the case of C#, a value like 0.05 without the suffix would be automatically treated as a double data type, which is not what you want to happen in this case. By adding the suffix, you take control of your code and communicate clearly with the computer about how you want your data to be handled.

Technically speaking, there is some error involved in trying to represent decimal numbers with a computer. This is because there is an infinite quantity of possible numbers that can be imagined, but a computer has limited capacity to represent such numbers. Thus, some rounding error is introduced when a number is converted into computer form. Therefore, a floating-point value approximates, rather than perfectly represents, a number. Nevertheless, for most game applications, the rounding error introduced is inconsequential.

On the other hand, if you were creating high-profile banking applications or launching rockets into space, you would be much more concerned with precision.

Double Precision (double)

A double-precision value, like a floating point, represents partial, fractional, or decimal values. It is designated by the double keyword. However, a double has more precision than a float, because it can represent numbers with 15–16 digits. This approximates a range of values from $\pm 5.0 \times 10^{-324}$ to $\pm 1.7 \times 10^{308}$ (Microsoft Corporation 2015c). Therefore, a double may be a better choice than a float when a high degree of precision is required.

For example, one cutting-edge way to control a digital game is by using an eye tracker. An eye tracker is a hardware device that detects where someone looks on a computer screen. It can be used as an alternative way to interact with games, rather than using a mouse, keyboard, or handheld controller. Yet, eye tracking is not a perfect process. The hardware is capable of estimating where someone looks, but there is some slight error involved in determining the exact on-screen coordinates that a player is focusing on. Still, it is important for the controls in a game to be as precise as possible to enhance usability. Thus, when storing the coordinates for where a player is looking, an eye tracker is likely to use a double data type rather than a float. This provides added precision in a situation that requires extreme detail.

For circumstances where you require the exceptional precision offered by 15–16 digits, and the 7 digits offered by a float are insufficient, you will want to use the double data type. That said, for most game applications, including those in this book, it is not necessary to use a double. While the double adds precision, it comes at the cost of using more memory and processing power from the computer. Therefore, you should only elevate your data type to a double when you truly need to. Furthermore, be aware that even larger and more precise data types exist than the double, such as the decimal data type in C#. Although they are only used in rare circumstances that require the highest degree of detail in representing numbers, you should know that other data types exist.

Similar to float, it is best to explicitly indicate when you want the computer to treat a value as a double. This can be done by adding a lowercase d or uppercase D to the end of any double value you set. For example, if you want to represent Luna's speed with a double, you should use a value of 0.05d or 0.05D. Likewise, you can clearly identify variables that use the double data type by prefixing their names with the letter d, as in dSpeed.

Character String (string)

The character string is an interesting data type for a couple of reasons. First, it can be used to store information that closely represents our human language, including letters, words, numbers, and symbols. Second, unlike the other data types we've seen, a character string is actually composed of a collection of smaller pieces.

These pieces, known as characters, represent one single part of the character string. For example, in the character string "I have coded 1,000 lines!" the letter *a* is a character. The spaces, punctuation, and numbers are also characters. Indeed, characters have their own data type, which uses the `char` keyword. The `char` data type can be used to represent a wide range of Unicode characters, which include a variety of common letters, numbers, and symbols used in computer software (Microsoft Corporation 2015b). For our purposes, it is good to know that characters are the foundational building blocks of strings. However, for our practical development, we will focus on using strings, rather than creating individual characters.

In C#, you can assign the character string data type to a variable using the `string` keyword. When setting the value of a character string, you must enclose the data within a pair of double quotes, " and ". For instance, Luna might have a string variable called `race`, whose value would be "Dark Elf". You can think of strings as containers that hold text information, in contrast to the other data types, which store numbers or true/false values. Multiple strings can be manipulated and compared in a variety of ways (Microsoft Corporation 2015f). When you need to represent information as text, use a character string. For example, character strings are useful for names, text information that will displayed to players, and data that will be logged during the development process to verify that your game is working properly. You may choose to prefix your `string` variable names with *s* (sRace), *txt* (txtRace), or a similar convention.

❚❚ Hint: How Computers Think

Recall that the Boolean data type can represent only one of two values: `true` or `false`. Similarly, at the most fundamental level, computers only understand two values. This is known as a *binary* or *base 2* number system. All information stored in a computer's memory can ultimately be traced back to a collection of 0s and 1s. Like a single switch or a lever, a binary digit, or *bit*, can only have a value of 0 or 1. A bit is the purest form of information stored in a computer.

You may have heard of the term *byte* before. A byte is a series of 8 bits. Using its 8 bits, each of which equals 0 or 1, a byte can represent things like a single letter Q or the number 255. To create things like decimal numbers or strings of words, the computer puts a series of bytes together in a specific pattern. From a byte, we derive other computer memory terms you may have heard of before, such as *kilobyte* (1,000 bytes), *megabyte* (1,000,000 bytes), and *gigabyte* (1,000,000,000 bytes). Each of these structures is built upon collections of individual bits holding values of 0 or 1.

Imagine yourself inside a massive building filled with many billions of tiny switches along its walls. Every slightest action, like taking a step or saying a word, causes many of the switches to flip, revealing a new unique pattern among the collection of switches in the building. Using these switches, any state of the world can be uniquely represented for an instant, before it is updated once again by subsequent actions. This is what it is like to be inside a computer's memory. Every time you load a web page, save a file, or type a letter, your computer is reconfiguring its bits to represent the present state of its memory.

Truthfully, the computer understands nothing more than 0 or 1. Since writing directly in bits would be nigh impossible and dreadfully tedious for humans, we use computer languages as the compromise between 0s and 1s and the natural languages we speak among people. A computer is incapable of genuine autonomous thought, and although it processes mathematics quickly, it cannot rightfully be considered to be smart. Rather, it is a coder like you who has to tell the computer what to do. The computer will faithfully try its best to do whatever you tell it to. It will never defy you. Thus, as a coder, your challenge is to become proficient in solving problems, such that you can tell a computer exactly what you want it to do. With your code, a computer is transformed into a useful and powerful tool for achieving your goals.

Generally speaking, computers are more efficient at processing data that closely resemble their own representation of information as compared to data that humans can readily interpret. Hence, data types like `bool` and `int` tend to be processed faster and use less memory in the computer than data represented as `float`, `double`, or `string`. On the other hand, using strings and decimal numbers, which resemble our familiar words and numbers, may be more intuitive for you than representing information in other forms. For certain applications, such as programming graphics and physics engines, using optimized code at every opportunity is critical. However, for the coding involved in this book, which focuses primarily on the player-facing user experience, you should not experience any major performance differences based on the data types you choose. Just be aware that different data types have different implications for interpretability and how taxing they are on the computer. Do what is comfortable for you today and helps you solve problems successfully. The important thing is that you can use code to create great games. As you continue to learn and become more proficient in coding, you will find yourself experimenting with different approaches and developing your own personal style.

Figure 2.1 Lily is a dryad, a spirit of nature and protector of the forest.

▮ Challenge Extension: Data Types

At this point, you should be able to come up with reasonable data types for Luna's variables and justify why you chose them. An extended challenge is offered for additional practice. You can complete this challenge by looking at the LilyStats script in your code editor. As with LunaStats, a number of variables have been defined, but are currently missing data types. Again, your challenge is to complete the variable definitions by providing suitable data types.

By the way, *Lily* (Figure 2.1) is another character who Luna may encounter on her journey through the surface world. Lily is a dryad, which is a spirit of nature that has a particular affinity for trees. Her hair is like leaves and her skin resembles the bark of the tree from whence she came. She loves her forest home and will protect it at all costs. Go forth and code Lily's variables!

▉ Example Solution: Data Types

Your challenge was to provide data types for Luna's variables in the LunaStats script. One interpretation of the suitable data types for these variables is provided. The data types, which have replaced the comments from the challenge file, are in bold.

```
//character's first name
private string _firstName;

//character's last name
private string _lastName;

//character's race
private int _race;

//character's current happiness level
public int happy;

//character's current energy level
public int energy;

//character's current experience points
public int exp;

//character's movement speed
private float _speed;

//pct exp bonus when grouped with others
private float groupExpBonus;

//whether character is overjoyed
private bool _isJoyful;

//whether character is fatigued
private bool _isFatigued;
```

The first and last name variables clearly need to hold text, and therefore strings are the best choice. For race, a string could be used. However, we might also code the races in our game using integers like 0 = dark elf, 1 = dryad, 2 = dwarf, and 3 = orc. The happiness, energy, and experience variables can all be represented by whole numbers, which makes integers suitable. If, for some reason, our game needed to use decimals for these variables, we could use floating-point values instead. Meanwhile, due to our need for fine-grained control over Luna's speed, a float is necessary. Since the group experience bonus is represented as a percentage value, a float is again the optimal choice. Lastly, our joyful and fatigued variables both have only two states and therefore are best represented by Boolean values. A similar thought process has been applied to assign the data types for the LilyStats script.

```
//forest from which character originates
private string _origin;

//color of leaves
private string _leafColor;

//type of leaves; 0 = blade, 1 = vine, 2 = moss
private int _leafType;

//type of tree bark; 0 = birch, 1 = cherry, 2 = oak
private int _barkType;

//pct health of leaves
public float leafHealth;

//pct leaf health regeneration rate per day
private float _regenRate;

//current temperature of leaves, in Celsius
public float leafTemp;

//whether wilting due to temperature
private bool _isWilting;

//whether character sheds leaves
private bool _isDeciduous;

//whether character needs water nutrients
private bool _isThirsty;
```

Your own data types may vary slightly from these example solutions. For instance, you may have used integers where floats were used or vice versa. The important thing is that you can justify your choices with reasonable explanations. Your data types should accurately represent the kind of information that is stored in your variables. Furthermore, take a moment to consider any variables where your data types differed from the offered solutions. Think about how the information in those variables could be stored as both the data type you chose and the one presented in the example solution. By taking multiple perspectives on these variables, you can gain additional insights on how to choose your data types.

▎▊ Challenge: Defining Variables

Now that you have successfully typed a variety of variables, why not try designing some of your own? Let's introduce a new character that Luna might encounter on her journey through the surface world. *Larg* (Figure 2.2) is a friendly orc from the western mountains. Being very unlike his brutal, ignorant kin, Larg was outcast from his society. Ultimately, he was forced to flee down the mountain to avoid a gruesome fate. Today, he peacefully dwells upon the surface among people of all kinds. Nevertheless, he owes his physical might to his orc heritage.

At the moment, Larg is completely without variables to define his characteristics. Your challenge is to define 10 different variables that represent him. Once you have designed the characteristics for Larg, open up the LargStats script and code the variables.

Figure 2.2 Larg is a peaceful orc who was outcast by his brutal kin.

▌ Hint: Access Levels

Previously, you set the data types for a number of variables in the LunaStats and LilyStats scripts. If you take a look back at the variables in those files, you will notice that one component precedes the data type. This is the access level, which determines the extent to which a variable can be referenced and modified by external code.

Imagine that script A would like to be able to ask script B for a value from one of its variables. If script B's variable has its access level set to `public`, then script A will be allowed to retrieve the requested information. On the other hand, if script B doesn't want script A to ask about its variables, then it should use the `private` access level.

Basically, a `private` variable can only be accessed from inside the script in which it was created. Hence, only code within a given script can access its own `private` variables. Meanwhile, a `public` variable can be accessed from any script. This means that the variable can be referenced to determine its value or even have its value modified by an external script. Thus, any code within or outside of a given script can access that script's `public` variables. To distinguish between `private` and `public` variables in your code, it is customary to add a leading underscore to the name of all `private` variables, as in `_aPrivateVar`. In contrast, `public` variables have no such marking, as in `aPublicVar`. This makes it easy to distinguish between `public` and `private` variables as you are working through your code.

For the time being, think of `private` as the default access level for variables. Most often, you do not want or need external code to access a script's variables. Consider a character's name. Typically, this would not be something that another character could change. Therefore, a `private` access level would make sense. On the other hand, there are some cases where you do need to share information between scripts or allow external scripts to modify variable values. Consider a character's health. This value is expected to increase or decrease frequently during gameplay as a result of interactions with other characters. In cases like this, use a `public` access level to allow other scripts to retrieve and modify a variable's value. Similar to data types, there are even more access levels available in computer languages. You may encounter these in special circumstances and advanced coding applications. However, for our purposes, `public` and `private` will be suitable.

Hint: Naming Variables

The final component required to create a variable is its name. The name follows the access level and data type on the code line that declares the variable. In C#, there are certain rules that must be followed when naming variables:

- Alphanumeric characters are valid (A–Z, 0–9), as in `LevelScore01`.

    - However, a number may not be the first character, as in `9Lives`.

- Underscores may be used, as in `_is_Magic`.

    - Other special characters, such as *, !, or %, may not be used, as in `wow!*Magic*`.

In addition to the required naming rules, you should adopt a style for creating meaningful variable names. To start, ensure that your variable names accurately represent how they are used. The name you choose should reflect things like the data contained in the variable and the broader purpose of the variable in the game. For instance, Luna is likely to encounter other heroes in the surface world who will want to join in the adventure. Therefore, we might want to have a variable that represents how large the player's hero group is. Accordingly, a name like `iGroupSize` would clearly identify an integer variable that tells us how many members are in the group. An included comment could explicitly describe the variable on the line where it was created. Thereafter in the code, the name serves as its own reminder of the variable's purpose.

Let's consider a few of the most common variable naming styles, all of which can help you create easy-to-read code. In *Camel Case*, a variable name starts with a lowercase letter. Subsequently, each new word in the variable begins with a capital letter. Hence, if our group size variable were named `groupSize`, we would be using Camel Case. Meanwhile, *Pascal Case* was a similar technique, whereby the variable name starts with an uppercase letter. Subsequently, each new word also begins with an uppercase letter. Thus, if our group size variable employed Pascal Case, it would be named `GroupSize`. These styles make your code easier to read and interpret. It is highly recommended that you use either Camel Case or Pascal Case to name your variables. If you need extra evidence, try reading the following sets of variables. Track which set takes you more time to read and which is easier to interpret.

- Set A (poor style)
  - `_ maxgroupsize`
  - `YELLINGVOL`
  - `highScorerank`
  - `lEvEloNe`
- Set B (good style)
  - `isLevelEnded`
  - `PlayerClass`
  - `runSpeed`
  - `CanCastSpells`

Either of Camel Case or Pascal Case is appropriate. Each will help you to create meaningful variable names. Regardless of which style suits you best, always be sure to create valid and meaningful variable names. By using effective naming practices, you will make it easier for yourself, as well as others, to read, recognize, and remember your code.

▮ Hint: Declaring Variables

You know about access levels, data types, and naming. That's everything you need to fully declare a variable. The general format for creating a variable is as follows:

```
accessLevel dataType variableName;
```

Of course, we want to include a comment as well, either above or at the end of the line, to describe our variable. For example, to declare the strength of Larg, we could use this code:

```
//base strength (str) stat
//determines how much weight character can lift
private int iStr;
```

Besides the comments, access level, data type, and variable name, notice that a semicolon (;) is included at the very end of the variable declaration line. This is used not only when creating variables, but also for ending all statements in your C# code. So, you will become very familiar with semicolons. A semicolon in C# is a bit like the period at the end of a sentence. It completes one full instruction to the computer. Like a sentence, a computer statement can be formatted differently and spread out across multiple lines visually. However, once the computer sees the semicolon, it knows that the statement is complete and can be evaluated.

For instance, this would also be a valid, albeit not recommended, way to declare Larg's strength variable.

```
//base strength (str) stat
//determines how much weight character can lift
private
                    int
     iStr
        ;
```

▮ Challenge Extension: Defining Variables

There's one more character to become acquainted with, although he hardly needs any introduction. *Pink Beard* (Figure 2.3) is a wild and adventurous dwarf. He originally hails from the lavish dwarven city of Goldstone, located deep within the eastern mountains. His lively and energetic personality eventually became too much for his people, who generally carry a formal and reserved attitude. Thus, the dwarves sent Pink Beard out on a pilgrimage to their ancient homeland upon the surface. It was their hope that Goldstone would enjoy at least a few months of peace and quiet before he returned. Pink Beard is noted for his namesake beard of bright pink whiskers, as well as the absurdly large sunglasses that he wears, even when underground. For additional practice, think of 10 variables that capture Pink Beard's unique personality and talents. Then open the PinkBeardStats script and code them.

▮ Example Solution: Defining Variables

It was up to you to fully design and declare 10 variables to represent Larg and Pink Beard. Example solutions are provided to demonstrate how you may have solved this challenge. In addition to the data types, which you have practiced extensively already, this challenge requires you to choose access levels and variable names.

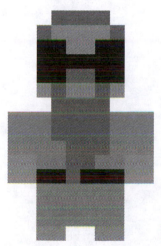

Figure 2.3 Pink Beard is an energetic dwarf on a pilgrimage to find his people's ancient homeland.

```
//excerpt from LargStats.cs

//number of fangs character has, usually 1 to 4
private int _numFangs;

//physical might; for strength-based calculations
public int str;

//maximum weight character can lift, in kg
private int _maxWeight;

//length of fangs, in cm
private float _fangLength;

//time to recharge super strength, in seconds
private float _superStrRest;

//multiplier for super strength
private float _superStrBonus;

//whether currently using super strength
private bool _isSuperStr;

//whether one parent was race other than Orc
private bool _isHalfOrc;

//whether character has Orcish unibrow
private bool _hasUnibrow;

//whether character has Orcish underbite
private bool _hasUnderbite;


//excerpt from PinkBeardStats.cs
//family name
private string _surname;

//worshiped deity in Dwarven culture
private string _deity;

//forge specialty; 0 = tools, 1 = armor, 2 = jewelry
private int _forgeType;

//current grumpiness level
public int _grumpyLevel;

//amount of gold carried
public int gold;

//length of beard, in cm
public float beardLength;

//height of character, in cm
private float _height;

//weight of character, in kg
private float _weight;

//whether sunglasses are currently worn
private bool _isGlassesOn;

//whether beard can be rubbed for luck
private bool _isLuckyBeard;
```

Recall that a `private` access level is most often suitable, except for cases where a variable's value needs to be modified or referenced in an external script. As for variable names, it is best to keep them brief, informative, and consistently formatted. Also, remember to include comments to explain the meaning behind your variables. If you can reason through your variables in this manner, you are on the right track to becoming a proficient coder.

▌ Challenge: Initializing Variables

Currently, we have four characters and a collection of several variables that represent each of them. Your final challenge for this chapter is to initialize each and every variable with a reasonable starting value. Also, include a meaningful comment with each variable to explain why you assigned the value that you did. To get started, find the `Start()` function in each character's script. This is where you will initialize each character's variables.

▌ Hint: Initialization

To *initialize* a variable is to give it a starting value. A critical thing to know about variables is that they should never be used without having been initialized. In some languages, a variable that has not been initialized will contain random or no information. This would cause an error, should you try to access the variable in your code. In other languages, a variable may automatically receive a default value at creation. Although it may prevent outright errors from appearing, you don't want the computer making assumptions on your behalf. If the computer assumes a value that you did not intend, your code will not run as designed. Instead, you want to be in control of your code and explicitly tell the computer what you want to make happen. Many common bugs and errors arise when people try to access information in variables that have not been initialized. Therefore, it is wise to always initialize your variables with meaningful values prior to accessing them in any other part of your code.

To initialize a variable, you simply set it to a valid value based on its data type. When choosing a value, think of what a reasonable starting point would be in the context of your game. A few examples are provided. Note the use of the variable name, followed by an equal sign, a value, and a semicolon to end the line.

```
//examples of initialized variables

//the character's name must be set at the start
_firstName = "Luna";

//all characters begin game with full health of 100
health = 100;

//character will not be fatigued to start
isFatigued = false;
```

▌ Hint: Unity's `Start()` Function

`Start()` is a special function in Unity. It is used to control the timing of execution for code. Specifically, any code in the `Start()` function will run after a script is enabled, but before other functions in the game loop (Unity Technologies n.d.). The `Start()` function is called only one time. Since our variables need to be initialized once and must be assigned values before they are used later in the code, the `Start()` function is an excellent place to handle initialization. In fact, `Start()` is a good place to put any code that only needs to be used once and must execute prior to the main body of your script.

Besides initializing variables, `Start()` is commonly used to call one-time setup functions. For example, imagine beginning a new level in a game. There might be certain things that need to be set up before the level begins, such as score counters, timers, obstacles, and object positions. The initial preparation of such items could be handled in separate functions that get called from within `Start()`. This helps to keep the code clean and more organized.

▌ Hint: Comments

You may have noticed certain descriptions placed throughout the sample code and challenge files provided with this book. Whenever a single line contains a double slash (//) or multiple lines are contained within slashes and asterisks (/* and */), a comment is being designated. Comments are special sections in our code. They are ignored by the computer when it compiles our code into a functioning program. Although they do not alter the function of our programs, comments are an absolutely vital part of coding. This is because comments allow us to insert notes and descriptions into our code using human language.

Recall that human language and computer language are different enough as to be difficult to interpret between one another. A computer cannot understand human language. A human has to do a bit of translation to understand computer language. Therefore, we use comments to leave notes, descriptions, and explanations in our code using human language. This makes it easier for us, as well as others, to understand how our code works. Try to interpret the meaning of the following code:

```
float deltaMoveX = _newDir.x * _speed;
```

Without knowing the context or purpose in which the code was written, it is difficult to accurately assess what the code does. You may be able to make a reasonable guess as to what the code does, but with a great deal of uncertainty. In contrast, try to interpret the same code after comments have been added:

```
//calculate change in movement based on user input direction and
  player speed
float deltaMoveX = _newDir.x * _speed; //x axis change
```

Suddenly, the comments have made the intent of this code clear. The comment above the code gives a general picture of what is happening. A player's

---

2. Characters and Characteristics

movement is being calculated based on speed and direction. Meanwhile, the end-of-line comment clarifies that this particular formula is calculating the x axis movement. Armed with this information, the code can be readily understood. A `float` variable called `deltaMoveX` stores the change in x movement, which is calculated as the new x direction times the player's speed. Thanks to the comments, this code is easy to understand in terms of its purpose and function.

Comments are best placed immediately above the code they are describing. When adding brief, extended details, you may choose to include a comment at the end of a line as well. Just make sure the comment is placed after the semicolon, so it will not interfere with the functional code on the line. Both techniques were demonstrated in the preceding `deltaMoveX` example. To create single-line comments like these, simply use two forward slashes (//). Anything that comes after the slashes will be ignored. This allows you to add any necessary notes to your code in human language without disrupting the function of your program.

```
//a single-line comment can be placed above the code it describes
isCommented = true; //a comment can also be placed at the end of a
   line
```

Besides single-line comments, you can also write multiline comments. These can be spread out over several lines of code and wrapped into blocks, like paragraphs. Multiline comments are useful when extended descriptions are required that cannot easily fit within a single line. To begin a multiline comment, use the /* characters. To end a multiline comment, use the */ characters. Everything between these opening and closing characters will be treated as a comment. This allows for more details to be added to the code in an easy-to-read format. For instance, the header of each script in this book contains a basic description of the file's purpose, as well as copyright information. Note the use of a multiline comment and line breaks to form a sort of paragraph.

```
/*
LunaStats
Defines the stats for Luna.

Copyright 2014 John M. Quick.
*/
```

You should use comments abundantly in your code. Every nontrivial line or action taken in your code needs to have a descriptive comment. When you want to describe what a particular line of code will do, add a comment directly above the code. When you just need to make a small note or add bonus details, add a comment to the end of the line. If you need to include a detailed explanation or summarize a complicated process, make use of a multiline comment.

Comments are critical for demonstrating your understanding of code and recalling it at a later time. As you make more and more games, you will want to refer back to problems you solved in the past, rather than expending the time and energy to duplicate existing work. With good commenting practices, you will rapidly reuse your existing code, so you can focus on learning new and more complex techniques.

▐ Example Solution: Initializing Variables

Reasonable example initialized values are offered for each character's variables. Your values will naturally vary. Just be sure that your initialized values match the data types of their corresponding variables. In addition, these values should reflect what you expect the characters to start their adventure with in your game world.

```
//excerpt from LunaStats.cs
void Start() {

        //first name
        _firstName = "Luna";

        //last name
        _lastName = "Lunaurora";

        //0 = Dark Elf
        _race = 0;

        //start with moderate happiness
        happy = 5;

        //start with full energy
        energy = 10;

        //start with no experience
        exp = 0;

        //suitable speed in game world units
        _speed = 0.05f;

        //25% bonus exp when grouped
        groupExpBonus = 0.25f;

        //not overjoyed to start
        _isJoyful = false;

        //not fatigued to start
        _isFatigued = false;

} //end function

//excerpt from LilyStats.cs
void Start() {

        //from the Southern Forests
        _origin = "South";

        //has green leaves
        _leafColor = "Green";

        //grows vines
        _leafType = 1;

        //skin is made of birch wood
        _barkType = 0;

        //start at max health (100%)
        leafHealth = 1.0f;
```

```
        //regenerate 10% of health per day
        _regenRate = 0.1f;

        //comfortable outdoor temperature
        leafTemp = 24.0f;

        //healthy to start
        _isWilting = false;

        //does not shed
        _isDeciduous = false;

        //energized to start
        _isThirsty = false;

} //end function


//excerpt from LargStats.cs
void Start() {

        //this Orc has 1 fang
        _numFangs = 1;

        //default starting strength for Orcs
        str = 10;

        //by default, 10 times strength
        _maxWeight = 100;

        //5cm, a rather long fang
        _fangLength = 5.0f;

        //30s to recharge ability
        _superStrRest = 30.0f;

        //strength is doubled
        _superStrBonus = 2.0f;

        //must be activated by player
        _isSuperStr = false;

        //full-blooded Orc
        _isHalfOrc = false;

        //two, distinct eyebrows
        _hasUnibrow = false;

        //makes fang stick out even more
        _hasUnderbite = true;

} //end function


//excerpt from PinkBeardStats.cs
void Start() {

        //family known for distinct laughter
        _surname = "Loudlaff";
```

```
    //legendary hero of tunneling
    _deity = "Dugodurr";

    //master of jewelry crafting
    _forgeType = 2;

    //not grumpy to start
    _grumpyLevel = 0;

    //brought some savings along for journey
    gold = 100;

    //30cm beard
    beardLength = 30.0f;

    //150cm height
    _height = 150.0f;

    //100kg weight
    _weight = 100.0f;

    //currently wearing glasses
    _isGlassesOn = true;

    //beard can be rubbed for luck
    _isLuckyBeard = true;

} //end function
```

Summary

You have risen to the challenge and fulfilled the entire process of designing, declaring, and initializing variables. You are well on your way to setting up the foundations of your very own game. At this point, you should be able to succeed in all of these coding tasks:

- Design stats for game characters

- Define variables to represent different characteristics

- Write valid and meaningful variable names

- Select the appropriate data types for variables

- Set the appropriate access levels for variables

- Initialize variable values

- Use Unity's Start() function

- Write meaningful single-line and multiline comments to identify the purpose of code

In Chapter 3, we will return to the surface world and continue coding Luna's quest. Although you have defined and initialized variables, you will see that there are many more ways in which these values can be manipulated to make exciting things happen within the game world.

References

Microsoft Corporation. 2015a. bool (C# Reference). https://msdn.microsoft.com/library/c8f5xwh7.aspx (accessed January 30, 2015).

Microsoft Corporation. 2015b. char (C# Reference). https://msdn.microsoft.com/library/x9h8tsay.aspx (accessed January 30, 2015).

Microsoft Corporation. 2015c. double (C# Reference). https://msdn.microsoft.com/library/678hzkk9.aspx (accessed January 30, 2015).

Microsoft Corporation. 2015d. float (C# Reference). https://msdn.microsoft.com/library/b1e65aza.aspx (accessed January 30, 2015).

Microsoft Corporation. 2015e. int (C# Reference). https://msdn.microsoft.com/library/5kzh1b5w.aspx (accessed January 30, 2015).

Microsoft Corporation. 2015f. string (C# Reference). https://msdn.microsoft.com/library/362314fe.aspx (accessed January 30, 2015).

Unity Technologies. n.d. MonoBehaviour.Start. http://docs.unity3d.com/ScriptReference/MonoBehaviour.Start.html.

3 The Bounds of the World

Thanks to you, Luna is up and running along the surface world. It's time to start coding more features and characteristics of our game. We'll start by defining the boundaries of the game world. This requires us to dive into the topic of collision detection. Collisions are one of the most fundamental components of game development. It's most unlikely that you will ever create or play a game that does not involve collisions. With the ability to code collisions, you will be able to introduce all kinds of interactivity into your games.

▐ Goals

By the end of this chapter, you will be able to apply these coding techniques:

- Prevent a game character from moving outside the screen

- Logically determine how objects collide in two-dimensional (2D) space

- Manipulate variable values using math and equality operators

- Modify variable values using expressions

- Convert between screen and world coordinates in Unity

- Access Unity game components from within your code

▌ Required Files

In this chapter, you will need to use the following files from the *Chapter_03 > Software* folder.

- *Challenge > Assets > Scenes > Map.unity* to run, modify, and test your solution

- *Challenge > Assets > Scripts > UserMove.cs* to code your solution to the challenge

- *Demo > Mac/PC > PlayerBounds* to demonstrate how your completed solution should work

- *Solution > UserMove.cs* to compare your solution to the provided example solution

▌ Challenge: Detecting Boundary Collisions

Return to your original challenge project from Chapter 1, *PlayerMove*, and run it in Unity. This was the challenge in which you got Luna moving for the first time. If you move her to the edge of the screen in any direction, she just keeps on going! There is nothing stopping her from disappearing into oblivion. Nor is there anything to console the poor players who might have lost their hero to this case of incomplete coding. In contrast, try running the demo for this chapter by double-clicking on *PlayerBounds*. Here, you will see that Luna stops whenever she reaches the edge of the screen on all four sides. She cannot pass the boundaries of the game world and cannot be lost in the mysterious space beyond. We want her to stay with us at all times, so this is a good thing. Ultimately, your challenge is to implement boundary collisions that keep Luna visible on the screen at all times.

Before you begin trying to code a solution, recall the pseudocode and process mapping techniques we previously discussed. It is time to put these techniques to work. If you can solve the challenge using one or more of these methods first, you will be in a much better position to efficiently and effectively translate your thoughts into code. After you have solved the logic of this challenge, begin working to remedy the situation in the PlayerBounds project. Inside this project, open the UserMove script in your code editor. Look for the series of four `if` statements inside the `MoveObject()` function. To solve this challenge, you need to replace the `true`/*REPLACE WITH POSITION CHECK*/ and /*UPDATE NEWX/Y POSITION*/ comments with the appropriate code to stop Luna from moving outside the boundaries of the screen. Meanwhile, you can run the Map scene in Unity to test your code. To help you focus on the logic behind this challenge and translate your solution into code, several hints are provided.

▌ Hint: 2D Collisions

When we originally thought about how Luna could move, we pictured the world as a 2D coordinate plane. Once again, this visual will help us understand how to prevent her from moving outside the boundaries of our world. Whereas before we had a limitless coordinate system stretching in all directions, we now are placing boundaries at the edges of the screen. Therefore, you can draw out your coordinate system with Luna in the middle just like before (Figure 3.1). To represent the boundaries, simply draw a rectangle around the sides of your grid. These indicate the top, bottom, left, and right edges of the screen. We know that our completed code should ensure Luna never moves past these boundaries.

However, one big question remains to be answered: How do we know when Luna collides with a boundary? More generally, how do we know when two objects collide in 2D space? Think about this question for a moment and see if you can reason out a response.

Since our world can be represented as a 2D coordinate plane, all objects inside the world have x and y coordinates. These coordinates tell us where every object is at a given time. In the case of Unity, we previously discussed the `Transform` component, along with its `Vector3 position` variable, which stores the x and y coordinates of an object. Hence, at any given moment, we know exactly where Luna is, as well as any other object in our game. We can also think of our boundaries as having x and y coordinates. So, how do we know if two objects are colliding or not? Basically, two objects are colliding in 2D space when they share the same coordinates to some degree. In other words, two objects are colliding when they overlap one another.

Once again, it would be helpful to visualize this situation. Imagine there is an invisible box around Luna. Draw it on your diagram. You have already drawn lines to represent the boundaries of the screen. Thus, you can begin to understand how Luna will collide with the screen boundaries using your diagram. At the same time, think in terms of the x and y coordinates of these objects.

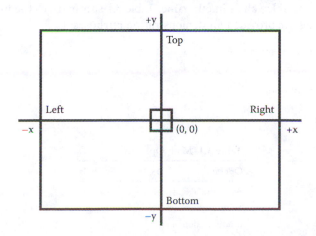

Figure 3.1 The game world is conceptualized as a 2D coordinate plane. The boundaries of the screen have been drawn to represent where Luna's movement should be stopped.

For instance, we know that Luna has collided with the rightmost boundary once her x position is greater than or equal to the screen's right edge x position. Following the same logic, take a moment to see if you can reason out the left, top, and bottom collisions.

▐ Hint: Operators

By now, you should be able to come up with the logic behind the challenge of keeping Luna within the screen's boundaries. So, let's transition into the code portion of this challenge. We know that we want to compare Luna's x and y values to the four edges of the screen to check for collisions. To do this, we will need to make some calculations and comparisons in our code. This is where operators come into play. While there are many types of operators available to you in C#, the two types of immediate importance to this challenge are the math and equality operators.

Math Operators

The math operators in C# are those that you are already familiar with from, well, math. In a sense, a computer is just a high-powered calculator. It can perform all kinds of operations and calculations many times per second. At the most basic level, we have addition, subtraction, multiplication, and division. Each has its own symbol in code. A plus sign (+) indicates addition and a minus sign (−) represents subtraction. Furthermore, an asterisk (*) represents multiplication, whereas a forward slash (/) indicates division. One unique math operator that is common in computer languages is modulus, which is represented by the percent sign (%). Essentially, the modulus operator returns the remainder of the division between two numbers. Thus, 5 % 3 calculates the remainder of 5 divided by 3, which is 2. Modulus is useful for iterating through lists of objects, among other things. Using these math symbols, we can perform calculations with numbers and modify variable values in our game. Table 3.1 summarizes the math operators. Examples are provided for demonstration purposes:

```
//math operator examples

//addition
//add one and one
1 + 1
```

Table 3.1 Math Operators

Operators	Symbols
Addition	+
Subtraction	−
Multiplication	*
Division	/
Modulus	%

```
//subtraction
//reduce Luna's energy by 5
energy - 5


//multiplication
//double Luna's speed
_speed * 2


//division
//calculate the aspect ratio of the screen
Screen.width / Screen.height


//modulus
//get the second digit in a number
25 % 10 //gives us 5
```

Equality Operators

You are probably familiar with several equality operators from your prior experience in math. Equality operators help us compare values to one another, such as checking whether two numbers are the same or whether one is higher than the other. Often, equality operators are used within conditional statements to determine whether a section of code should be executed. For example, when checking Luna's position against the screen boundaries, you want to ask whether her coordinates are greater than or equal to any of the boundaries. If so, you won't allow her to move beyond the boundary. If not, you simply allow her to keep moving as normal. The most common C# equality operators are shown in Table 3.2. Again, each has its own code symbol. Note that when you want to set a value of a variable, you use a single equal sign (=). This is called *assignment*. However, if you want to ask whether two values are equal to one another, a double equal sign is used (==). Examples are provided:

```
//equality operator examples


//equal
//set the speed variable
_speed = 0.01f
```

Table 3.2 Equality Operators

Operators	Symbols
Equal (assignment)	=
Equal (comparison)	==
Not equal	!=
Greater than	>
Less than	<
Greater than or equal to	>=
Less than or equal to	<=

```
//equal comparison
//are the numbers equal?
1 == 2 //false

//not equal
//are the numbers not equal?
1 != 2 //true

//greater than
//does Luna have energy left?
energy > 0

//less than
//is Luna below the maximum level?
currentLevel < maxLevel

//greater than or equal to
//does Luna have enough gold to buy this item?
gold >= price

//less than or equal to
//is Luna's energy fully recharged?
energy <= maxEnergy
```

▌ Hint: Expressions

Like mathematical expressions, computer programming expressions contain a series of values, variables, and operators that can be evaluated. You have already learned about values, variables, and operators. With expressions, you can combine any quantity of these elements to calculate, modify, or compare values in your code. One important thing to note is that expressions are evaluated in a particular order (Microsoft Corporation 2015). This depends on the precedence given to each type of operation. For instance, multiplication is handled before addition. Items within parentheses are always evaluated first, so this gives you a degree of control over how your code is evaluated. In the case where there is a tie for precedence, expressions are evaluated from left to right by default. Table 3.3 summarizes the precedence for evaluating expressions in C#. A series of examples is provided. Try to calculate the values yourself to make sure you understand the order in which expressions are evaluated.

Table 3.3 Expression Evaluation Precedence Ordered from First to Last

Operators	Symbols
Parentheses	( )
Multiplication and division	* / %
Addition and subtraction	+ –
Greater and less than	< <= > >=
Equal (comparison)	== !=
Equal (assignment)	=

```
//expression examples
//what is the value of each line?

x = 1 + 2 + 3 //6

x = 10 / 2 + 3 //8

x = 10 / (2 + 3) //2

10 * 2 - 5 < (5 * 2) + 5 //false

6 * 4 >= 2 * 12 / 2 //true

1 + 3 * 5 == 2 * (4 + 4) //true
```

▮ Hint: Screen Size in Unity

The screen size is the last piece of the puzzle you need. Once you can get the width and height of the screen, you will be able to perform your boundary collision checks and keep Luna inside the game world. In the case of Unity, retrieving and making use of the screen dimensions requires a bit of explanation. This is due to the fact that Unity has several different kinds of coordinate systems. Often, you will need to convert between them in your code to make sure you are using consistent values. For this challenge, we will need to reconcile two of Unity's coordinate systems.

World Coordinates

One way that Unity represents space is through the world coordinate system. You can think of world coordinates as measuring things that are inside the game world itself. For example, Luna is inside the game world, along with many other characters and objects. In our own terms, we might describe Luna as a sprite with a width of 64 pixels and a height of 64 pixels. However, in Unity's world coordinate system, she is 0.64 units wide and 0.64 units tall. This equates to a conversion of 100 between pixels to world units. That is, 64/100 = 0.64.

Indeed, Unity has a setting for art assets that are imported into any project. This setting is called `Pixels Per Unit` and carries a default value of 100. Take a look in the *Assets* > *Textures* folder of your Unity project. Click on the *DarkElf* image. Then, direct your attention to the Inspector window. A few lines down you will find the `Pixels Per Unit` setting and see that it has defaulted to a value of 100. The reason this conversion is important is because you want to always use consistent units in your code. Otherwise, things will not work as you intend. Since Unity understands the game world in its own units, you want to make sure to use these units in your code. Therefore, if you needed to refer to Luna's size, you would want to use a value of 0.64 units, rather than 64 pixels. For another example, peek back at the UserMove script. You can see that Luna's `_speed` variable is set to a value 0.05f. This value is in world coordinates. It basically tells the computer that we want Luna to move at a rate of 0.05f world units. By the way, it is possible to change Unity's `Pixels Per Unit` setting. However, unless you have a specific reason to do so, it is generally recommended that you retain the default setting and make the necessary unit conversions in your code where required.

Screen Coordinates

Another way that Unity represents space is through screen coordinates. In this case, the *screen* refers to the Unity player window. You use the Unity player window whenever you press the *play* button to test your project and see it run in the Game window. Based on the resolution of your monitor and how you arrange your Unity interface, the player window can adopt a variety of sizes. Similarly, you also see the player window whenever you run a compiled Unity game. For instance, all of the demo projects included with this book are run within a Unity player window. If you hold the command (Mac) or control (PC) key and double-click to open a demo, Unity allows you to choose from a wide variety of resolutions, such as 1024 × 768 and 800 × 600. Your resolution choice ultimately defines the size of the player window. In the event you run a game in full-screen mode, the size of the player window is equivalent to the monitor resolution.

Furthermore, Unity's screen size is measured in pixels along the width and height of the player window. For instance, a resolution of 1024 × 768 means the screen is 1024 pixels wide and 768 pixels tall. In Unity, you can retrieve the width of the player window, in pixels, using the `Screen.width` command. Likewise, you can retrieve the height of the player window, in pixels, using the `Screen.height` command. Thus, if your Unity player window has a resolution of 1024 × 768 pixels, `Screen.width` returns a value of 1024 and `Screen.height` returns 768 (Figure 3.2).

The major benefit of being able to access the screen size is that we can make our software resolution independent with relative ease. Imagine how many versions of the same game code you would need to write for it to play well on all the different shapes and sizes of mobile devices in the world today. Similarly, consider how hard it would be to make a desktop game that looks right on all the various monitors that people own, some of which are 5, 10, or even 15 years old. Thankfully, we can use the `Screen.width` and `Screen.height` commands to retrieve the current screen size our game is being played on, regardless of what

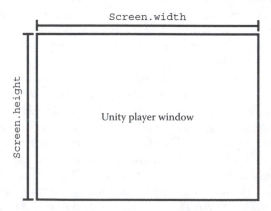

Figure 3.2 Unity's screen size is measured in pixels according to the size of the player window. By default, divide any pixel measurement by 100 to convert it into Unity world units.

device or resolution is being used. This is what allows us to efficiently handle many devices with a single set of code. Instead of coding our game with a single resolution in mind, we can make our code adapt to a wide variety of situations. To do so, we still have to be conscious of the different coordinate systems at work within Unity. Thus, to make effective use of the `Screen.width` and `Screen.height` commands, we must remember to convert these pixel values into world units. This will ensure all measurements and values are consistent throughout our code.

Converting Screen Coordinates to World Coordinates

We know that we can retrieve the screen dimensions using Unity's `Screen.width` and `Screen.height` commands. At the same time, we know that Unity's `Pixels Per Unit` conversion is 100. Therefore, to begin identifying where our boundaries are in terms of world units, we can make the following conversion:

```
//width of screen in world units
Screen.width / 100

//height of screen in world units
Screen.height / 100
```

By dividing our screen dimensions by Unity's `Pixels Per Unit` value, we have translated our screen width and height into world units. Recall that position values, such as Luna's 2D coordinates at any given time, are measured in world units as well. Now we are able to accurately compare Luna's position to the boundaries of our screen! Recall that the origin of the Unity world is at the point (0, 0), which lies in the center of the screen. Can you calculate the point that represents the right edge of the screen? Try drawing a diagram to visualize the situation.

From the provided code and hints, you should now have everything you need to make your boundary collision checks. Try once again to write the code necessary to compare Luna's position against the top, bottom, left, and right sides of the screen. Furthermore, stop her from moving outside these boundaries, when necessary, by updating the values of newX and newY.

▮▮ Example Solution: Boundary Collisions

Our challenge was to detect boundary collisions and prevent Luna from moving beyond the edges of the screen. Solving this problem requires us to apply operators and expressions in two ways. Take a moment to examine the logic behind this solution, which is depicted in pseudocode.

```
//left edge of player is past left side of screen
IF player's x position IS LESS THAN negative one half the screen
    width
THEN set player's x position EQUAL TO negative one half the screen
    width
```

```
//right edge of player is past right side of screen
IF player's x position IS GREATER THAN one half the screen width
THEN set player's x position EQUAL TO one half the screen width

//top edge of player is past top side of screen
IF player's y position IS GREATER THAN one half the screen height
THEN set player's y position EQUAL TO one half the screen height

//bottom edge of player is past bottom side of screen
IF player's y position IS LESS THAN negative one half the screen
    height
THEN set player's y position EQUAL TO negative one half the screen
    height
```

Inside the UserMove script, return to the `if` statements that you modified in the `MoveObject()` function.

```
//check x axis
//left edge of player is past left side of screen
if (true/*REPLACE WITH POSITION CHECK*/) {

    //stop player at edge
    /*UPDATE NEWX/Y POSITION*/

} //end if

//right edge of player is past right side of screen
if (true/*REPLACE WITH POSITION CHECK*/) {

    //stop player at edge
    /*UPDATE NEWX/Y POSITION*/

} //end if

//check y axis
//top edge of player is past top side of screen
if (true/*REPLACE WITH POSITION CHECK*/) {

    //stop player at edge
    /*UPDATE NEWX/Y POSITION*/

} //end if

//bottom edge of player is past bottom side of screen
if (true/*REPLACE WITH POSITION CHECK*/) {

    //stop player at edge
    /*UPDATE NEWX/Y POSITION*/

} //end if
```

First, you need to complete the `if` statements by checking Luna's position against the screen boundaries. In this script, Luna's position is represented by the newX and newY variables. Essentially, newX and newY represent Luna's new position based only on the user input direction and speed. However, there are times when newX and newY might fall outside the boundaries of the game world. Therefore, we are using `if` statements to check for such circumstances. Thus, inside the parentheses following the `if` keyword, you should compare the `newX` and `newY` variables against their associated edges of the screen. This will determine whether Luna's new position is valid (inside the boundaries) or invalid (outside the boundaries). Second, in the event you determine that Luna is about to move outside a given boundary, you need to set her `newX` or `newY` position equal to the boundary instead. This positions her at the edge of the screen, rather than allowing her to move past it. You can accomplish this by setting the affected `newX` or `newY` variable inside the brackets of the `if` statement.

An example solution is provided, with the updated code in bold. Consider the first two `if` statements, which check Luna's `newX` position against the left and right edges of the screen.

```
//excerpt from MoveObject() function

//check x axis
//left edge of player is past left side of screen
if (newX < -0.5f * Screen.width / 100) {

    //stop player at edge
    newX = -0.5f * Screen.width / 100;

} //end if

//right edge of player is past right side of screen
if (newX > 0.5f * Screen.width / 100) {

    //stop player at edge
    newX = 0.5f * Screen.width / 100;

} //end if
```

We know Luna has collided with a boundary on the x axis if her `newX` position is less than (more negative than) the left edge of the screen or greater than (more positive than) the right edge of the screen. Notice that we use `Screen.width/100` to convert our screen width into world coordinates, which match the units of Luna's position. We also multiply the screen width by 0.5f, which is equivalent to taking one-half of its value. You may recall that the origin point for our game world is at the center of the screen, while `Screen.width` gives us the entire length of the screen. Thus, if we want to get to the edges, we need to calculate only half of the screen width from the center. For the left edge, we take a negative value, since the left edge of the screen is less than zero on the x axis. Conversely, we take a positive value for the right edge of the screen, which is greater than zero on the x axis. These calculations are visualized in Figure 3.3.

In the event that Luna's `newX` value exceeds one of these boundaries, we update the `newX` value inside the brackets of the `if` statement. In both cases, we simply set her `newX` position equal to the screen boundary value that we checked. That is, rather than allowing Luna to continue moving as originally

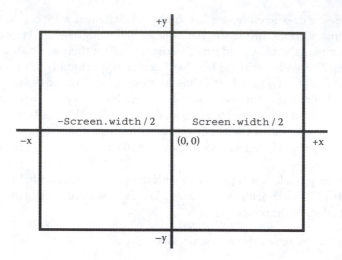

Figure 3.3 Calculate the left and right edges of the screen by considering its overall width and the origin of the game world.

planned, we explicitly tell her newX value to equal the boundary instead. Similar logic and code are applied to handle the top and bottom boundary collisions.

```
//excerpt from MoveObject() function

//check y axis
//top edge of player is past top side of screen
if (newY > 0.5f * Screen.height / 100) {

    //stop player at edge
    newY = 0.5f * Screen.height / 100;

} //end if

//bottom edge of player is past bottom side of screen
if (newY < -0.5f * Screen.height / 100) {

    //stop player at edge
    newY = -0.5f * Screen.height / 100;

} //end if
```

Since the top and bottom collisions involve movement along the y axis, we are concerned with Luna's newY position and the height of the screen. Again, Screen.height provides the entire height of the screen, in pixels, so we need to divide by 100 and multiply by 0.5f to calculate half of the height, in world units. The top boundary is greater than zero on the y axis, so a positive value is used. In contrast, the bottom boundary is less than zero on the y axis, so a negative value is used. Once again, should Luna's newY value exceed one of the boundaries, we set it equal to that boundary. Subsequently, Luna's y position will remain fixed at the edge of the screen, rather than being allowed to move past it.

■ Challenge: Accounting for the Character

If you run your code as currently written, you might notice a slight problem. While Luna is indeed stopped at the edges of the screen, she isn't stopped at the position we might expect. It appears that about half of her hangs over the edge. Naturally, we don't want half of Luna to disappear into oblivion, while half of her remains on the screen. We would prefer Luna to stay with us in the game world at all times. Therefore, we need to make one final adjustment to our calculations. This involves taking the dimensions of the character into account when making our boundary checks. Hence, your new challenge is to account for the width and height of the character, such that she stays entirely on the screen. See if you can reason out the logic behind how this adjustment will work before proceeding to the hints. Once again, drawing a diagram would be most helpful in this situation.

■ Hint: Origin Point

Click on the Player object in the Hierarchy tab of your Unity project. Then, direct your attention to the Scene tab. Zoom in, if necessary, and you will see that Luna has a small circular marker at her center (Figure 3.4).

This marker indicates that the origin point for our Player object is in the center. That is, the point (0, 0) for our Player object is set to the center of the object, as opposed to some other position, such as the top-left or bottom-left corner. This explains why our code needs to be expanded to compensate for the size of our character. In our previous code, we were comparing Luna's center position to the edges of the screen. That is why half of her would disappear over the edge of the screen. If we want to keep Luna entirely on the screen, we need to compensate for the fact that her origin point is in the center. What width and height values do you think you should use to adjust your calculations? Let Figure 3.5 assist you in forming a logical solution.

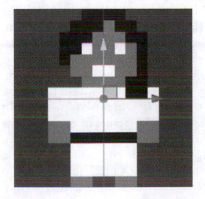

Figure 3.4 In the Scene window, we can see that Luna's origin point lies at her center.

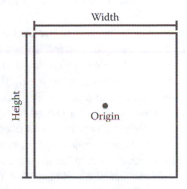

Figure 3.5 Luna's origin point is in the center. Thus, we can calculate her edges by extending half her width on the x axis and half her height on the y axis.

▮ Hint: Game Components in Unity

Perhaps you have noticed that we need to factor half the width and half the height of Luna into our boundary collision checks. Along the x axis, we need to subtract or add half of Luna's width to accurately check her position against the right and left edges of the screen. Similarly, we need to use half of Luna's height to properly check her position against the top and bottom edges of the screen. See if you can determine the points that represent Luna's left, right, top, and bottom edges. How would you compare these values to the left, right, top, and bottom edges of the screen?

The final piece of the puzzle involves retrieving Luna's dimensions, so we can incorporate them into our code. Recall that Luna is represented by a 64 × 64 pixel sprite. We could simply convert this to world units (divide by 100) and use a value of 0.32 in our code. However, it is generally best not to use such *hard-coded* values. This is true because hard-coded values make our code less versatile. For instance, suppose we were to represent half of Luna's height and width with a value of 0.32, but later changed the size of Luna's sprite. Our boundary collision code would be completely broken, since 0.32 no longer accurately represents Luna's dimensions. Wouldn't it be better if we could use a single command to access Luna's width and height, regardless of her sprite size? Better yet, is there a way for us to access the size of any character's sprite, regardless of what size that character is? Indeed, there is a way.

Click on the Player object in the Hierarchy window of your Unity project once again. To Unity, Player is considered to be a GameObject. A GameObject is like a container that can hold all kinds of things related to our game. In fact, almost everything in our game world will be associated with a GameObject in some way, whether it's a character, obstacle, environment, special effect, or script. With the Player object selected, turn your attention to the Inspector window (Figure 3.6).

Here, you will see the familiar Transform component. In Unity, a *component* is something that can be added to a GameObject in order to provide additional functionality. Any time you attach a component to a GameObject, it is like saying, "I want this feature to be added to this object." A Transform is one component that every GameObject has. The Transform gives the object a position and scale in the game world. Yet, a wide variety of other components can also be added to a GameObject. Still focusing on the Inspector tab of the Player object, you will notice that a pair of additional components are present. One is the UserMove script. This is where we have been writing all of our code. However, our code only applies to the Player object once it has been attached as a component. Hence, by attaching the UserMove script to the Player object, you are telling Luna to be controlled according to the code found within the script. The other component attached to our Player object is a SpriteRenderer. In Unity, a SpriteRenderer is used to display a 2D graphic. In our case, this SpriteRenderer is what makes Luna appear as she does on the screen. Without it, she would be invisible. The SpriteRenderer also grants Luna dimensions, based on the fact that the sprite is a 64 × 64 pixel image. Thus, to solve our current challenge, we need to retrieve Luna's width and height from the SpriteRenderer component of the Player GameObject in our scene. Subsequently, we must use those dimensions in the code of the UserMove script, which is also attached to the Player GameObject.

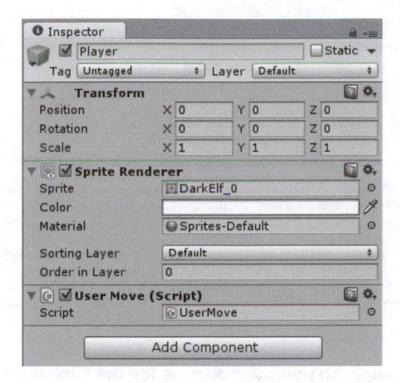

Figure 3.6 In the Unity scene, Luna is represented by the Player `GameObject`. This `GameObject` has `Transform`, `SpriteRenderer`, and script components.

Conveniently, Unity provides us with a simple way to access the components attached to a `GameObject` using code. From within a given script, we can use the `gameObject` command to reference the `GameObject` to which that script is attached. For instance, if we type the `gameObject` command into our UserMove script, we are referring to the Player `GameObject` in our Unity scene. Furthermore, we can access other components attached to the same object as our script, such as a `SpriteRenderer`. For example, we can access the Player object's `SpriteRenderer` component from our UserMove script by typing `gameObject.GetComponent<SpriteRenderer>()`. Moreover, we can even access the variables within the different components this way. Thus, to get the dimensions of the Player `GameObject` via its `SpriteRenderer`, we can type `gameObject.GetComponent<SpriteRenderer>().bounds.size.x` for the width and `gameObject.GetComponent<SpriteRenderer>().bounds.size.y` for the height. These relationships are summarized in the following sample code:

```
/*
Luna is made up of the
Player GameObject and its
attached components in our
Unity project.
*/
```

```
//from inside the UserMove script
//access the Player GameObject
gameObject

//access the SpriteRenderer
gameObject.GetComponent<SpriteRenderer>()

//access the SpriteRenderer's width
gameObject.GetComponent<SpriteRenderer>().bounds.size.x

//access the SpriteRenderer's height
gameObject.GetComponent<SpriteRenderer>().bounds.size.y
```

With this code, you are able to access Luna's dimensions. Therefore, you can adjust your boundary collision code to account for her center origin point, width, and height. Thus, you can finally prevent Luna from moving past the edges of the screen, regardless of her size. Dive into the code and implement your solution!

On a side note, be aware that you will regularly use the notation demonstrated in this challenge to access the components of `GameObjects`. It is quite common to retrieve information about the objects in your game world from within your code. You will become familiar with this approach throughout the challenges in this book, as well as your continued game development. This is only the beginning.

▌ Example Solution: Accounting for the Character

The final step in completing our boundary collision checks requires us to account for Luna's size. To do so, we access the width and height of the `SpriteRenderer` component attached to the Player `GameObject` in Unity. Using these dimensions, we can adjust our existing boundary checks, like so. The code added for this step is in bold.

```
//excerpt from MoveObject() function

//check x axis
//left edge of player is past left side of screen
if (newX - 0.5f * gameObject.GetComponent<SpriteRenderer>().bounds.
    size.x < -0.5f * Screen.width / 100.0f) {

    //stop player at edge
    newX = -0.5f * Screen.width / 100.0f + 0.5f * gameObject.
        GetComponent<SpriteRenderer>().bounds.size.x;

} //end if

//right edge of player is past right side of screen
if (newX + 0.5f * gameObject.GetComponent<SpriteRenderer>().bounds.
    size.x > 0.5f * Screen.width / 100.0f) {

    //stop player at edge
    newX = 0.5f * Screen.width / 100.0f - 0.5f * gameObject.
        GetComponent<SpriteRenderer>().bounds.size.x;

} //end if
```

```
//check y axis
//top edge of player is past top side of screen
if (newY + 0.5f * gameObject.GetComponent<SpriteRenderer>().bounds.
    size.y > 0.5f * Screen.height / 100.0f) {

    //stop player at edge
    newY = 0.5f * Screen.height / 100.0f - 0.5f * gameObject.
        GetComponent<SpriteRenderer>().bounds.size.y;

} //end if

//bottom edge of player is past bottom side of screen
if (newY - 0.5f * gameObject.GetComponent<SpriteRenderer>().bounds.
    size.y < -0.5f * Screen.height / 100.0f) {

    //stop player at edge
    newY = -0.5f * Screen.height / 100.0f + 0.5f * gameObject.
        GetComponent<SpriteRenderer>().bounds.size.y;

} //end if
```

While the values for the boundaries of the screen have remained the same, two major aspects of our collision code have changed. First, within the parentheses of each `if` statement, we have offset our `newX` and `newY` checks by half of Luna's size. For the x axis, we use one-half of Luna's width. For the y axis, we use one-half of Luna's height. Similar to how we halved the width and height when finding the edges of the screen, we again take half of Luna's dimensions when locating her personal boundaries. Again, this is due to the fact that Luna's origin point is at her center. Since the `gameObject.GetComponent<SpriteRenderer>().bounds.size.x` and `gameObject.GetComponent<SpriteRenderer>().bounds.size.y` commands return Luna's entire width and height, we have to halve them to get the distance from her center point to her edges. Relative to her personal origin, Luna's left side is negative, while her right side is positive. Likewise, Luna's top side is positive, while her bottom side is negative. These calculations are visualized in Figure 3.7.

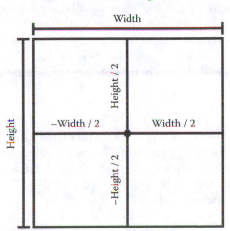

Figure 3.7 Luna's edge calculations relative to her center origin are shown.

With these implementations, we are now accurately checking Luna's left, right, top, and bottom sides against the left, right, top, and bottom edges of the screen.

The second adjustment to our code lies inside the brackets of our `if` statements. Here, after we have detected a collision, we must set Luna's position to be adjacent to the related boundary. In our prior code, we did not compensate for Luna's center origin point and allowed half of her to disappear from

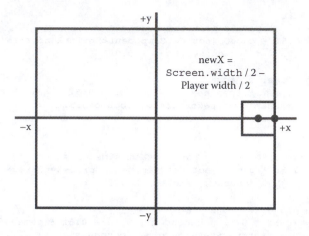

Figure 3.8 Previously, half of Luna would move off screen. However, by adjusting for her center origin point, we can ensure that she remains fully visible. In this example, we subtract half of her width from her x position to align her to the right edge of the screen.

the screen. However, with our adjustments, she will stay completely on the screen and her sides will touch the edge. To make this happen, we modify our newX and newY values to factor in half of Luna's size. For example, when moving right, Luna's right half would previously hang over the edge. Instead of letting this happen, we subtract an additional one-half of her width from the newX variable. This ensures that her right side is fully on the screen and touching the rightmost boundary. See Figure 3.8 for a visualization of this calculation.

Similar logic and calculations are applied to handle the left, top, and bottom collisions. To align Luna to the left edge of the screen, we add half of her width to newX. Next, to align Luna to the top edge of the screen, we subtract half of her height from newY. Last, to align Luna to the bottom edge of the screen, we add half of her height to newY. Each of these calculations compensate for the fact that Luna's origin is at her center and ensures that she is positioned exactly at the edge of the screen where we want her to be. Before you proceed, make sure you understand how the logic and code in this solution work. Drawing your own diagrams will aid you in interpreting this solution.

Summary

If you run your project in Unity and test it now, you will see that Luna stops just at the edges of the screen and does not move past them. Meanwhile, when she is not near the edges, she can move freely without interruption. Congratulations on completing this challenge. You have successfully implemented your first 2D collisions! You should now be familiar with all of these coding methods:

- Prevent a game character from moving outside the screen

- Logically determine how objects collide in 2D space

- Manipulate variable values using math and equality operators

- Modify variable values using expressions

- Convert between screen and world coordinates in Unity

- Access Unity game components from within your code

The excitement is just beginning as we continue to bring our game world to life. In Chapter 4, you will grant Luna special—dare we say, magical—powers.

Reference

Microsoft Corporation. 2015. C# Operators. http://msdn.microsoft.com/library/6a71f45d. aspx (accessed February 3, 2015).

4 Sprinting and Sneaking

Luna can move along the surface world, and we can ensure she will stay within the boundaries of the screen. With these fundamentals in place, let's give Luna some interesting things to do. For your first challenge, you will give Luna the ability to sprint at a faster speed than normal. Afterwards, you will grant her the magical power of invisibility. Creating these abilities will expose you to a variety of critical coding methods, such as the game loop and conditional statements. Let's get to work, so Luna can start doing awesome things in the game world.

▋ Goals

By the end of this chapter, you will be able to apply these coding techniques:

- Allow a character to sprint according to user input and energy limitations

- Make a character invisible based on user input and time-based limitations

- Implement frame-based and time-based systems

- Perform function calls

- Use Unity's `Update()` function to manage the game loop

- Apply conditional statements, including `if` and `switch`, along with Boolean operators

- Adjust variable values using the increment and decrement operators

- Modify variable access using getters and setters

- Use Unity's `GetComponent` command, along with dot notation, to access variables

- Manage game states with Boolean flags

- Create local variables within functions

▮ Required Files

In this chapter, you will need to use the following files from the *Chapter_04 > Software* folder:

- For the Making Luna Sprint challenge, see these files in the *PlayerSprint* folder:

  - *Challenge > Assets > Scenes > Map.unity* to run, modify, and test your solution

  - *Challenge > Assets > Scripts > UserSprint.cs* to code your solution to the challenge

  - *Demo > Mac/PC > PlayerSprint* to demonstrate how your completed solution should work

  - *Solution > PlayerSprint.cs* to compare your solution to the provided example solution

- For the Making Luna Invisible challenge, see these files in the *PlayerInvis* folder:

  - *Challenge > Assets > Scenes > Map.unity* to run, modify, and test your solution

  - *Challenge > Assets > Scripts > UserInvis.cs* to code your solution to the challenge

  - *Demo > Mac/PC > PlayerInvis* to demonstrate how your completed solution should work

  - *Solution > PlayerSprint.cs* to compare your solution to the provided example solution

Challenge: Making Luna Sprint

Your first challenge will be to grant Luna the ability to sprint. You will need to design and implement a particular system for handling this ability. As always, it is recommended that you begin by process mapping or pseudocoding to establish the logic behind your solution. Thereafter, you should begin to code it. To assist you with taking on this challenge, let's cover the basics of how your system should work once it is completed. Take a look at the UserSprint script in your code editor. In this file, you are provided with the following variables to start:

```
//the normal speed at which the player moves
private float _normalSpeed;

//the speed at which the player sprints
private float _sprintSpeed;

//the speed at which the player is currently moving
private float _currentSpeed;

//whether the player is currently sprinting
private bool _isSprinting;

//the player's remaining energy
private int _energy;
```

You should be able to manage your sprinting system using only these variables. Besides these, you are only given empty functions to work with. Specifically, you will need to initialize the variables in `Start()`, call functions from within `Update()`, and complete the `CheckUserInput()` and `CheckEnergy()` functions. Overall, your challenge is to find a way to manipulate the given variables so Luna can sprint. To make sure we are on the same page, here are some guidelines on how your sprint system should work:

1. Luna should start sprinting when a specific keyboard key is held.

2. Luna should stop sprinting when a specific keyboard key is released.

3. Luna can only sprint when she has energy.

4. When she is sprinting, Luna's energy should gradually reduce.

5. Should Luna's energy run out while sprinting, she should stop sprinting.

6. When she is not sprinting, Luna's energy should gradually increase.

Using these guidelines and the provided variables, work on sorting out the logic for your solution. Once you have a sound logic established, begin to code your solution. Let the upcoming hints provide you with additional guidance.

Hint: Function Calls

Calling a function is a bit like calling a person by name. For humans, calling someone's name gets her attention. If you are calling someone, you are probably providing or requesting something. Likewise, calling a function in a computer language requires you to use the name of the function in your code. Depending on the circumstances, you can be providing data to a function, requesting data from a function, or asking a function to do something. In the current challenge, you only need to ask a function to execute its code. To do this, you type the name of the function, followed by parentheses. For example, to call the `CheckUserInput()` function, you would use the following code. An example for the `CheckEnergy()` function is also provided.

```
//call the check user input function
CheckUserInput(); //this function's code is executed at this
    point

//call the check energy function
CheckEnergy(); //this function's code is executed at this point
```

Since a function's code is executed at the moment it is called, and prior to any subsequent code, it is important to think about when you need to call functions. The order in which you call different functions is important as well, because certain things need to happen in your code before others. Another consideration to make is whether your function needs to run continuously throughout the program, at specific times, or only once. Conditions like these will impact when you choose to call a function.

■ Hint: The Unity `Update()` Function

`Update()` is a special function in Unity. Unlike the `Start()` function, which is called only once, `Update()` is called many times per second. Therefore, we use `Update()` to handle things that need to happen repeatedly throughout our game. Any code placed inside the update function will repeat every *frame* (Unity Technologies n.d.b).

If you've ever worked with movies or animations, you may be familiar with frames. Indeed, movies were invented based on the concept of frames. A movie is not truly a smooth flow of continuous action as we perceive it to be. Instead, a movie is made of many individual still images, called frames. When these frames are placed back-to-back and swapped at a high rate of speed, our eyes perceive motion. The *frame rate*, measured in frames per second (fps), is commonly used to describe how fast these still images are swapped. For movies, animations, and games, you may have heard of common frame rates, such as 24, 30, and 60 fps. Games, in particular, are often recommended to run at 30 to 60 fps. However, depending on an individual player's hardware, how optimized the game code is, and other factors, the actual frame rate will vary.

In a movie, a frame is one still image that gets combined with many others to form a moving picture. However, in a game, each individual frame captures the state of our world at a given instant. As we put many frames together, things gradually happen within our game world. For example, when we make Luna move, we are taking advantage of frames and the `Update()` function. If you look back at the UserMove script, you will see that the `MoveObject()` function has been placed within `Update()`. This means that `MoveObject()`

is being called many times per second. Inside the `MoveObject()` function, we use a speed and direction to update Luna's position on the screen. Thus, in a single frame, we only make the slightest adjustment to Luna's position. Yet, since we are updating Luna's position many times per second, we perceive her as moving smoothly across the screen. Hence, our `MoveObject()` code is designed to adjust Luna's position one time within a single frame. We then leverage the `Update()` function to ensure that her position is updated over and over throughout the game.

The `Update()` function can be used for more purposes than just motion. Recall that a frame represents the state of our game at a given moment. Depending on the style of game, we may be doing many things within that moment, such as checking collisions, creating and destroying objects, accepting user input, making artificial intelligence (AI) decisions, and more. When all of these game actions have taken place within a single frame, we have completed one *game loop*. The game loop is a common term used to describe one complete cycle of events in a video game. Most games are designed such that all of the continuous actions that take place are handled with a single frame in mind. Subsequently, to produce the actual gameplay, these actions are repeated many times per second. In Unity, `Update()` is the built-in function that we use to manage our game loop. Any time you have code that needs to run continuously throughout your game, you want to put it inside `Update()`. Things like moving objects, checking collisions, determining game states, and accepting user input are all good candidates for inclusion in the `Update()` function.

In fact, the current challenge requires you to call functions that handle user input and energy from within the `Update()` function of the UserSprint script. Why? Well, you need to constantly watch for user input to determine whether the player is trying to sprint or not. At the same time, you need to constantly update Luna's energy level based on whether she is sprinting (drain energy) or not sprinting (recharge energy). Be sure to add these two function calls to `Update()` in your UserSprint script.

▌ Hint: Conditional Statements

Conditional statements are one of the most fundamental components of all computer programming. They can be used for a variety of purposes, such as introducing limits, comparing values, and checking states. The key feature of conditional statements is that they control *when* and *whether* code is executed. Without them, all of your program's code would always be executed. However, using conditional statements, you can specify the circumstances under which events happen in your game.

Interestingly enough, you already made use of conditional statements in your previous challenge. When you checked Luna's boundaries against the edge of the screen, you put code inside the parentheses of an `if` statement.

Recall that your task at that time was to compare Luna's position against the edges of the screen. While you did not write the structure of the `if` statements, you applied the conditions that would determine whether the code inside executes. For example, inside the parentheses of one `if` statement, you asked whether Luna's x position is greater than the right edge of the screen (newX > 0.5f * Screen.width / 100.0f). The answer to this question can only be true or false at a given moment. If it is false, the code within the brackets of the if statement is not run. In contrast, when the condition within the parentheses of the if statement is true, the code within the brackets is executed. In our example, this means that Luna's movement is stopped at the right edge of the screen if, and only if, her x position attempts to go beyond the right edge of the screen. As you can see, the if statement helps us to control when and whether things happen in our game world.

Let's consider the basic anatomy of the if statement. It begins with the keyword if. Next come two parentheses. A condition that can evaluate to true or false must be placed within these parentheses. Then come two brackets. Any code placed within these brackets will execute whenever the condition evaluates to true.

```
if ( /*Place true/false condition here.*/ ) {

    /*
    Code that executes when the statement
    is true should be placed here.
    */
}
```

Take an example from your current challenge. Perhaps you want to use the CheckUserInput() function to determine whether the player is holding the sprint key. If so, you can update the _isSprinting variable. Your code might look something like this:

```
//if player holds shift key
if (Input.GetKey(KeyCode.LeftShift)) {

    //toggle sprinting flag
    _isSprinting = true;

} //end if
```

This code uses an if statement to check whether the left shift key is being held. When the key is being held, it updates the _isSprinting variable to true. Otherwise, nothing happens. However, sometimes we want other things to happen. Fortunately, we can extend our if statements using another keyword, else. The else keyword can be used to add additional conditions via else if. It can also be used to apply a catchall condition via else alone. This is the basic structure for an if statement with multiple conditions.

```
if ( /*condition*/ ) {

    //code that executes when condition is true

}

/*
If the original condition was false,
the statement will proceed to check
```

```
the first else if condition.
*/

else if ( /*condition*/ ) {

        //code that executes when condition is true

}

/*
Any number of additional else if
statements could be placed here,
between the starting if and the
ending else. They will be checked
in order from top to bottom. If
any condition is found to be true
along the way, the if statement
stops there and executes the code.
*/

else {

        /*
        This code executes only if none of
        the previous conditions in the if
        and else if statements were true.
        */

}
```

A multicondition `if` statement must start with a basic `if` condition. There can only be one, and it must be placed at the very start. By comparison, there can be any number of `else  if` conditions. These are structured identically to the basic `if` condition, except that the keyword `else` comes before `if`. Lastly, a single, optional, `else` condition may come at the very end. Note that this ending `else` statement contains no parentheses or condition. This is because the ending `else` statement executes only when all of the other conditions are false. You can think of this `else` as a default circumstance that represents what happens if none of the special conditions are true. It can also be used to handle exceptional circumstances, such as errors. Let's expand upon our `CheckUserInput()` example by using a multicondition `if` statement:

```
//if player holds shift key
if (Input.GetKey(KeyCode.LeftShift)) {

        //toggle sprinting flag
        _isSprinting = true;

} //end if

//if player releases shift key
else if (Input.GetKeyUp(KeyCode.LeftShift)) {

        //toggle sprinting flag
        _isSprinting = false;

} //end if
```

```
//handle default or error cases
else {

        /*
        If there is something we need to do
        when the key is not being held
        or released, we can do it here. For
        example, we might print a message
        to the console.
        */

        Debug.Log("Sprint key neither held nor released");

}
```

Our updated if statement checks not only for when the left shift key is being held, but also for when it is released. Using else if, when the key is released, the _isSprinting variable is updated to false. Meanwhile, our ending else statement simply prints a confirmation message to the Unity Console window using the Debug.Log() command (Unity Technologies n.d.a).

That concludes your introduction to the if statement. You now have the ability to create more powerful game features and control how your code operates. Before continuing with the challenge, we'll cover another common conditional statement, called switch.

The switch statement is another technique that you can use to apply conditions to your code. Given a single variable, switch checks the variable's value against a series of mutually exclusive possible values. These possible values are called *cases*. Once a case is determined to be true, the code inside that case is executed. Let's look at the basic C# switch statement structure.

```
switch ( /*variable*/ ) {

    case /*one possible value*/:

        //code that executes when case is true

        break;

    case /*another possible value*/:

        //code that executes when case is true

        break;

    /*
    Any number of additional cases
    could be placed here, before
    the ending default case, so
    long as each checks for a
    unique possible value.
    */

    default:

        //code that executes when no other cases are true

        break;

}
```

The statement begins with its namesake keyword, switch. A single variable should be placed within the parentheses that follow. Inside the opening bracket, a series of cases form the body of the statement. For each case, the case keyword must be followed with a constant value (that is, not an expression, calculation, or anything other than a solitary value) and a colon. Placed within each case is code that will run in the event that case is true. This interior code can be unique to each case. Afterwards, each individual case is ended with the break keyword and a semicolon. The break keyword tells the switch statement to stop executing and allows the program to move on to subsequent code that lies outside of the statement. Hence, once we have found the one true case in a switch statement, we want to execute its code and move on to other things, rather than continuing to search through any subsequent false cases. This is what break does for us. Note that there can be any number of case statements, as long as each one checks for a unique value. Once all of the cases have been listed, the default case completes the body of the switch statement. For the default case, the default keyword is followed by a colon, then the code that will execute, the break keyword, and a semicolon. Unlike the case statements, default has no value to check for. Instead, the default case automatically executes when no other provided case is true. Therefore, default is quite similar to the ending else from the if statement. Similarly, the default case can be used to handle things like errors or exceptional circumstances. You should always include a default case in your switch statements. Lastly, following the default case, a closing bracket signals the end of the entire switch statement. Let's take a look at a partial example that you might apply to your CheckEnergy() function in the current challenge.

```
//check whether sprinting
switch (_isSprinting) {

    //is sprinting
    case true:

        //insert code to modify player's energy and speed
        break;

    //not sprinting
    case false:

        //insert code to modify player's energy and speed
        break;

    //default
    default:

        //insert code to handle errors or other exceptions
        break;

}
```

The demonstrated switch statement checks the current value of the _isSpriting Boolean variable. If it is true, that means the player is currently sprinting. Therefore, it would be good to place code that increases Luna's speed and drains her energy here. Conversely, in the false case, Luna is not sprinting.

Thus, her speed and energy should be adjusted accordingly. Finally, a default case is provided to complete the statement. You can use a `switch` statement like this in the `CheckEnergy()` function for your current challenge. Of course, you will need to add a bit of your own code to handle Luna's speed and energy according to whether she is or is not sprinting.

Most of the time, `switch` is functionally identical to the `if` statement. Yet, the `switch` statement has a unique structure and usage limitations that do not apply to `if` statements. In some instances, you might find that you like the cleanliness and organization of a `switch` statement. However, it is limited to checking a single variable across a set of mutually exclusive possible values. This makes it much less versatile than the `if` statement, which can easily handle expressions and comparisons between multiple values at once. As you develop your personal coding style, you should experiment with both statements and determine the circumstances in which you prefer to use each one.

You have been introduced to the basics of the `if` and `switch` statements. These are some extremely powerful coding tools that open up a new world of possibilities for your development of games. Get some practice with these coding methods by applying them to solve your current challenge.

▌ Hint: Increment and Decrement Operators

We previously discussed the use of math and equality operators. Among the many additional operators available in C# are the increment (++) and decrement (--) operators. These members of the unary operator family are handy for making fast, shorthand adjustments to our variables. The increment operator adds 1 to a variable, whereas the decrement operator subtracts 1 from a variable. Thus, rather than typing out a longer expression, we can use these operators whenever we need to adjust a value by just 1. The following sample code demonstrates this point:

```
//increment the _energy variable by 1
//3 different ways, from long to short
_energy = _energy + 1
_energy += 1
_energy++
```

As you can see, the increment operator is the shortest to type, although each line has the same outcome. While they are fast and easy to use, the downside is that the increment and decrement operators only modify a value by 1. Therefore, if we need to use a value other than 1, we will need to use a longer expression. Table 4.1 summarizes the increment and decrement operators. Code samples are provided for demonstration purposes:

Table 4.1 Increment and Decrement Operators

Operators	Symbols
Increment	++
Decrement	--

```
//increment
//add one to energy
_energy++

//decrement
//subtract one from energy
_energy--
```

You may have inferred from the code samples that these operators can help solve your current challenge. Do not hesitate to use them to increase and decrease your `_energy` variable as Luna sprints and rests. Furthermore, even beyond this challenge, you will find the increment and decrement operators useful in many coding situations.

▮ Hint: Getters and Setters

Let's take a moment to discuss an interesting situation that appears in our current challenge. This is the first challenge in which you have worked with two separate scripts. In addition to the UserMove script from our earlier challenge, you are now coding the UserSprint script. Therefore, this is a good time to point out that your scripts can communicate with one another. Scroll to the very bottom of the UserSprint script. Here, you will find a getter and setter declaration for the `_currentSpeed` variable.

```
//getters and setters
public float currentSpeed {
    get { return _currentSpeed; }
    set { _currentSpeed = value; }
}
```

Our `_currentSpeed` variable is normally private, meaning it cannot be accessed or modified by other scripts. However, with a getter and setter, even a private variable can be used in external scripts. As you can see, the getter and setter declaration begins by defining a public version of the same variable, but with a new name. To make a getter, which allows other scripts to access the variable's value, we start a line with the `get` keyword. Within the brackets for the getter, we add any code that we want to execute whenever a script accesses the variable. In the most basic case, we simply provide the value of the variable. This requires using the `return` keyword, followed by the original variable name. To make a setter, which allows other scripts to modify the variable's value, we start a line with the `set` keyword. Within the brackets for the setter, we put the code that needs to execute whenever a script modifies the variable. In the simplest case, we merely update the value of the variable. This is done by assigning the original variable equal to the `value` keyword. The `value` keyword generically represents a value that may be assigned to the variable. From this, we can derive the basic syntax for getters and setters as follows. Of course, the `dataType` should be replaced with a real data type, such as `bool`, `float`, or `int`. Meanwhile, the `publicVarName` and `_privateVarName` will be variable names of your choice that vary from script to script.

```
//create a getter and setter
//define a public version of a variable with a data type and name
public dataType publicVarName {

    //create a getter with the get keyword
    //the return keyword is followed by the private variable
    get { return _privateVarName; }

    //create a setter with the set keyword
    //set the private variable equal to the value keyword
    set { _privateVarName = value; }

}
```

Getters and setters can be used in more advanced ways beyond this basic format. You can put additional code within your get{} and set{} functions to create custom behavior. For example, you could not only get the value of a variable, but also increment a counter to keep track of how many times it has been accessed by another script. Further, instead of only setting a variable's value, you could also trigger a related animation. Besides introducing custom behavior when our variable values are retrieved or modified, getters and setters allow private variables from one script to be accessed by other scripts. Typically, we don't want other scripts to modify our private variables. Yet, sometimes we need to give other scripts some degree of access. For instance, our UserMove script needs to retrieve Luna's speed from the UserSprint script. Continue to the next hint to find out exactly how this is done.

▌ Hint: Unity's GetComponent Command and Dot Notation

In previous challenges, Luna's speed was set to a fixed value in the UserMove script. However, with the introduction of the sprint ability, her speed can change during gameplay. Since the code managing her speed is now in the UserSprint script, but the code that manages her movement is still in the UserMove script, we must allow these scripts to communicate. To establish a connection, our UserMove script uses the getter in the UserSprint script to retrieve Luna's current speed. Open the UserMove script in your code editor and go to the beginning of the MoveObject() function. There, you will find this line of code:

```
//retrieve speed from sprint script
_speed = gameObject.GetComponent<UserSprint>().currentSpeed;
```

Recall that _speed is the variable in UserMove that factors into Luna's movement calculation. In the above line of code, currentSpeed is the public version of the private _currentSpeed variable in UserSprint. Since we defined currentSpeed publicly in a getter, UserMove is able to access it. In this manner, UserMove can retrieve Luna's current speed from UserSprint at any time and update its movement calculations accordingly.

Besides the _speed and currentSpeed variables in the provided line of code, there are a couple of other things you might be curious about. So, let's dissect the rest of the line to learn more about manipulating objects in Unity. For one, take note of the `gameObject` command. In Unity, whenever you type `gameObject` from a script (note the lowercase letter at the start of the command), you are referencing the Unity `GameObject` to which the script is attached. For example, if you click on the Player object in your Unity project and look at the Inspector window, you will see that the UserMove script is attached to it. Therefore, when you type `gameObject` into your UserMove script, you are referencing the Player object in the Unity scene. This `gameObject` command applies similarly to all Unity scripts. Thus, any time you want to access a script's parent `GameObject`, use the `gameObject` command.

Following `gameObject` is another useful Unity command, called `GetComponent`. This command allows you to retrieve any of the components attached to a GameObject. For instance, our Player object has a `Transform`, `SpriteRenderer`, UserMove script, and UserSprint script attached to it. All of these can be accessed from within a script using the `GetComponent` command. To do this, start by typing `GetComponent`. Within a pair of less than and greater than symbols, you put the type of object you are retrieving. Afterwards, a pair of parentheses signal the end of the command. In our code sample, the UserMove script is accessing the Player's UserSprint script. Therefore, UserSprint is the data type defined and the full command becomes `GetComponent<UserSprint>()`. Similarly, you can access other components attached to the Player, such as the `SpriteRenderer`. To do this, you would type `GetComponent<SpriteRenderer>()`. In fact, you already used this technique to find Luna's dimensions in the previous challenge. Overall, `GetComponent` is another tool you will want to keep in mind when working in Unity. It allows you to get the individual components attached to an object. After that, you can use your code to manipulate them.

Lastly, notice that we used `gameObject` and `GetComponent` together to form `gameObject.GetComponent<UserSprint>()`. Afterwards, we added a period (dot) and the name of the variable we wanted to access (`.currentSpeed`). This is known as *dot notation*. Basically, we can use dot notation to access a variable inside a script or component. Here, we used `gameObject.GetComponent<UserSprint>().currentSpeed` to access the `currentSpeed` variable inside the UserSprint script attached to the Player GameObject. Likewise, you can see another example of dot notation at the bottom of the `MoveObject()` function. There, we use `gameObject.transform.position` to set the `position` variable of the `Transform` component attached to the Player object. Dot notation is a handy way to access things inside things, such as variables inside scripts or functions inside objects. You will encounter and apply dot notation often in your C# coding.

With all that said, we have toured a variety of exciting code techniques in our challenge to make Luna sprint. We have learned about function calls, the `Update()` function, conditional statements, increment and decrement operators, getters and setters, and several ways to access information in Unity! You should apply these coding tools to solve the current challenge before proceeding to the example solution.

▎ Example Solution: Making Luna Sprint

Before describing the example solution, we should review the requirements for this challenge:

1. Luna should start sprinting when a specific keyboard key is held.

2. Luna should stop sprinting when a specific keyboard key is released.

3. Luna can only sprint when she has energy.

4. When she is sprinting, Luna's energy should gradually reduce.

5. Should Luna's energy run out while sprinting, she should stop sprinting.

6. When she is not sprinting, Luna's energy should gradually increase.

The associated logic is visualized in Figure 4.1.

We'll break these requirements down step-by-step to see how they can be translated into code. Naturally, to begin your solution, you need to initialize the variables in `Start()` and call the appropriate functions in `Update()`, like so:

```
void Start() {

      //normal speed in world coordinates
      _normalSpeed = 0.05f;

      //double normal speed
      _sprintSpeed = 2.0f * _normalSpeed;

      //default to normal speed
      _currentSpeed = _normalSpeed;

      //default to not sprinting
      _isSprinting = false;

      //maximum energy level to start
      _energy = 100;

} //end function
```

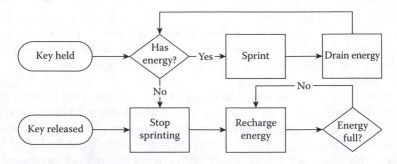

Figure 4.1 A process map illustrates the logic behind Luna's sprint ability.

```
void Update() {

        //check user input
        CheckUserInput();

        //check energy
        CheckEnergy();

} //end function
```

You may have selected different values for your variables. However, it makes sense that the sprint speed is higher than the normal speed, that the player begins at normal speed, and that the player is not sprinting at the beginning. Meanwhile, `CheckUserInput()` and `CheckEnergy()` both need to run continuously throughout our game and should be called within `Update()`. Returning to our requirements list, the first two items specifically address key presses and therefore pertain to our `CheckUserInput()` function.

```
private void CheckUserInput() {

        //if player holds shift key
        if (Input.GetKey(KeyCode.LeftShift)) {

                //toggle sprinting flag
                _isSprinting = true;

        } //end if

        //if player releases shift key
        else if (Input.GetKeyUp(KeyCode.LeftShift)) {

                //toggle sprinting flag
                _isSprinting = false;

        } //end if

} //end function
```

In this function, we use an `if` statement to check whether the left shift key is being held. If so, Luna's state is updated by setting the `_isSprinting` variable to `true`. If not, we use `else if` to check whether the player has released the left shift key. If so, Luna's state is returned to normal by setting the `_isSprinting` variable to `false`. In total, this function succinctly handles all user input related to Luna's sprint ability and simply updates her state accordingly. Continuing, the final four requirements can be handled in the `CheckEnergy()` function.

```
private void CheckEnergy() {

        //check whether sprinting
        switch (_isSprinting) {

                //is sprinting
                case true:

                        //energy remains
                        if (_energy > 0) {
```

```
                    //drain energy
                    _energy--;

                    //update speed
                    _currentSpeed = _sprintSpeed;

            } //end if

            //energy depleted
            else if (_energy <= 0) {

                    //set to min
                    _energy = 0;

                    //update speed
                    _currentSpeed = _normalSpeed;

            } //end inner if

            //each case of a switch statement requires a
                break
            break;

        //not sprinting
        case false:

            //energy is less than max
            if (_energy < 100) {

                    //replenish energy
                    _energy++;

                    //update speed
                    _currentSpeed = _normalSpeed;

            } //end if

            //energy is at max
            else if (_energy >= 100) {

                    //set to max
                    _energy = 100;

                    //update speed
                    _currentSpeed = _normalSpeed;

            } //end inner if

            break;

        //all switch statements should have a default condition
        default:
            break;

    } //end switch

} //end function
```

This is our most complex code to date. Did you know that you can put an `if` statement inside of a `switch` statement? That is what's happening here. For that matter, you can also put `switch` inside of `if`, `if` inside of `if`, `switch` inside of `switch`, and so on. You may have used some combination of techniques like this in your own solution, or perhaps you used completely separate statements throughout. When we put multiple statements inside of one another, they are called *nested* statements. This is perfectly valid code and allows us to apply multiple combinations of conditions at once. However, it is best to limit nesting to just a couple of statements at a time, since any more will render our code illegible. Now that this nesting situation has been exposed, let's step through the code to figure out how it works.

```
//excerpt from CheckEnergy() function

//check whether sprinting
switch (_isSprinting) {

    //is sprinting
    case true:

        //energy remains
        if (_energy > 0) {

            //drain energy
            _energy--;

            //update speed
            _currentSpeed = _sprintSpeed;

        } //end if

        //energy depleted
        else if (_energy <= 0) {

            //set to min
            _energy = 0;

            //update speed
            _currentSpeed = _normalSpeed;

        } //end inner if

        //each case of a switch statement requires a break
        break;
```

It all begins with a `switch` statement that checks the current value of the `_isSpriting` Boolean variable. The first case we arrive at is the `true` condition. When Luna is sprinting, we use a nested `if` statement to check if her energy is greater than 0. Recall that she cannot sprint if she doesn't have energy (requirement 3). If she does have energy, then her energy is decremented and her speed is set to sprint (requirement 4). On the contrary, if her energy falls below the minimum of 0, we stop reducing it and return her speed to the normal level (requirement 5). The *true* case, as with all cases, ends in a *break*.

```
//excerpt from CheckEnergy() function

//not sprinting
case false:

        //energy is less than max
        if (_energy < 100) {

                //replenish energy
                _energy++;

                //update speed
                _currentSpeed = _normalSpeed;

        } //end if

        //energy is at max
        else if (_energy >= 100) {

                //set to max
                _energy = 100;

                //update speed
                _currentSpeed = _normalSpeed;

        } //end inner if

        break;
```

The next switch case handles when the _isSprinting variable is false. We know that we want Luna's energy to recharge whenever she is not sprinting (requirement 6). Therefore, a nested if statement within this case asks whether Luna's energy is less than the maximum value of 100. If so, Luna's energy is incremented and her speed remains at the normal level. On the other hand, if her energy exceeds the maximum, we stop increasing it and maintain her normal speed.

```
//all switch statements should have a default condition
default:
        break;
```

Lastly, the default case handles the unexpected situation that _isSprinting winds up being neither true nor false. While unlikely, this could happen if someone mistakenly changed _isSprinting from bool to another data type or stored the wrong kind of data in the variable. Hence, we always maintain the default case for good measure. In the end, with just a single switch statement and two nested if statements, we were able to manage Luna's speed and energy. Combined with our user input function, we have successfully granted Luna the ability to sprint. Our UserSprint script is officially complete.

▌ Challenge: Making Luna Invisible

While we're in the mood of granting special powers, why not allow Luna to become invisible? Your second challenge is to grant Luna invisibility. As with the sprint ability, you need to implement a logical system to handle invisibility.

To help you get started, we will cover the basics of how your invisibility system should function. Take a look at the UserInvis script in your code editor. In this file, you are provided with these variables:

```
//whether the player can currently use invisibility
private bool _canInvis;

//whether the player is currently invisible
private bool _isInvis;

//the duration of the invisibility effect
private float _duration;

//the cooldown time
private float _cooldown;

//the time at which the most recent invisibility/cooldown cycle
    started
private float _startTime;
```

You can create a fully functional invisibility system with only these variables. Furthermore, you are provided with two empty functions to complete, CheckUserInput() and CheckInvis(). Below are summary guidelines on how your invisibility system should work:

1. Luna should become invisible when a specific keyboard key is pressed once.

2. Luna should become visible after the duration of her invisibility has ended.

3. After Luna becomes visible again, the cooldown period begins.

4. Luna can only go invisible again after the cooldown period has ended.

Work on solidifying your logic before you begin to code. As you put your solution into place through code, let these hints provide you with additional assistance.

▌▌ Hint: Boolean Flags

Boolean flags, or simply flags, are variables used to control conditions in our code. Since a Boolean variable can only be true or false at a given moment, it is convenient to use such variables to identify different game states. With a single Boolean flag, you can represent two states, such as win or lose. If you put two flags together, you can achieve a total of four unique states. When used effectively, flags give you extra control over your code by determining if and when certain events take place. Therefore, flags are an excellent complement to conditional statements.

For your current challenge, two flags are provided in the UserInvis script. These are _canInvis and _isInvis. The former should be used to determine whether Luna can or cannot become invisible, whereas the latter tells us whether Luna is or is not invisible at this moment. Think about the requirements for this challenge and how these flags can help you manage Luna's possible states. Luna should become invisible when a key is pressed (requirement 1), but only if the cooldown has ended (requirement 4). Surely, the _canInvis flag can be used to make Luna invisible if the key is pressed and she is able to become invisible at that moment. Furthermore, when Luna is invisible, we should keep track of the ability's duration, since she can only stay invisible for so long. Likewise, when Luna is not invisible, we must keep track of the cooldown period to know when she can use her ability again. Thus, the _isInvis flag can be used to guide whether we should keep track of Luna's invisibility duration or the ability's cooldown period at a given time. In total, with _canInvis and _isInvis, you are able to manage Luna's ability to become invisible. Be sure to make use of these flags in your solution.

■ Hint: Boolean Operators

Boolean operators are among the many operators in C# that help us to realize our logic through code. One Boolean operator is the *conditional and*. It is represented by a double ampersand symbol, &&. When this is used inside a conditional statement, like if, it allows multiple conditions to be evaluated at once. For example, consider the following code:

```
if (x == 5 && y > 0)
```

This if statement asks whether the variable x equals 5 *and* the variable y is greater than 0. The entire statement only evaluates to true if both conditions are true. If either x does not equal 5 or y is less than or equal to 0, the entire statement would evaluate to false. Hence, the code within this if statement will only run when both conditions are true. This is the effect of the && operator. It allows us to apply multiple conditions to a single statement and check whether all of them are true. You are not limited to using a single && operator per statement. Therefore, you are free to chain together multiple conditions this way. However, it is good practice to limit yourself to using just a few at a time for better code readability and organization.

Another Boolean operator is the *conditional or*, which is represented by a pair of vertical bars, ||. When used in a conditional statement, the statement will evaluate to true if either of the conditions is true. For instance, consider this code:

```
if (x == 5 || y > 0)
```

Here, if x equals 5 *or* y is greater than zero, the entire statement will evaluate to true. Unlike the && operator, which required both conditions to be true, the || operator only requires one of the conditions to be true. Hence, if x equals 4, but y equals 1, the example code would still evaluate to true using the || operator. Like the && operator, || can be used many times within a single conditional statement.

Yet another related operator worth mentioning is the *logical not*. Surprisingly, it is represented by an exclamation mark, !. When placed in front of a condition, this operator means to take the opposite of that condition. Consider that our conditional statements are being evaluated as either true or false. Therefore, to take the opposite is to take false when a statement is true or true when a statement is false. This is demonstrated in the following code sample:

```
//imagine a light switch is represented by the isOn Boolean variable

//the switch is turned on
isOn //true
!isOn //false

//the switch is turned off
isOn //false
!isOn //true
```

As you can see, applying the ! operator simply takes the opposite true or false value of whatever it precedes. Moreover, we previously discussed the use of this operator with the equal sign in an earlier chapter. To reiterate, when != is used, a condition will be true whenever one value is not equal to another. Along with && and ||, the ! operator can be used in conjunction with Boolean flags and conditional statements to add more control to your code. Furthermore, be aware that these operators can be used together in a variety of combinations. Can you interpret the meaning of this example statement? Under which circumstances would it evaluate to true?

```
if (x == 5 && y > 0 || z != 10)
```

In this code sample, all three operators are used together. For the statement to be true, x must equal 5 *and* y must be greater than 0 *or* z must not equal 10. Hence, if x is 5 and y is greater than 0, the statement is true. Likewise, if z does not equal 10, the statement is true. But, if x does not equal 5 or y is less than or equal to 0 and z equals 10, then the statement is false. Clearly, these operators open many avenues for managing game states and conditions in your code. Table 4.2 summarizes the Boolean operators.

In terms of your current challenge, you can use Boolean operators and flags together to great effect. Remember our guidelines that Luna should become invisible when a key is pressed (requirement 1) and that she can only become invisible if the cooldown has ended (requirement 4). Inside the CheckUserInput() function, we might represent those conditions like so:

```
//if player presses key and is able to go invisible
if (Input.GetKeyDown(KeyCode.I) && _canInvis == true) {

    /*
    Code to be executed if statement
    is true should be placed here.
    */

} //end if
```

Table 4.2 Boolean Operators

Operator	Symbol
Conditional and	&&
Conditional or	||
Logical not	!

This code uses the && operator to check for both a key press and the ability to become invisible. Only if Luna is currently able to become invisible and the player presses the corresponding key will we proceed to execute the necessary code for her ability. You may want to apply this approach to the CheckUserInput() function in your solution. Think about what code should go inside this if statement. Also, be aware that there may be opportunities to use Boolean operators and flags inside the CheckInvis() function for this challenge.

▐ Hint: Unity's `Time.time` Command

In Unity, the Time.time command returns the time, in seconds, since the game started running (Unity Technologies n.d.c). This time is sampled at the start of a given frame. From a logical standpoint, you can think of Time.time as being the time *right now*. Therefore, whenever you need to know the time at a given instant, use Time.time.

To begin the current challenge, you were provided with the _startTime variable. This represents the time at which the most recent invisibility or cooldown cycle started. From our guidelines, we know that Luna stays invisible for only a limited amount of time (requirement 2) and that a cooldown period follows before she can become invisible again (requirement 3). Thus, we need to keep track of how long Luna has been invisible in order to make her visible at the right time. Likewise, we have to keep track of how long the cooldown period has lasted in order to allow her to use her ability again. Therefore, the first thing we need to know is when exactly Luna last changed states. To do this, we can update the _startTime variable whenever Luna becomes invisible or visible. Unity's Time.time command allows us to accomplish this task, like so:

```
/*
At the moment Luna becomes invisible or
becomes visible after being invisible, we
should update our start time variable
*/
_startTime = Time.time;
```

Remember that Time.time gives us a value that represents the present moment. This is perfect for updating our _startTime variable each time Luna changes states from being visible to invisible or vice versa. In your solution, make sure that you are updating _startTime whenever a new invisibility or cooldown cycle begins.

▐ Hint: Local Variables

You have created and made use of many variables in your challenges. Thus far, all of these have been *global* variables. Global variables are defined within the *class* section of a script, but outside of any particular function. Since they do not belong to a specific function, they exist throughout an entire script and can be accessed by other scripts. In contrast, *local* variables are defined within a single function. Such variables only exist within a given function and cannot be accessed outside of it. This relationship is demonstrated by the following code sample, which depicts a common class script setup in C# and Unity:

```
//an example class script
public class ClassName : MonoBehaviour {

    //global variables go here
    private bool isGlobal; //this is an example of a global
        variable

    //an example function
    private void ExampleFunction() {

        //local variables go here
        bool isLocal; //this is an example of a local
            variable

    } //end function

} //end class
```

In this code sample, the global variable lies within the brackets of the class definition. Meanwhile, the local variable is contained within the brackets of an individual function. Further, note that the local variable does not have an access level, such as `public` or `private`, associated with it. This is because a local variable cannot be accessed anywhere but inside its own function. Therefore, it would be irrelevant to assign an access level. On a related point, local variables have no need for getters or setters, because there is nothing outside their own function that can retrieve or modify them. Local variables freely exist within their own functions and nowhere else within our code. With these exceptions noted, local variables are similar to global variables in terms of declaration and usage. To declare a local variable, simply list the data type followed by a valid variable name and a semicolon. You can assign values to local variables the same way as with global variables. Local variables can also be manipulated using operators and everything else we've learned so far. The major difference is that a local variable can only be utilized within the function in which it was created.

You may be curious when to use global and local variables. A sound guideline is to use local variables wherever you can and only use global variables when you truly need them. In other words, whenever you can accomplish what you need to inside the body of a function, do so using local variables. Yet, when the need arises to communicate across functions or throughout multiple scripts, you have to use global variables. A reason that local variables are generally preferred is that they consume less computer memory. They have a very short lifespan, since they are only created inside a single function, and then destroyed after the function has executed. In contrast, global variables exist for the entire lifetime of a script, which often means the entire duration of the program. Therefore, global variables are perpetually consuming computer resources. If you use too many of them, your game may not run as efficiently, especially on less powerful hardware. Too many global variables can also make it difficult to keep track of the information flowing through your code. Thus, think of global variables as things you must use to communicate throughout and across different scripts. For everything that can be accomplished in one place, try to use local variables instead.

The current challenge provides you with an opportunity to showcase your understanding of local variables. In a previous hint, you updated the _startTime variable using Time.time. This makes sure that the beginning of the latest invisibility or cooldown cycle has been stored for later use. This variable is global because it marks a specific point in time that needs to be referenced many times over in the future. Hence, it needs to live on longer than a single function. After updating the _startTime whenever Luna changes visibility, the other thing we need to do is keep track of how long her current state has lasted. This is where our local variable comes into play. The CheckInvis() function is responsible for managing these states, so we'll put the code there. Using a single local variable, we can check how long it has been since we last updated _startTime.

```
//calculate the duration of the current invisibility/cooldown cycle
float cycleDuration = Time.time - _startTime;
```

Inside our CheckInvis() function, we create a local variable called cycleDuration. We set this variable equal to Time.time (the time right at this moment) minus the _startTime (a time that we saved in the past). Thus, the difference is equal to the total amount of time since Luna last switched states. By using our global _startTime variable and temporarily recreating our local cycleDuraton variable each time the CheckInvis() function is run, we are constantly keeping track of how long it has been since Luna last became visible or invisible. But, how do we know whether Luna is currently visible or invisible? Don't forget that you have the _isInvis flag to keep track of that. Moreover, if you know Luna's current state and how long she has been in that state, how do you know if it is time to switch? That is what our _duration and _cooldown variables are for. If Luna is invisible and the cycleDuration has exceeded the _duration, you should make her visible and reset _startTime. Similarly, if Luna is visible and the cycleDuration is greater than the _cooldown, you should allow her to use her ability again by updating _canInvis. See if you can translate this logic into code as you build the CheckInvis() function.

Hint: Unity SpriteRenderer Visibility

The final task necessary to complete this challenge is to actually make Luna invisible. We can do this by accessing and manipulating the SpriteRenderer component attached to our Player GameObject. In an earlier challenge, you used the size of Luna's SpriteRenderer (that is, GetComponent<SpriteRenderer>(). bounds.size) to retrieve her dimensions and check for collisions at the screen boundaries. Similarly, you need to access the SpriteRenderer component again in this challenge. However, this time, you will modify a different property of that component.

All Unity components have an `enabled` property. Essentially, this is a Boolean flag that tells whether the component is or is not active. If it is active, it is free to do whatever it does. If it is not active, it is unable to do anything. The job of a `SpriteRenderer` is to display a 2D image. If it is enabled, the image will be displayed. If it is not enabled, the image will not be displayed. As you may have predicted, we can enable or disable Luna's `SpriteRenderer` component to make her visible or invisible. Here is the code that you can use to do it:

```
//access the SpriteRenderer of the Player GameObject
//use the enabled property to modify Luna's visibility

//make Luna visible
gameObject.GetComponent<SpriteRenderer>().enabled = true;

//make Luna invisible
gameObject.GetComponent<SpriteRenderer>().enabled = false;
```

As we have done before, we use the `gameObject` command to access the Unity `GameObject` that our current script is attached to. In this case, our UserInvis script is attached to the Player object. From there, we use the `GetComponent<SpriteRenderer>()` command to access the `SpriteRenderer` component attached to the Player object. Lastly, via dot notation, we access the `enabled` flag within the `SpriteRenderer`. To make Luna visible, set the `enabled` variable to `true`. To make Luna invisible, set the `enabled` variable to `false`. From here, it is just a matter of knowing when you want to make Luna visible or invisible and doing so at the appropriate times.

That's everything you need to know to successfully solve the current challenge and grant Luna the ability to become invisible. Use the power of flags, operators, local variables, and time itself to make it happen. Once you have your version working, proceed for a walk-through of the example solution.

▥ Example Solution: Making Luna Invisible

Now that we've looked at each piece of the puzzle and you have put together your own solution, let's walk through a demonstration of how Luna can be given the power of invisibility. The requirements for the invisibility system are listed:

1. Luna should become invisible when a specific keyboard key is pressed once.

2. Luna should become visible after the duration of her invisibility has ended.

3. After Luna becomes visible again, the cooldown period begins.

4. Luna can only go invisible again after the cooldown period has ended.

Subsequently, the logic for the example solution is visualized in Figure 4.2.

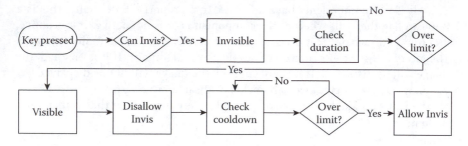

Figure 4.2 A process map illustrates the logic behind Luna's power of invisibility.

To begin, you need to initialize your variables in `Start()` and call the appropriate functions in `Update()`.

```
void Start() {

        //default to able to use
        _canInvis = true;

        //default to visible
        _isInvis = false;

        //one second duration
        _duration = 1.0f;

        //two second cooldown
        _cooldown = 2.0f;

        //start from current time
        _startTime = Time.time;

} //end function

void Update() {

        //check user input
        CheckUserInput();

        //check invisibility
        CheckInvis();

} //end function
```

Your values may differ from the ones shown in this example. Here, we assume that Luna is not invisible to start and will not become so until the player presses a key. Therefore, `_canInvis` is `true` and `_isInvis` is `false`. The `_duration` of invisibility is set to 1 second, while the `_cooldown` period is set to 2 seconds. We initialize the `_startTime` to the present for good measure. Afterwards, we call the `CheckUserInput()` and `CheckInvis()` functions in `Update()`. This is because we need to repeatedly check for key presses and determine Luna's invisibility state throughout the duration of the game. Next, we'll move on to the `CheckUserInput()` function:

```
private void CheckUserInput() {

        //if player presses key and is able to go invisible
        if (Input.GetKeyDown(KeyCode.I) && _canInvis == true) {
```

```
//toggle flags
_canInvis = false;
_isInvis = true;

//make player invisible by disabling renderer
gameObject.GetComponent<SpriteRenderer>().
    enabled = false;

//update start time
_startTime = Time.time;

    } //end if

} //end function
```

As we have done before, we will use the `CheckUserInput()` function to handle key presses from the player. To activate invisibility, a key must be pressed once (requirement 1). Thus, we use `Input.GetKeyDown()` to register the first frame in which the I key (`KeyCode.I`) is pressed. However, in this system, Luna cannot become invisible again until after a cooldown period ends (requirement 4). Hence, our `if` statement uses the `&&` operator to require both a key press and the `_canInvis` flag to be `true`. If either condition is not true, the inner code will not execute. For example, if the player is already invisible and the player presses the I key, nothing would happen. Yet, supposing the player triggers the ability when Luna is able to become invisible, we immediately switch our Boolean flags: `_canInvis` becomes `false`, while `_isInvis` becomes `true`. Then we physically make Luna invisible on the screen by disabling the `SpriteRenderer` component attached to the Player object. Finally, we update the `_startTime` to `Time.time` to mark the beginning of a new invisibility cycle. In `CheckUserInput()`, we have handled taking user input and kicking off Luna's invisibility. Then, we use `CheckInvis()` to further manager her states.

```
private void CheckInvis() {

    //calculate the duration of the current invisibility/cooldown
        cycle
    float cycleDuration = Time.time - _startTime;

    //player is currently invisible and
    //invisibility duration has been exceeded
    if (_isInvis == true && cycleDuration > _duration) {

        //toggle flag
        _isInvis = false;

        //update visibility
        gameObject.GetComponent<SpriteRenderer>().enabled =
            true;

        //update start time for cooldown
        _startTime = Time.time;

    } //end if
```

```
        //player is currently visible and
        //cooldown duration has been exceeded
        else if (_isInvis == false && cycleDuration > _cooldown) {

                //toggle flag
                _canInvis = true;

        } //end else if

} //end function
```

You may remember our discussion of local variables. We need to perpetually keep track of how long Luna has been invisible or how long her cooldown period has lasted to manage her states appropriately (requirements 2 and 3). To do this, we use the `cycleDuration` local variable in coordination with `Time.time` and `_startTime`.

```
//excerpt from CheckInvis() function

//calculate the duration of the current invisibility/cooldown cycle
float cycleDuration = Time.time - _startTime;
```

The calculated `cycleDuration` applies regardless of whether we are calculating how long Luna has currently been invisible or how long she has been in a cooldown period. By taking `Time.time` (the time right now) and subtracting the `_startTime` saved when Luna last switched states, we calculate the total amount of time since Luna last switched states. In the `if` statement that follows, we compare this value against the `_duration` or `_cooldown` as necessary, depending on whether she `_isInvis` or not at the present moment. Using `_isInvis` in this manner allows us to assign a different length of time to Luna's invisibility and cooldown periods.

```
//excerpt from CheckInvis() function
//player is currently invisible and
//invisibility duration has been exceeded
if (_isInvis == true && cycleDuration > _duration) {

        //toggle flag
        _isInvis = false;

        //update visibility
        gameObject.GetComponent<SpriteRenderer>().enabled = true;

        //update start time for cooldown
        _startTime = Time.time;

} //end if
```

In the initial `if` condition, if Luna is invisible for longer than the allowable amount of time, we immediately set `_isInvis` to false and enable the `SpriteRenderer` to show her on the screen. Since this signifies the beginning of a cooldown period, we also reset the `_startTime`.

```
//excerpt from CheckInvis() function

//player is currently visible and
//cooldown duration has been exceeded
else if (_isInvis == false && cycleDuration > _cooldown) {

    //toggle flag
    _canInvis = true;

} //end else if
```

In the `else if` case, should Luna be visible for long enough that the required cooldown period has been exceeded, we change the `_canInvis` flag to `true`. This allows the player to decide when to make Luna invisible again by pressing the required key. With that, the entire process of managing Luna's invisibility is complete.

Summary

You have granted Luna the powers of super sprint speed and magical invisibility. With these additions, our character is coming to life and your coding skills are rapidly developing. Having completed this chapter, you should be able to do all of these amazing things with your code:

- Allow a character to sprint according to user input and energy limitations

- Make a character invisible based on user input and time-based limitations

- Implement frame-based and time-based systems

- Perform function calls

- Use Unity's `Update()` function to manage the game loop

- Apply conditional statements, including `if` and `switch`, along with Boolean operators

- Adjust variable values using the increment and decrement operators

- Modify variable access using getters and setters

- Use Unity's `GetComponent` command, along with dot notation, to access variables

- Manage game states with Boolean flags

- Create local variables within functions

In your next challenge, you will apply what you have learned so far to start enhancing the surface world that Luna resides in.

References

Unity Technologies. n.d.a. Debug.Log. http://docs.unity3d.com/ScriptReference/Debug. Log.html (accessed February 16, 2015).

Unity Technologies. n.d.b. MonoBehaviour.Update. http://docs.unity3d.com/ ScriptReference/MonoBehaviour.Update.html (accessed February 16, 2015).

Unity Technologies. n.d.c. Time.time. http://docs.unity3d.com/ScriptReference/Time-time.html (accessed February 16, 2015).

5 Collectables

Luna is moving, sprinting, and sneaking through the surface world. Thus far, our game world consists of no more than an empty screen with boundaries at the edges. In this challenge, you will start bringing the game world to life. One way to do this is through the introduction of collectable objects. Once you know how to create collectables, you can add a variety of useful objects to your game world. Example game collectables include powerups, equipment, health, and treasure, just to name a few. Let's begin building our world by introducing collectable objects.

▌ Goals

By the end of this chapter, you will be able to apply these coding techniques:

- Create objects that can be collected by a game character

- Manipulate variables with primitive and composite data types

- Utilize tags to access objects in Unity

- Detect Axis-Aligned Bounding Box (AABB) collisions between objects

- Destroy objects in Unity

▎ Required Files

In this chapter, you will need to use the following files from the *Chapter_05 > Software* folder:

- *Challenge > Assets > Scenes > Map.unity* to run, modify, and test your solution

- *Challenge > Assets > Scripts > Collectable.cs* to code your solution to the challenge

- *Demo > Mac/PC > Collectable* to demonstrate how your completed solution should work

- *Solution > Collectable.cs* to compare your solution to the provided example solution

▎ Challenge: Collecting Objects

In this challenge, you will create a type of collectable object. Whenever Luna moves across one of these collectables, the object should be removed from the screen. You can think of this as simulating the act of Luna coming across a collectable in the game world and choosing to pick it up. Naturally, this process will involve detecting collisions between Luna and the collectable object. You successfully detected collisions in a past challenge when you kept Luna within the boundaries of the screen. You should leverage this knowledge to help you detect the necessary collisions in this challenge. Here is a summary of the requirements for this challenge:

1. The Collectable script, which is attached to each collectable object, should continuously check for collisions with Luna.

2. The CheckCollisions() function retrieves Luna's current position and uses it to check for collisions with the collectable.

3. If a collision is detected between a collectable object and Luna, the collectable object is destroyed.

Open the challenge project and the Map scene in Unity. In the Hierarchy window, click on the arrow beside the Middleground object to display its contents (Figure 5.1). You will see that four different collectable objects have been added to the scene. Each one has the Collectable script component attached to it. Your coding for this challenge will be done within this script. Hence, as you

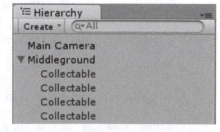

Figure 5.1 Expand the Middleground to see the collectable objects in the scene.

are solving the problem, make sure to think in terms of what needs to happen when Luna encounters a single collectable object. Once your solution is complete, it will apply to any number of collectables that are added to the game world.

For this challenge, you will work entirely within the Collectable script. You are required to declare and initialize any variables, call the appropriate functions in `Update()`, and complete the `CheckCollisions()` function. Remember that inside `CheckCollisions()`, you will need to determine whether or not Luna is colliding with the collectable object. If so, make sure to remove the object from the game world. Think through the logic of this problem before you dive into the code. It may be especially helpful for you to draw out how you will determine the collisions between Luna and the collectable objects. Furthermore, facilitate your problem solving with the provided hints.

▎ Hint: Primitive and Composite Data Types

To date, you have used variables with *primitive* data types in your code. These include the `bool`, `int`, `float`, and `double` variables that you are familiar with, as well as a few others in the C# language. These data types are called primitive because they cannot be broken down into any simpler form than they already are. That is, a `bool` is already as basic as it gets. It cannot be divided into any other data types. The same goes for other primitive data types.

In contrast, *composite* data types can be broken down into a collection of simpler data types. In fact, all composite data types are formed through a combination of other data types. Think back to our earlier discussion of strings. The `string` data type was singled out as different from `bool`, `int`, `float`, and `double`. This is because a `string` is actually a collection of characters, which are of the `char` primitive data type. Hence, a `string` is a composite data type that is made up of several primitive characters. As it happens, we often make use of composite objects that are created from a mixture of variables with primitive and composite data types.

For example, you can think of the Player `GameObject` in our Unity scene as being composite. It is made up of a collection of components, such as `SpriteRenderer`, `Transform`, and UserMove script. Each of these components is in turn made up of its own variables, which have primitive data types like `bool` and `int`, as well as composite data types, like `Sprite` and `Vector3`. Generally, this process of creating complex objects out of collections of simpler ones is known as *composition* in coding terminology. It basically means that you can mix and match several data types to produce increasingly complicated objects in your code. In this way, individual variables are like the building blocks that add up to much larger and more complex objects when they are put together.

The great ability that we gain from composition is that we are no longer limited to using primitive data types for variables. Instead, nearly any object in our game can itself become a variable that can be manipulated in our code. That means any character, any script, or any component inside our game world can be put at our fingertips. Furthermore, we can represent almost anything in our game world by assembling the right combination of variables. Therefore, we gain much greater control over the destiny of our game and can do more sophisticated things with our code thanks to composition.

In the current challenge, you have the opportunity to try out some composite data types for yourself. Let's consider a starting point for our `CheckCollisions()` function. We need to determine whether there is a collision between Luna and the collectable. To make the code behind our calculations easier to read, it would be useful to store this information in local variables. Recall that Luna is represented in Unity by the Player object. Player is of the `GameObject` data type, which is a special container that Unity uses for many types of things in our game world. Our collectable is also a `GameObject`. Indeed, `GameObject` is a composite that can be made up of many components, such as a `Transform`, `SpriteRenderer`, and scripts. You may also remember that the `Transform` component of every `GameObject` has a `position` variable, which is of the `Vector3` type. Moreover, `Vector3` is a composite that is made up of three primitive `float` variables that represent the x, y, and z coordinates of an object. The positions of both Luna and our collectable object are stored in `Vector3` variables. Likewise, we will need to adjust for our objects' center origin points when checking collisions. We can retrieve this information from their `SpriteRenderer` components and store it in `Vector3` variables. Thus, to gather all of the information we need to make our collision calculations, we can create local variables with the composite data types of `GameObject` and `Vector3`.

Conveniently, whenever you want to create variables with composite data types, you follow the same rules as with primitive data types. That is, you must declare the data type and provide a valid variable name in your code. To set up the necessary variables at the beginning of your `CheckCollisions()` function, you might use the following code. Can you think of the next thing you should do with these variables to determine whether Luna and the collectable are colliding?

```
//store the objects from the Unity scene in local variables

//player in scene
GameObject thePlayer;

//collectable
GameObject theCollectable;

//player position
Vector3 playerPos;

//collectable position
Vector3 collectPos;

//player size
Vector3 playerSize;

//collectable size
Vector3 collectSize;
```

▮ Hint: Unity Tags

In the previous hint, we set up the basic variables we need to detect a collision between Luna and a collectable. The next step is to find the position of both objects. Since the Collectable script is attached to a collectable object, we can easily retrieve information about the collectable using the `gameObject` command, as we have done before. However, we cannot do the same for Luna, since the Collectable script is not attached to her. We need another way to access our Player `GameObject` in the Unity scene. Thankfully, we can use Unity's tag system.

In Unity, you can apply custom tags to objects. Go to your Unity project and look at the Hierarchy window. Inside the Middleground object, you will find several collectable objects. If you click on one of the collectables and turn your attention to the top of the Inspector window, you will find a *Tag* dropbox. Inside that dropbox, you will see that the collectable object has been assigned a tag called *Collectable*. Similarly, if you look at the Player `GameObject`, you will see that it has been tagged as *Player* (Figure 5.2).

Figure 5.2 The *Player* tag has been applied to the Player object.

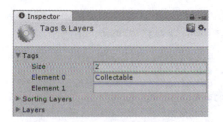

Figure 5.3 Custom tags can be created in the *Tags & Layers* panel.

Figure 5.4 The custom *Collectable* tag has been applied to the collectable objects in the scene.

Furthermore, if you click on the dropbox, you can see several choices that can be applied to any object. In addition, you can click on the *Add Tag …* option to create your own custom tags. Doing this will open the *Tags & Layers* view inside the Inspector window (Figure 5.3).

There you can add or remove tags, which can later be applied to your objects in the Tag dropbox (Figure 5.4). To prove this, try adding your own custom tag, creating a new `GameObject`, and adding your tag to that object now.

Using Unity's tag system, we can categorize and organize our objects. For example, we might use a unique tag like *Player* to identify the one and only character the player controls in our game. On the contrary, we might group several similar objects using tags, as we have done by using the *Collectable* tag on all of our collectable objects. Besides identification, the major benefit we get from tagging objects is the ability to retrieve them anywhere in our code. Unity has a built-in function called `GameObject.FindWithTag()`. This allows us to find any single object by providing the function with its tag. To do so, we type a `string` value into the function's parentheses that matches the tag applied to the object. Here is a basic example:

```
//find a single GameObject using its tag
//find the object with the tag called "tagString"
GameObject.FindWithTag("tagString");
```

Our current challenge requires us to retrieve Luna's position, so we can determine whether she is colliding with a collectable. Since we know that Luna has been assigned the *Player* tag, we can retrieve her using the GameObject. FindWithTag() function. In addition, using dot notation, we can access variables inside the GameObject we find. Thus, we can access the position variable of the Transform component, as well as the size variable of the SpriteRenderer component, attached to the Player GameObject. That gives us everything we need to start checking collisions. Building from the previous hint, our variables should look like this. The additions are shown in bold.

```
//store the objects from the Unity scene in local variables

//player in scene
//find the object with the "Player" tag
GameObject thePlayer = GameObject.FindWithTag("Player");

//collectable
//this script is attached to a collectable
//therefore, we use the gameObject command
GameObject theCollectable = gameObject;

//player position
//use dot notation to access the player's position
Vector3 playerPos = thePlayer.transform.position;

//collectable position
//use dot notation to access the collectable's position
Vector3 collectPos = theCollectable.transform.position;

//player size
//use dot notation to access the player's size
Vector3 playerSize = thePlayer.GetComponent<SpriteRenderer>().
    bounds.size;

//collectable size
//use dot notation to access the collectable's size
Vector3 collectSize = theCollect.GetComponent<SpriteRenderer>().
    bounds.size;
```

▌▌ Hint: Axis-Aligned Bounding Box Collisions

With the necessary information in hand, it is time to write our collision detection code in the CheckCollisions() function. You may want to refer back to the earlier challenge in which you prevented Luna from moving outside the boundaries of the screen. Similarly, in this challenge, you will need to use the position of Luna's top, bottom, left, and right edges to determine whether she is colliding in the game world. However, instead of comparing with the edges of the screen, you will compare against the top, bottom, left, and right edges of a collectable object. Hence, you are calculating whether two objects are colliding in two-dimensional (2D) space, no matter where they are placed on the screen.

Note that our player and collectable objects are treated as rectangles for the purposes of collision detection. Of course, their sprites do not fill an entire rectangle or take on that exact shape. Yet, they have invisible rectangles around them, which are used to determine their top, bottom, left, and right edges for collisions. These invisible rectangles are called *bounding boxes*. You can see a visual representation of the bounding boxes of our player and collectable objects in Figure 5.5.

Furthermore, these bounding boxes are always *axis aligned* for the purposes of our collision calculations. Once again, imagine that our game world is on a 2D coordinate plane. To be axis aligned means that our bounding boxes are always perfectly parallel with our axes. That is, the top and bottom edges of the bounding box are parallel to the x axis, while the left and right edges are parallel to the y axis. This remains true no matter what happens to the contents of the box. For instance, if you were to rotate Luna's sprite at any angle, her bounding box would retain its axis alignment.

Since we are calculating collisions with bounding boxes that are always axis aligned, this method is called Axis-Aligned Bounding Box (AABB) collision detection. It is a common form of 2D collision detection applied in games. AABB collisions are easy to implement and do not require advanced physics calculations. They are also relatively easy on computing resources. However, AABB is not the most accurate form of collision detection. Depending on factors, such as how well your sprites fill a rectangular shape, the speed at which objects move, and the amount of precision required in your collisions, AABB may or may not yield visibly pleasant results. For the purposes of our game, AABB collisions will be suitable. Luna and the collectables are relatively square in shape. Also, a collectable will disappear as soon as Luna moves over it. This will give the player a fairly good impression that the objects collided smoothly.

If you have not worked out the logic for AABB collisions yet, take the time to do so. Remember that you must detect collisions between the top, bottom, left, and right edges of each object's bounding box. Based on these edges, how will you know when the objects are colliding on the x axis or the y axis? Think in terms of your conditional statements as well. What conditions must be true for you to be completely sure that the objects are colliding? Drawing a diagram like the one shown in Figure 5.6 should help you to discover the necessary calculations.

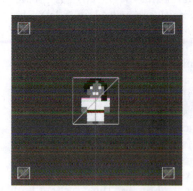

Figure 5.5 The bounding boxes of the player and collectable objects are visualized.

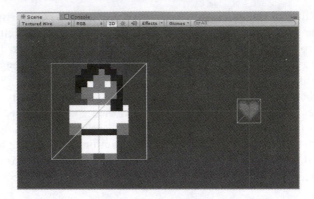

Figure 5.6 The player's and a collectable's bounding boxes are shown. What calculations and conditions must be applied to determine whether these objects are colliding?

To help you get started, let's look at how we might check for an x axis collision between Luna and a collectable object:

```
//check object collisions
//x axis position comparisons
if (
    //right edge of player beyond left edge of collectable
    (playerPos.x + 0.5f * playerSize.x >=
    collectPos.x - 0.5f * collectSize.x)

    &&

    //left edge of player before right edge of collectable
    (playerPos.x - 0.5f * playerSize.x <=
    collectPos.x + 0.5f * collectSize.x)
)
```

We previously stored the positions of Luna and the collectable in the `playerPos` and `collectPos` variables. We also stored their sizes in `playerSize` and `collectSize`. To determine whether these positions overlap on the x axis, we can check whether Luna's right edge is greater than or equal to the collectable's left edge. Simultaneously, Luna's left-edge position must be less than or equal to the collectable's right edge. If both of these conditions are true, we know that the objects are colliding on the x axis. See Figure 5.7 for a visual depiction of this calculation.

As we have become accustomed to, we make adjustments in our code by half the width of each object. Again, this is due to the fact that the objects have a center origin point. Thus, the right edge of an object is its x position plus one-half of its width. Meanwhile, the left edge of an object is its x position minus one-half of its width.

This sample code only tells part of the story. While the x portion of your collision check could be true, note that the objects' y axes may not be colliding. For example, both objects could have the same x coordinate, but one object could be at the top of the screen while the other is at the bottom. Thus, without both x and y alignment, you cannot be certain that a collision has occurred. This means you will need to add extra conditions to verify your collisions. See if you can expand this code and write your own collision detection for the y axis.

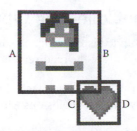

Figure 5.7 The player and the collectable are colliding on the x axis if the player's left edge (A) is less than the collectable's right edge (D) and the player's right edge (B) is greater than the collectable's left edge (C). What conditions must be true for a y axis collision?

▎■ Hint: Unity `Destroy()` Function

The final step in this challenge is to remove the collectable from the screen after Luna has collided with it. To accomplish this, we can use Unity's `Destroy()` function. The `Destroy()` function removes a `GameObject`, or one of its components, from the game world (Unity Technologies n.d.). Ultimately, it will be removed from the computer's memory, thereby freeing up resources for other activities. This is why destroying our collectable is better than using another method to make it disappear, such as disabling its `SpriteRenderer`. On the other hand, destroying an object is permanent, so it cannot be retrieved or used again afterwards. Therefore, you want to use `Destroy()` once you are certain that an object no longer has a purpose in the game. Conversely, you should not destroy anything you need to use again at a later time. Furthermore, since destroying is permanent and disallows subsequent use, you should always make sure that `Destroy()` is the very last thing you do to an object.

To use `Destroy()`, we must provide the `GameObject` or individual component that we want to destroy. We do this by placing the object inside the parentheses of the function. Often, functions accept information, such as a value or variable, inside parentheses. The individual pieces of information provided to a function are commonly called *arguments* or *parameters*. After an argument is passed in through its parentheses, a function is able to use that information to perform operations. In the case of `Destroy()`, Unity accepts whatever object or component we provide to it. Afterwards, it takes care of destroying the object and releasing it from the computer's memory.

Thus, to finish off our Collectable script, we should destroy the collectable object once Luna has collided with it. All we need to know is what, exactly, to pass into the `Destroy()` function as an argument. Since we know that our Collectable script is attached to a collectable object in our Unity scene, we can simply use our familiar `gameObject` command. Recall that `gameObject` refers to the Unity `GameObject` that the script is attached to. Our Collectable script is attached to a collectable object. Therefore, `gameObject` points directly to the collectable we need to destroy. Here's the code needed to remove the collectable once and for all:

```
//remove the collectable object from the game
//destroy the GameObject this script is attached to
Destroy(gameObject);
```

▮ Example Solution: Collecting Objects

Conceptually, the logic behind this challenge is somewhat simple to arrive at (Figure 5.8). As a reminder, here are the requirements again:

1. The Collectable script, which is attached to each collectable object, should continuously check for collisions with Luna.

2. The CheckCollisions() function retrieves Luna's current position and uses it to check for collisions with the collectable.

3. If a collision is detected between a collectable object and Luna, the collectable object is destroyed.

While the logic may appear simple, AABB collisions can be quite tricky to figure out the first time around. The good news is that you can now apply AABB collisions widely throughout your future work in making games.

Let's discuss the sample solution provided for collectable objects that Luna can collect in the game world. Interestingly, this solution requires no global variables to be created or initialized. Only the CheckCollisions() function needs to be called inside Update(). Otherwise, everything happens within the CheckCollisions() function.

```
void Update() {

    //check collisions
    CheckCollisions();

} //end function
```

In the previous hints, we already discussed accessing the player and collectable objects, as well as their relevant attributes.

```
//excerpt from CheckCollisions() function

//check collisions
private void CheckCollisions() {

    //get the relevant scene objects
    //player in scene
    GameObject thePlayer = GameObject.FindWithTag("Player");

    //collectable this script is attached to
    GameObject theCollect = gameObject;
```

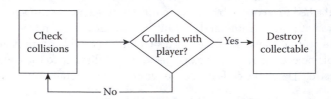

Figure 5.8 A process map illustrates the logic behind the example solution.

```
//player position
Vector3 playerPos = thePlayer.transform.position;

//collectable position
Vector3 collectPos = theCollect.transform.position;

//player size
Vector3 playerSize = thePlayer.
    GetComponent<SpriteRenderer>().bounds.size;

//collectable size
Vector3 collectSize = theCollect.
    GetComponent<SpriteRenderer>().bounds.size;
```

Subsequently, this information is used to implement AABB collision detection in a single `if` statement (albeit a rather large one). To reiterate, in all of the statement's conditions, we adjust by the half width or height of the objects to account for their center origin points. To ensure a collision has occurred, we must know that the objects are overlapping on both the x and y axes. Therefore, we can start by checking that Luna's right-edge x position is greater than or equal to the collectable's left edge. Simultaneously, Luna's left-edge x position must be less than or equal to the collectable's right edge. If both conditions are true, we know the objects are aligned on the x axis.

```
//excerpt from CheckCollisions() function

//check object collisions
if (
    //x axis position comparisons
    //right edge of player beyond left edge of collectable
    ((playerPos.x + 0.5f * playerSize.x >=
    collectPos.x - 0.5f * collectSize.x)

    &&

    //left edge of player before right edge of collectable
    (playerPos.x - 0.5f * playerSize.x <=
    collectPos.x + 0.5f * collectSize.x))
```

However, we also need to check the y axis to determine whether there is indeed a collision. Thus, we check whether Luna's top-edge y position is greater than or equal to the collectable's bottom edge, and whether Luna's bottom-edge y position is less than or equal to the collectable's top edge. If both of these conditions are true, we have y axis alignment between the objects.

```
//excerpt from CheckCollisions() function
//continued from preceding code sample

    &&

    //y axis position comparisons
    //top edge of player beyond bottom edge of collectable
    ((playerPos.y + 0.5f * playerSize.y >=
    collectPos.y - 0.5f * collectSize.y)

    &&
```

```
        //bottom edge of player below top edge of collectable
        (playerPos.y - 0.5f * playerSize.y <=
        collectPos.y + 0.5f * collectSize.y))

) {
```

Logically speaking, we cannot be sure that a collision is happening unless all four of the stated conditions are true. This is why we use so many && symbols in the code of our if statement. If all four conditions are true, we have both x and y overlap between the objects, and therefore a collision. Once we verify the collision, our only task is to destroy the collectable, thereby removing it from the game world.

```
//excerpt from CheckCollisions() function

//destroy object
Destroy(gameObject);
```

Having completed these steps, all three requirements for the challenge are satisfied. For additional clarity, the entire CheckCollisions() function is provided in one place.

```
private void CheckCollisions() {

    //get the relevant scene objects
    //player in scene
    GameObject thePlayer = GameObject.FindWithTag("Player");

    //collectable this script is attached to
    GameObject theCollect = gameObject;

    //player position
    Vector3 playerPos = thePlayer.transform.position;

    //collectable position
    Vector3 collectPos = theCollect.transform.position;

    //player size
    Vector3 playerSize = thePlayer.
       GetComponent<SpriteRenderer>().bounds.size;

    //collectable size
    Vector3 collectSize = theCollect.
       GetComponent<SpriteRenderer>().bounds.size;

    //check object collisions
    if (
        //x axis position comparisons
        //right edge of player beyond left edge of collectable
        ((playerPos.x + 0.5f * playerSize.x >=
        collectPos.x - 0.5f * collectSize.x)

        &&

        //left edge of player before right edge of collectable
        (playerPos.x - 0.5f * playerSize.x <=
        collectPos.x + 0.5f * collectSize.x))

    &&
```

```
        //y axis position comparisons
        //top edge of player beyond bottom edge of collectable
        ((playerPos.y + 0.5f * playerSize.y >=
        collectPos.y - 0.5f * collectSize.y)

        &&

        //bottom edge of player below top edge of collectable
        (playerPos.y - 0.5f * playerSize.y <=
        collectPos.y + 0.5f * collectSize.y))
    ) {

        //destroy object
        Destroy(gameObject);

    } //end if

} //end function
```

Summary

In this relatively brief challenge, you have made some big additions to your game coding toolkit. You now know how to implement collectables, which can represent many different objects, such as powerups, equipment, health, and treasure. You also know how to detect AABB collisions between objects in 2D space. AABB collisions are widely used in games, and you will be certain to apply them in many of your own creations. At this point, you should feel comfortable coding all of these game elements:

- Create objects that can be collected by a game character

- Manipulate variables with primitive and composite data types

- Utilize tags to access objects in Unity

- Detect Axis-Aligned Bounding Box (AABB) collisions between objects

- Destroy objects in Unity

In Chapter 6, you will continue to expand your coding skills by learning how to spawn numerous objects inside the game world.

Reference

Unity Technologies. n.d. Object.Destroy. http://docs.unity3d.com/ScriptReference/Object.Destroy.html (accessed October 16, 2014).

6 Spawning Objects

You have created an object for Luna to collect on her journey through the surface world. It would be nice if your code could make several of these objects all over the map, rather than having to place them into the world one by one. Indeed, you can. Cloning and spawning objects is a very common task in game coding. You will want to do this almost any time you need multiple copies of an object. In this challenge, you will focus on spawning many collectables with randomized positions. Once you get the hang of spawning, you can apply this technique to a variety of game items, such as obstacles, enemies, and treasure.

▮ Goals

By the end of this chapter, you will be able to apply these coding techniques:

- Spawn multiple objects inside the game world

- Instantiate prefabs in Unity

- Randomize position values for spawned objects

- Organize spawned objects under a common parent

- Apply type casting to specify a variable's data type

- Write for and while loops

▐ Required Files

In this chapter, you will need to use the following files from the *Chapter_06 > Software* folder:

- *Challenge > Assets > Scenes > Map.unity* to run, modify, and test your solution

- *Challenge > Assets > Scripts > CollectableSpawn.cs* to code your solution to the challenge

- *Demo > Mac/PC > CollectableSpawn* to demonstrate how your completed solution should work

- *Solution > CollectableSpawn.cs* to compare your solution to the provided example solution

▐ Challenge: Spawning Collectables

Your challenge is to spawn a number of collectable objects on the map. Your code will be placed entirely within the Spawn() function of the CollectableSpawn script. Also note that the CollectableSpawn script is attached to the Middleground GameObject in the Unity scene. Two variables have been provided for you in the script.

```
//number of objects to spawn; defined in Unity Inspector
public int numSpawns;

//prefab defined in Unity Inspector
public GameObject prefab;
```

The numSpawns variable tells our script how many different objects to create every time the Spawn() function is called. Meanwhile, prefab tells our code which of our objects is being cloned. Interestingly, both of these variables are initialized in the Unity Inspector window, rather than inside our code. You can verify this by looking at the Middleground object in the Unity editor. Then, find the CollectableSpawn script attached to it in the Unity Inspector window. There, you will see two boxes: one for numSpawns and one for prefab (Figure 6.1).

Conveniently, whenever we make a variable public in one of our scripts, Unity will make it appear in the Inspector window. Filling in the box beside a variable's name allows us to define its value. This is an alternative to initializing the variable's value in our code, like we previously have. For certain variables, it is helpful to use the Unity Inspector method. However, note that this method only works in Unity, can only handle certain types of public variables, and cannot be used with private variables. Therefore, most of the time, you will want to initialize your variable values as normal inside their scripts. You can always initialize variables in your code. However, in some special circumstances, it is helpful to provide values through the Unity Inspector instead. You will explore one of those circumstances in this challenge as you work to clone objects.

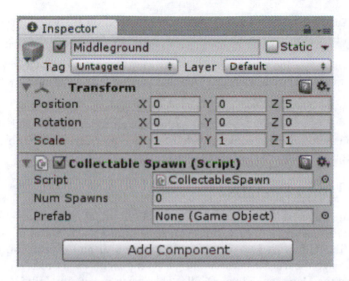

Figure 6.1 The CollectableSpawn script's numSpawns and prefab variables can be set from inside the Unity Inspector window. Similarly, whenever a variable is made public inside a script, it will automatically appear in the Unity Inspector and can be given a value there.

Besides the two variables, you are also provided with a familiar Update() function. This function checks for an R key press. If the key is pressed, the Spawn() function is called. This handy function makes it easy for you to debug your spawn code. Any time you want to test it, simply press the R key to create more objects.

```
void Update() {

    //check for key press
    if (Input.GetKeyDown(KeyCode.R)) {

        //spawn objects
        Spawn();

    } //end if

} //end function
```

Although a few things have been provided for you, you will need to learn about some new coding techniques to solve this challenge. Namely, you must be able to clone prefabs in Unity, as well as write for and while loops. These requirements explain exactly how your final code should function once it is completed:

1. Each spawn should be cloned from a specified object, based on the value given to the prefab variable.

2. Each spawn should have a randomly generated position. Ensure that spawns are placed completely within the boundaries of the screen.

3. Each spawn should be organized under a common parent object.

4. Spawn a specified number of prefabs, based on the value given to the numSpawns variable.

5. Use a for loop to manage the spawning of your objects. Once you have it working, write a while loop that yields an identical outcome.

From these guidelines, make sure to work out the logic behind how your solution will function. Once you have gathered your thoughts, proceed to implement your solution. Hints are provided to guide you, especially with the new coding concepts required by this challenge.

▌ Hint: Unity Prefabs

Prefabs are a special kind of object in Unity. With prefabs, we are able to save a GameObject with all of its various components as a single entity in our game project. This allows us to reuse the same object over and over again, without going through the trouble of assembling its components each time.

Open the Map scene of your CollectableSpawn project in Unity. If you look inside the Project window, within the *Assets* folder, you will find a folder named *Prefabs*. Click on this folder to reveal its contents. For this project, we already have two prefabs named Collectable and Player. Naturally, these represent Luna and the collectable objects in our game world. You can click on these prefabs and look at the Inspector window to see their underlying components and settings. These prefabs were originally made by creating an empty GameObject in the Hierarchy window and then configuring the necessary components in the Unity Inspector. After the objects were finished, they were dragged into the *Prefabs* folder. Subsequently, Unity automatically converted them into prefabs for later use.

Try making your own prefab now. Select *GameObject > Create Empty* from the top menu bar in Unity (Figure 6.2). A new object will be added to the Hierarchy window.

File	Edit	Assets	GameObject	Component
	Create Empty			Ctrl+Shift+N
	Create Empty Child			Alt+Shift+N
	3D Object			▶
	2D Object			▶
	Light			▶
	Audio			▶
	UI			▶
	Particle System			
	Camera			

Figure 6.2 Create a new GameObject in Unity by accessing the *GameObject > Create Empty* menu option.

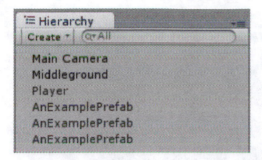

Figure 6.3 Several prefabs have been dragged out of the *Assets > Prefabs* folder and into the Hierarchy window. These are all identical copies of the original prefab.

Feel free to rename the object and add any components you like. Change some of the settings on the components as well. When you are finished, click on the object and drag it into the *Assets > Prefabs* folder. Next, go back to the Hierarchy and delete the original object you created. Then, drag and drop the prefab object from your *Prefabs* folder and into your Hierarchy window a few times. As you can see, several copies of the object are made, all with the exact configuration that you specified in the original (Figure 6.3). You may delete these objects from the Hierarchy.

This is the basic process that you can follow to create any kind of prefab for your Unity games. As you can see, *Assets* is a special kind of folder. Unity will turn any `GameObject` you drag into that folder, or any subfolders, into a prefab. The benefit of using a prefab is that you can configure a `GameObject` once and then clone it easily. In addition, whenever you change the settings of the original prefab, all copies of that prefab will automatically update. Furthermore, we can create and manipulate prefabs in our code. All of these features make using prefabs a great way to save time and organize the various objects in our game.

▉ Hint: Unity Prefab Instantiation

Before we consider how to handle prefabs in our code, let's look at one more thing in our Unity project. Click on the Middleground object in the Hierarchy and find its components in the Inspector window. You will see that our CollectableSpawn script has been added to it. As mentioned before, we have two public variables in this script that can be set via the Unity Inspector. One of them has the `GameObject` type and a name of `prefab`. This variable is used to define which of the objects saved in our *Assets > Prefabs* folder will be associated with our script. As you can see, the Collectable prefab has been selected. To assign a prefab to a public variable like this one, you can either drag the object from the *Assets > Prefabs* folder into the variable's box or click on the circular icon next to the box and select from the possible options (Figure 6.4).

Recall that our prefabs were originally created with the `GameObject` type. While Unity has saved them as a special kind of prefab object, they are still recognized as being of the `GameObject` data type. Therefore, our code will always use the `GameObject` data type when working with prefabs. That is why our `prefab` variable is designated with the `GameObject` data type in the CollectableSpawn script.

Now that you know what prefabs are, how they can be created, and how they can be assigned, let's learn to clone them in our code. To create a copy of a prefab and add it to your game world, you can use Unity's `Instantiate()` function.

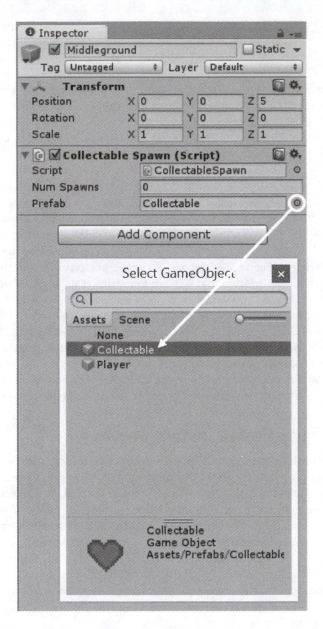

Figure 6.4 Assign a prefab to a public variable in the Unity Inspector window by clicking on the circular icon beside the variable's box and selecting it from the list.

The `Instantiate()` function must be provided with an object to clone. This happens to be the prefab we want to duplicate. Remember our discussion of function arguments from the preceding challenge? The object passed into the `Instantiate()` function is an argument. Besides receiving information as arguments, functions can also *return* information. Some functions not only take in information to make calculations, but also give information back when they are finished. `Instantiate()` is one of those functions. It will accept a prefab object that we provide to it and return to us a new copy of that object. Since the `Instantiate()` function returns to us a cloned prefab, we can create a new `GameObject` variable to store it. You can think of this variable as *catching* what is sent back from the function, like how one basketball player catches a ball passed from another. After we have stored the clone in a variable, we can proceed to manipulate other aspects of it, such as its position and parent. Below is the specific code needed to clone one of our collectable objects using the `Instantiate()` function.

```
//clone a prefab and store it inside a variable
GameObject newSpawn = (GameObject)Instantiate(prefab);
```

Here, we declare a variable of the type `GameObject` and give it the name newSpawn. We set this variable equal to the `Instantiate()` function, which has been provided with a prefab to clone. The `Instantiate()` function performs its duties and returns us a copy of the prefab. At the end, we have a clone of our original prefab stored inside the newSpawn variable. This fulfills the first requirement for the challenge.

You may be curious about the `(GameObject)` code directly in front of the `Instantiate()` function. What this does is specify the data type of the object returned by the `Instantiate()` function. In this case, we are saying the object returned by `Instantiate()` will be of the `GameObject` type. This process of specifying a variable's data type is known as *type casting*. You can perform a type cast by putting a data type inside parentheses just before a variable. This example is just one form of type casting, which is generally used to modify or identify data types. You can read more on type casting in the official documentation for the C# language (Microsoft Corporation 2015). Note that type casting is not an especially frequent task, but it is necessary from time to time, particularly when we want to specify or alter a variable's data type.

Moreover, if you read the documentation for Unity's `Instantiate()` function (Unity Technologies n.d.a), you will see that the function receives and returns variables of the `Object` type. This happens to be a generic, underlying type for all kinds of things in Unity. Therefore, it is referred to as a *base class*. Many different things, including every `GameObject`, inherit their features from the `Object` base class. When something inherits its features from a base class, it is known as an *inherited class*. Not only do inherited classes retain the features of the base class, but also they add their own unique features. Since `Instantiate()` deals with the `Object` base class, it is capable of cloning everything that inherits from the base class as well. This allows us to use a single function to clone many kinds of things in Unity. However, it also makes us responsible for defining exactly what kind of object we expect the function to return. This is why we must explicitly state that we consider the object returned by `Instantiate()` to be a `GameObject`. That way, our code knows that the object will have all of the unique features that a `GameObject` has and not just the generic features of the `Object` base class. Once we make this type cast, we can proceed to manipulate our newSpawn variable just like any `GameObject`.

▌ Hint: Random Number Generation

Randomness plays a role in nearly all games. Therefore, generating random numbers is a frequent coding task. In this challenge, we need to generate random x and y position values for our spawned objects (requirement 2). We can do this using Unity's built-in `Random.Range()` function (Unity Technologies n.d.b). `Random.Range()` accepts two arguments. The first is a minimum value and the second is a maximum value. You can pass either `int` or `float` values into this function. `Random.Range()` will take the minimum and maximum values, then return a randomly generated number that lies between them. If you provide `float` values, the range is inclusive, meaning that both the minimum and maximum value can themselves be generated. Hence, if you generate a random float between 0 and 1, your possible outcomes are 0, 1, or any value in between. However, if you provide `int` values to the `Random.Range()` function, the minimum is inclusive, while the maximum is exclusive. Therefore, if you provided `int` values of 1 and 5, a number between 1 and 4 would be generated. The basic format for using the `Random.Range()` function is demonstrated in this code sample:

```
//Unity's Random.Range() function
//accepts two arguments: min and max
//returns a random number between min and max

//float version
//generate a random number between 0 and 1
//store the returned value in a variable
float randFloat = Random.Range(0.0f, 1.0f);

//int version
//generate a random number between 1 and 9
//store the returned value in a variable
int randInt = Random.Range(1, 10);
```

You should be able to apply this sample code to solve the specific challenge of generating random positions for your spawned collectables. Remember that the position of our spawned collectable is stored as a `Vector3`, which uses `float` values to represent x, y, and z coordinates. The x and y will give us placement within our game world. We are not concerned with generating the z value, since we are working in two dimensions (2D). Further, you want to ensure that the objects are spawned completely within the boundaries of the screen (requirement 2). Therefore, be sure to factor in the screen size to your minimum and maximum values, as well as adjust for the center origin point of the spawned objects. Once you have your values generated, you can use them to set the spawned object's `transform.position` value. Take the opportunity to implement this randomization in your code to set the position of your `newSpawn` variable.

▌ Hint: Parent Objects in Unity

Your next step is to make sure that your spawned objects share a common parent object in the Unity scene (requirement 3). This will ensure that the cloned objects are neatly organized under a single parent, rather than cluttering up our

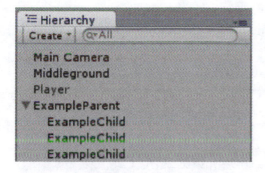

Figure 6.5 Children objects appear indented under their common parent object. Clicking on the arrow icon beside the parent collapses or reveals the child objects.

Hierarchy window and making a mess of the Unity interface. Furthermore, using a common parent makes it easier to manage all of the objects in our code. Recall that every `GameObject` in Unity has a `Transform` component. One variable of the `Transform` component is parent. By setting the parent of a `GameObject`, we assign it to be filed under another object. Once an object has been assigned a parent, it becomes a *child* of that parent. In the Unity Hierarchy window, we can visualize these relationships. A child object will always be placed beneath and indented relative to its parent (Figure 6.5). Moreover, the children inside a parent object can be hidden or revealed using the arrow symbol beside the parent's name. This parent and child system in Unity allows us to organize our objects into a clean, hierarchical format.

To assign an object to its parent, you set its `transform.parent` variable equal to the `Transform` of the intended parent object. See the following code for a demonstration:

```
//assign an object to a parent
//make the parentObject the parent of the childObject
childObject.transform.parent = parentObject.transform;
```

In this challenge, you want to set the parent of your `newSpawn` variable. The CollectableSpawn script is attached to the Middleground object in the Unity project. Since nothing else is contained within that object, the Middleground makes a suitable parent for our spawned collectables. Using the sample code above, as well as your prior knowledge of accessing objects in your code, you should be able to assign Middleground as the parent of `newSpawn`.

∎ Hint: `for` and `while` Loops

At this point, you should have written the necessary code to spawn a single collectable object, provide it with a random position, and assign it to a parent. For example, your `Spawn()` function code might look something like this:

```
//excerpt from Spawn() function

//clone prefab
GameObject newSpawn = (GameObject)Instantiate(prefab);

//calculate screen and object bounds
//use to ensure object is spawned on screen
float halfScreenW = 0.5f * Screen.width / 100.0f;
float halfScreenH = 0.5f * Screen.height / 100.0f;
```

```
float halfObjW = 0.5f * prefab.gameObject.
  GetComponent<SpriteRenderer>().bounds.size.x;
float halfObjH = 0.5f * prefab.gameObject.
  GetComponent<SpriteRenderer>().bounds.size.y;

//get random x and y position values
float randX = Random.Range(-halfScreenW + halfObjW,
  halfScreenW - halfObjW);
float randY = Random.Range(-halfScreenH + halfObjH,
  halfScreenH - halfObjH);

//store the original position
Vector3 randPos = newSpawn.transform.position;

//update position with randomized x and y values
randPos.x = randX;
randPos.y = randY;

//set random position
newSpawn.transform.position = randPos;

//set parent game object in Unity scene
newSpawn.transform.parent = gameObject.transform;
```

After instantiating the prefab and storing it in newSpawn, we set up a few local variables to store the half size of the screen and the object. We use these values to make adjustments inside the Random.Range() function to ensure our object will be spawned within the bounds of the screen. We store the object's original position in a Vector3 variable named randPos. The x and y values for randPos are updated to reflect the randomized x and y coordinates we generated. We then set the position of our newSpawn object equal to the randomly generated position. Lastly, we set the parent of newSpawn equal to the Transform of the GameObject attached to this script, which happens to be the Middleground object in our scene.

This Spawn() function code successfully creates one instance of a cloned object. If you were to test the game now, you would see that a single collectable is spawned every time you press the R key. However, when we are spawning objects in games, we often want to create many more than just one at a time. *Loops* are the fundamental coding technique that allow us to automatically and rapidly repeat actions many times over. For this challenge, we will explore two common kinds of loops: for and while.

for Loop

A for loop is composed of three major parts: an iteration variable declaration, a condition, and an increment (or decrement). The basic structure of a for loop follows:

```
for (iteration variable; condition; increment/decrement) {

    //any code placed here will execute each time the loop runs

}
```

The loop begins with the `for` keyword. Inside parentheses, each section is separated by a semicolon. The first part requires an iteration variable to be declared. It is common coding practice to use the letter *i* to represent the iteration variable. For subsequent loops inside the same function, use the letters *j*, *k*, and so on. The second part of the loop contains the condition. This is a statement that must evaluate to `true` for the code inside the loop to run. The third part of the loop increments or decrements the iteration variable. Thus, each time the loop is run, the iteration variable gets smaller or larger. Eventually, the loop ends when the iteration variable is incremented to the point that the condition is no longer `true`. Following the parentheses are two brackets. Any code placed within those brackets will execute each cycle of the `for` loop. Let's take a look at a basic example loop.

```
for (int i = 0; i < 10; i++) {

    Debug.Log("The value of i this cycle is: " + i);

}
```

Can you predict what this loop will print to the Unity Console window? Why not test it out in your own project? In this loop, we give the iteration variable `i` an initial value of 0. In the condition, we check that the value is less than 10. In the increment phase, which takes place at the end of one loop cycle and prior to the start of the next one, we add 1 to the iteration variable. Therefore, we would expect the loop to print the values 0, 1, 2, 3, 4, 5, 6, 7, 8, and 9. After 9, the value of the iteration variable gets incremented to 10 and the condition becomes `false`. Thus, the loop ends.

You can also write loops in reverse. That is, instead of counting upwards and incrementing the iteration variable, you can move downwards by decrementing it. Here is an example of such a loop. See if you can predict what values will be printed to the Unity Console window. Test the loop yourself to determine whether you had it right.

```
for (int i = 10; i > 0; i--) {

    Debug.Log("The value of i this cycle is: " + i);

}
```

As you can see, the reverse `for` loop simply starts the iteration variable at a maximum and decrements it. In the condition, we check that the iteration variable has reached a specified minimum value. You have already produced the code required to spawn a single collectable object. From here, you just need to put it inside a `for` loop. Rather than hard-coding a value, like the 10 shown in these example loops, be sure to utilize your `numSpawns` variable. This will allow your script to work properly no matter what number is specified in `numSpawns`. Go ahead and write your `for` loop. Test and retest it in your Unity project until you get it working. When your loop is working, you should expect to see a number of objects added to your screen equal to numSpawns every time you press the R key. Once you do, proceed to read about `while` loops.

while Loop

A while loop can be functionally identical to a for loop, but it takes on a slightly different format. The while loop has only one major component in its syntax, which is a condition. So long as the condition is true, the loop will keep running over and over. The basic structure is shown.

```
while (condition) {

        //any code placed here will execute each time the loop runs

}
```

With the for loop, the iteration variable and the increment step ensure that the loop will eventually stop running. However, the while loop has no such built-in mechanism that causes it to stop. This makes it easy to make the mistake of writing an *infinite loop*. A loop is infinite whenever its condition can never be false, and subsequently, it can never stop running. When this occurs, the computer will surely crash. To prevent an infinite loop situation and ensure our while loops are implemented properly, we must manually create our own way to exit the loop. This is typically done through an iteration variable or a Boolean flag. When using an iteration variable, a while loop turns out to be quite similar to a for loop. When using a Boolean flag, you can look for additional special conditions that should end the loop, rather than relying on the increment alone. Both examples are demonstrated in this code sample:

```
//while loop example with iteration variable
//create the iteration variable
int i = 0;

//define the while loop
while (i < 10) {

    //any code placed here will execute each time the loop runs

    Debug.Log("The value of i this cycle is: " + i);

    //increment the iteration variable
    //the loop will stop once i becomes 10 or greater
    i++;
}

//while loop example with Boolean flag
//create the flag variable
bool isComplete = false;

//define the while loop
while (isComplete == false) {

    //any code placed here will execute each time the loop runs

    Debug.Log("The value of isComplete this cycle is: "
        + isComplete);
```

```
    //check to see if a custom condition that
    //should end the loop is now true
    if (/*custom condition goes here*/) {

        //update the flag to end the loop
        isComplete = true;
    }
}
```

These are just a few basic examples of while loops. You can create more complex systems and conditions to iterate through your code as the need arises. At this point, you should be able to interpret what each of these example loops will print to the Unity Console window. You should also be capable of implementing a while loop to create an amount of collectable objects equal to the value of the numSpawn variable.

Prepared with your newfound knowledge, try applying loops to enhance your Spawn() function. If you have not already done so, start by writing a for loop that spawns a number of collectables equal to the value stored in the numSpawns variable. After you get it working, comment out the for loop and write an identical while loop that also spawns a number of collectables equal to numSpawns. When you are finished, a single call to your Spawn() function should create whatever number of collectable objects is specified in numSpawns. By achieving this, you will witness the power of loops to efficiently execute actions many times with a relatively small amount of code. You will also have fulfilled requirements 4 and 5 for this challenge.

▌▊ Example Solution: Spawning Collectables

Ultimately, the solution for this challenge involves pairing the instantiation code discussed in the earlier hints with the looping techniques demonstrated in the latest hint. The logic for a for loop solution is shown in pseudocode:

```
FOR counter = 0 IS LESS THAN specified number of spawns, each
iteration:
```

1. INSTANTIATE clone of prefab
2. Generate random x between negative half screen width plus half object width and positive half screen width minus half object width
3. Generate random y between negative half screen height plus half object height and positive half screen height minus half object height
4. Set clone's position EQUAL TO randomly generated position
5. Set clone's parent EQUAL TO object in scene
6. INCREMENT counter via FOR loop

The challenge requirements are listed again as a reminder of how your code should function:

1. Each spawn should be cloned from a specified object, based on the value given to the prefab variable.

2. Each spawn should have a randomly generated position. Ensure that spawns are placed completely within the boundaries of the screen.

3. Each spawn should be organized under a common parent object.

4. Spawn a specified number of prefabs, based on the value given to the numSpawns variable.

5. Use a for loop to manage the spawning of your objects. Once you have it working, write a while loop that yields an identical outcome.

The following code sample provides the entirety of the CollectableSpawn script's Spawn() function:

```
public void Spawn() {

        //calculate screen and object bounds
        //use to ensure object is spawned on screen
        float halfScreenW = 0.5f * Screen.width / 100.0f;
        float halfScreenH = 0.5f * Screen.height / 100.0f;
        float halfObjW = 0.5f * prefab.gameObject.
          GetComponent<SpriteRenderer>().bounds.size.x;
        float halfObjH = 0.5f * prefab.gameObject.
          GetComponent<SpriteRenderer>().bounds.size.y;

        //for loop
        //run loop a number of times equal to numSpawns
        for (int i = 0; i < numSpawns; i++) {

          //clone prefab
          GameObject newSpawn = (GameObject)Instantiate(prefab);

          //get random x and y values
          float randX = Random.Range(-halfScreenW + halfObjW,
            halfScreenW - halfObjW);
          float randY = Random.Range(-halfScreenH + halfObjH,
            halfScreenH - halfObjH);

          //store the original position
          Vector3 randPos = newSpawn.transform.position;

          //update position with randomized x and y values
          randPos.x = randX;
          randPos.y = randY;

          //set random position
          newSpawn.transform.position = randPos;

          //set parent game object in Unity scene
          newSpawn.transform.parent = gameObject.transform;

        } //end for

} //end function
```

The Spawn() function begins by setting up local variables to store the half-screen and object sizes. These are later used to ensure our objects are spawned completely within the bounds of the screen (requirement 2). This example solution applied a for loop (requirement 5). Note that the condition element of the loop asks whether the iteration variable i is less than numSpawns. The iteration variable starts at 0 and is incremented by 1 each cycle until it reaches the value of numSpawns and stops. Therefore, the loop runs a number of times equal to numSpawns (requirement 4). Inside the loop, we placed our code that clones a single object. That is, we instantiate a clone from our prefab (requirement 1), generate a random position (requirement 2), and assign a common parent object in the Unity scene (requirement 3). We only need to write the code to spawn a single object successfully inside our loop. Since the loop runs many times over, we eventually create many objects—hence the value of using loops rather than having to copy our spawn code over and over. The identical while loop is provided (requirement 5). The parts of the while loop that differ from the for loop are in bold.

```
//excerpt from Spawn() function

//while loop
//track total number of spawns made thus far
int totalSpawns = 0;
while (totalSpawns < numSpawns) {

    //clone prefab
    GameObject newSpawn = (GameObject)Instantiate(prefab);

    //get random x and y values
    float randX = Random.Range(-halfScreenW + halfObjW,
      halfScreenW - halfObjW);
    float randY = Random.Range(-halfScreenH + halfObjH,
      halfScreenH - halfObjH);

    //store the original position
    Vector3 randPos = newSpawn.transform.position;

    //update position with randomized x and y values
    randPos.x = randX;
    randPos.y = randY;

    //set random position
    newSpawn.transform.position = randPos;

    //set parent game object in Unity scene
    newSpawn.transform.parent = gameObject.transform;

    //increment counter
    totalSpawns++;

} //end while
```

The spawn code inside the while loop is identical to that in the for loop. However, we set up an iteration variable called totalSpawns outside the while loop. This keeps track of how many objects have already been spawned, starting from 0. The condition asks whether `totalSpawns` is less than `numSpawns`, which ensures that the loop will run a number of times equal to `numSpawns`. At the very end of the loop code, we manually increment `totalSpawns` by 1. This ensures that the loop ends once `totalSpawns` equals `numSpawns`, thereby making the condition `false`. Simultaneously, that is the point at which we have spawned the desired number of objects. In the end, the two loops have the same result in our game world. Yet, you have practiced two different methods of writing loops. In the future, you will apply both `for` and `while` loops in your code, so it is good to know how to use them.

Summary

You have risen to the challenge and spawned several collectables for Luna to find during her journey. With the ability to spawn objects, you can introduce a wide variety of things into your game world, including items, powerups, enemies, obstacles, and more. You have added all of these coding methods to your game-making toolkit:

- Spawn multiple objects inside the game world

- Instantiate prefabs in Unity

- Randomize position values for spawned objects

- Organize spawned objects under a common parent

- Apply type casting to specify a variable's data type

- Write `for` and `while` loops

With all of these objects being created and collected in the game world, it would be nice to keep track of them. Thus, your next challenge will involve managing groups of objects and creating an inventory of the things Luna has collected.

References

Microsoft Corporation. 2015. Casting and Type Conversions (C# Programming Guide). http://msdn.microsoft.com/library/ms173105.aspx (accessed February 23, 2015).

Unity Technologies. n.d.a. Object.Instantiate. http://docs.unity3d.com/ScriptReference/Object.Instantiate.html (accessed February 23, 2015).

Unity Technologies. n.d.b. Random.Range. http://docs.unity3d.com/ScriptReference/Random.Range.html (accessed February 23, 2015).

7 Taking Inventory

Luna is no longer alone in the surface world. She is surrounded by collectable objects, which we can spawn in vast amounts. As you know, many similar objects could be introduced into our game, such as additional characters, obstacles, or items. Until now, our collectables have been generically spawned and exist only for the purpose of one-time collisions. However, there is much more that we can do with the objects in our game. To unleash their full potential, we need to start identifying and keeping track of our objects over time. This will allow them to be a long-term part of the game. Imagine introducing things like special items, pieces of equipment, or extra heroes into your game. These kinds of objects need to stick around and play a role in our game long after the first time they are encountered. To explore how we can manage our in-game objects over time, this challenge will involve creating an inventory for Luna to store her collected objects in.

Goals

By the end of this chapter, you will be able to apply these coding techniques:

- Create an on-screen inventory system for a game character

- Store multiple objects simultaneously in an inventory

- Apply the C# using directive to access external namespaces

- Manage collections of objects using the C# `List`

- Utilize arguments that are passed into functions

- Access objects that are stored inside a C# `List`

- Add objects to and remove objects from a C# `List`

Required Files

In this chapter, you will need to use the following files from the *Chapter_07 > Software >* folder:

- *Challenge > Assets > Scenes > Map.unity* to run, modify, and test your solution

- *Challenge > Assets > Scripts > CollectableInventory.cs* to code your solution to the challenge

- *Demo > Mac/PC > CollectableInventory* to demonstrate how your completed solution should work

- *Solution > CollectableInventory.cs* to compare your solution to the provided example solution

Challenge: Keeping Track of Collectables in an Inventory

In this challenge, you will create a visible, on-screen inventory to store the objects that Luna collects. Open the CollectableInventory script in your code editor and the Map scene in Unity. Find the Middleground object in the Hierarchy window. As you can see in the Inspector, the CollectableSpawn script from the preceding challenge is attached. Therefore, you can press the R key whenever you want to spawn more collectables. This will help you test your solution to this challenge. Look inside the Foreground object and you will find the familiar Player object, as well as a new object, called Inventory. The Inventory object has the CollectableInventory script attached to it. You will work inside this script throughout the challenge. In addition, you will use the Inventory object to visually organize Luna's collectables. As you know, Luna can collect objects by colliding with them, as defined in our Collectable script. However, this time around, instead of destroying our collectables, we will add them to an on-screen inventory. The overall requirements for this challenge are listed:

1. Each object that the player collects must be stored in a `List`.

2. When an object is collected, it should be added to the `List`. It should also be positioned next to the previous item in the on-screen inventory.

3. When the player presses the T key, the last object in the on-screen inventory should be removed. It should also be removed from the `List`. If no objects exist, the key press should have no effect.

Most of the work for this challenge is ahead of you. Yet, a few things have been provided in the CollectableInventory script. You already have `Start()`, `Update()`, `AddItem()`, and `RemoveItem()` functions defined. Inside these functions, you will write the code that brings your inventory to life. Furthermore, you will need to declare and initialize any variables that you need. Before you get started, try to formulate the logic for how your code will work based on the given requirements. Since this challenge involves managing groups of objects for the very first time, you may want to read along with the hints as you put your solution together.

▌ Hint: The `using` Directive

Look to the top of your CollectableInventory script. You will find this line:

```
using UnityEngine;
```

This line makes use of the C# `using` directive (Microsoft Corporation 2015e). The `using` directive allows a script to access external *namespaces* (Microsoft Corporation 2015b). You can think of a namespace as an organized collection of code that lies outside of the script itself. Typically, we apply the `using` directive to gain access to the contents of a different namespace, so we can use its objects, functions, and other features in our own code. In fact, all of the scripts we write in C# and Unity are going to use these directives to some degree. You can find them near the top of every script associated with this book. For example, the previous example line of code accesses the UnityEngine namespace. This is what allows us to access all of the great features built into the Unity engine, such as `GameObject.FindWithTag()`, `gameObject.transform.position`, `Random.Range()`, and countless others.

In order to start grouping our objects and manipulating them in our inventory, we will need to add a new `using` directive to our script. Specifically, we have to access the *System.Collections.Generic* namespace (Microsoft Corporation 2015d). This namespace contains several classes related to collecting and organizing objects in our code. Most importantly for our current challenge, this namespace is required for us to create a C# `List`. You can add the directive to your script, like so. Place it just below the line that references the UnityEngine namespace:

```
using System.Collections.Generic;
```

On a side note, you will see a compiler error if you ever forget to include a `using` directive in your script. Typically, the error message will read something like this: *The type or namespace name [INSERT NAME] could not be found. Are you missing a using directive or an assembly reference?* This is a clear indication that your script does not currently have access to something important that it needs. Your first troubleshooting step should be to ensure you have all of the required `using` directives.

◼ Hint: The C# `List`

With access to the `System.Collections.Generic` namespace, you are free to create a `List`. A `List` is one of very many ways that you can collect, organize, and manipulate groups of objects in C#. In our current challenge, we need to be able to add and remove objects from our inventory in real time. A `List` is an excellent choice for handling this task.

Before diving into the implementation, let's discuss the basic properties of the C# `List`. A `List` stores a collection of objects with a specified data type (Microsoft Corporation 2015a). For instance, a `List` can contain a group of `int`, `bool`, `GameObject`, or similar values. However, in a single `List`, the data type of every object must be the same. In addition, every object in a `List` is associated with an *index* value. An index represents the position of the object inside the `List`. Note that a `List`, like most other collections of objects in computer coding, is *zero indexed*. This means that the first item in the `List` is represented by the index value of 0. Meanwhile, the second item has an index of 1, the third item has an index of 2, and so on. Unlike human counting, which typically begins at 1, computer code tends to start at 0 in most cases. Keep this in mind when working with `List`. You will get used to counting from 0 as you gain experience as a coder. The other key feature of a `List` is that it can increase and decrease in size as necessary throughout its life span. This means that objects can be added to or removed from a `List` at any time. Therefore, we can refer to a `List` as having a *variable length*. Later on, you will learn about other ways to handle groups of objects, some of which have a *fixed length* that cannot change over time. To summarize, the C# `List` stores multiple objects of the same data type, is zero indexed, and has a variable length.

Let's look at some basic code samples to better understand how `List` can be implemented. To declare a `List`, you must provide a data type and a variable name, like so:

```
//declare a List that stores integers
List<int> intList;

//declare a List that stores GameObjects
List<GameObject> goList;
```

After declaring a `List`, you need to initialize it. To accomplish this, use the new keyword to call the built-in `List` constructor function (Microsoft Corporation 2015c). This automatically provides us with an initialized `List`, which we can use in our code.

```
//initialize a List that stores integers
intList = new List<int>();

//initialize a List that stores GameObjects
goList = new List<GameObject>();
```

This covers the basics of the C# `List`. Why don't you declare and initialize your own `List` in the CollectableInventory script? Doing so fulfills the first requirement for this challenge, because this `List` will store the objects that Luna collects. Therefore, you can think of this `List` as the underlying code behind Luna's on-screen inventory.

▌ Hint: Add and Remove Functions

A convenient feature of the C# `List` is that objects can be added and removed using built-in functions. To automatically add an object to the end of a `List`, call the `Add()` function. Inside the parentheses of the `Add()` function, you should provide the object that you want to add to the `List`. Examples are provided to demonstrate how to use `Add()`.

```
//add an object to the end of a List using Add()

//add the integer 10 a List
intList.Add(10);

//add the Game Object attached to this script to a List
goList.Add(gameObject);
```

Alternatively, you can also insert an object at a specific index position in a `List` using the `Insert()` function. For `Insert()`, you must provide two arguments: the index position, followed by the object itself. `Insert()` does not overwrite any of the other objects in the `List`. It simply places an object at the specified index position and bumps any following objects to the next higher index. This principle is demonstrated:

```
//insert an object into a List using Insert()

/*
Assume that intList currently contains these
values: 1, 2, 3, 4, 5
*/

//insert the integer 10 at index 2
intList.Insert(2, 10);

/*
After the insertion, intList now contains
these values: 1, 2, 10, 3, 4, 5

Remember that Lists are zero indexed when
using the Insert() function!
*/
```

On the other hand, you can automatically remove the first occurrence of an object found in a `List` by calling the `Remove()` function. Inside the parentheses for `Remove()`, you must provide the object that you would like to remove. Note that `Remove()` only removes the very first matching object that it finds. Therefore, any additional instances of the same object would remain in the `List`.

```
//remove an object from a List using Remove()

/*
Assume that intList currently contains these
values: 1, 2, 1, 4, 1
*/
```

```
//remove the first instance of the integer 1
intList.Remove(1);

//Afterwards, intList contains: 2, 1, 4, 1

//remove the first instance of the integer 1
intList.Remove(1);

//Afterwards, intList contains: 2, 4, 1
```

As you can see, Remove() does not give a large degree of control when eliminating objects from a List. Fortunately, we can use RemoveAt() to specify an exact index value at which to remove an object. The RemoveAt() function only requires us to provide an index position. Subsequently, the function will remove the object that it finds at that index position in the List. Again, it does not overwrite or eliminate other objects. Instead, any objects that come later in the list will have their index value reduced to fill the gap left by the removed object.

```
//remove an object from a List using RemoveAt()

/*
Assume that intList currently contains these
values: 1, 2, 3, 4, 5
*/

//remove the integer 3, which is at index 2
intList.RemoveAt(2);

//After the removal, intList contains: 1, 2, 4, 5

//remove the integer 4, which is at index 2
intList.RemoveAt(2);

//After the removal, intList contains: 1, 2, 5

/*
Remember that Lists are zero indexed when
using the RemoveAt() function!
*/
```

With Add(), Insert(), Remove(), and RemoveAt(), you have several handy functions for manipulating any List. Turn to thinking about the current challenge. Part of the second requirement entails adding an object to your List whenever Luna collects it. Meanwhile, part of the third requirement entails removing the last item in the List whenever the player removes it from the on-screen inventory. Think about how you might accomplish these tasks using the List functions discussed in this section.

▌▌ Hint: Access by Index

You've added objects to a List and might be wondering how you can make use of them. One way to retrieve an object in a List is to access it by its index value. Recall that every object has an index position when it is added to a List.

To retrieve an object from a `List`, we use the `List` name, followed by square brackets that contain the index value. Consider these examples:

```
//access List objects by their index position

/*
Assume that intList currently contains these
values: 1, 2, 3, 4, 5
*/

//access the integers in intList by their index positions
//recall that the List is zero indexed
intList[0]; //this would retrieve the value 1 from intList
intList[1]; //2
intList[2]; //3
intList[3]; //4
intList[4]; //5
intList[5]; //this would cause an error
```

This is one of the convenient things about storing objects in a `List`. Since every object is assigned an index value when it is added, we can later retrieve any object by simply referring to its index position. As demonstrated, the object stored at the index position is what gets returned. After retrieval, you may choose to set the object equal to a local variable, pass it into a function as an argument, or use it in calculations.

Also, note the error line in the sample code. A common error that you may encounter when working with index values reads something like this: *Index out of range.* Whenever you see a message similar to this, it means that you attempted to access an invalid index position. For instance, in the sample code, our `List` has only five objects. Therefore, it has index values that range from 0 to 4. If we try to access an index position of 5, or anything else other than 0 to 4, we would cause an error. What the error message tells us is that the `List` does not have an index position for the given value. That is, we never added an object to that position, so that index was never created either. Hence, we would need to modify our code to ensure we only access valid index positions. Be aware of this error as you work with groups of objects and index values. Any time you see it, you will know to examine the index values in your code.

■ Hint: The `Count` Property

All Lists have a *length*, which indicates how many objects are contained inside. You can access the length of any `List` by calling its `Count` property. The value returned by `Count` will be equal to the total number of items in the `List`. Here is a demonstration:

```
/*
Assume that intList currently contains these
values: 12, 37, 92, 85, 64

Use the Count property to retrieve the total
number of objects in a List.
*/

intList.Count; //this would equal 5
```

You can use the Count of a List in a variety of useful ways. For example, perhaps you want to loop through all of the objects in the List. To do so without exceeding the maximum index position and causing an error, you could apply the Count in your condition.

```
/*
Assume that intList currently contains these
values: 12, 37, 92, 85, 64

This for loop uses Count in the
condition to ensure that only valid
index values are iterated through.
*/

for (int i = 0; i < intList.Count; i++) {

        //this would print 12, 37, 92, 85, 64 before the loop ends
        Debug.Log("The current index position is: " + i);

}
```

Another way that you might use the length of a List is to ensure that you have a valid index value before you use it to access an object. For instance, consider the following code sample:

```
/*
Assume we are gradually moving through
the values in our List one by one. Each
time our counter variable is incremented,
it would be good to ensure that a valid
index position exists to match it within
our List. If the counter exceeds the length
of the List, we can wrap back around to the
start of the List.
*/

//increment the index counter
indexCounter++;

//check whether the index value is valid
//valid index
if (indexCounter < intList.Count) {

        //print the retrieved object
        Debug.Log(intList[indexCounter]);

}
//invalid index
else if (indexCounter >= intList.Count) {

        //reset the index counter
        //return to start of List
        indexCounter = 0;

        //print the retrieved object
        Debug.Log(intList[indexCounter]);

}
```

These are just a few of the useful ways that you can apply the Count property to improve your code. Remember this property, as you will be applying it regularly whenever you are working with a C# List. You may even find a way to utilize it in the current challenge.

▮ Hint: Function Argument Usage

Previously, we passed arguments into functions and stored the values that were returned by functions. However, the current challenge gives us an opportunity to utilize an argument that has been passed into a function. Recall that an argument can be passed into a function, like so:

```
/*
When calling a function that accepts arguments,
you can pass one or more arguments into the
function by placing them inside the parentheses.
*/

//create a variable to pass into the function
int aValue = 0;

//pass the variable into the function
theFunction(aValue);
```

After an argument has been passed into a function, it can be manipulated by that function. Here is an example structure for a function that accepts a single argument:

```
/*
This function accepts an argument of the int data type.
That means any int value can be passed into the function.
Afterwards, the int can be used via the defined pseudonym.
*/

void theFunction(int theArgument) {

        /*
        Whenever this function is called, an int
        value must be passed into it. No matter
        what the value is, it can now be referred
        to using the pseudonym theArgument.
        */

        //for example, we could add one to the value
        theArgument++;

        //and print it
        Debug.Log(theArgument);
}
```

Interestingly, no matter what value is passed into a function as an argument, it is renamed by the function. In the sample code, our original variable was named aValue. However, when it is received by the function, it becomes known as theArgument. This renaming feature may seem obscure at first, but it is for a very convenient purpose. That is, we can write our function a single time in a single way using a single variable name for the argument. Regardless of what value or variable is originally passed into the function, it will always be understood by the function under its specified pseudonym. As such, our function is flexible enough to handle any variable name we might pass into it. We will further discuss creating our own functions that accept arguments at a later time. Right now, we only need to understand how to utilize the arguments passed into functions. The key point is that we can use the generic name the function provides to manipulate whatever argument is passed into it.

Let's examine how you can use arguments to support your solution to the current challenge. Open the Collectable script in your code editor and proceed to the bottom of the file. There, you will find this code:

```
//excerpt from Collectable script

//add object to inventory
//note: references CollectableInventory script
CollectableInventory theInventory = GameObject.
    FindWithTag("Inventory").GetComponent<CollectableInventory>();
theInventory.AddItem(gameObject);
```

This code searches for the Inventory GameObject in the Unity scene and accesses its attached CollectableInventory script. Then, it calls the AddItem() function from the CollectableInventory script. As an argument to the CollectableInventory's AddItem() function, it provides the GameObject to which the Collectable script is attached. Recall that the Collectable script is attached to each collectable object in the game. Therefore, when AddItem() is called with an argument of gameObject, the individual collectable that has just collided with Luna is passed to the CollectableInventory script. That way, the collectable can be placed into our on-screen inventory. Go to your CollectableInventory script and find the AddItem() function. The basic function code looks like this:

```
//add an object to the inventory
//note: the Collectable script references this function; when
  collected, the collectable is passed into this function, so it
  can be added to the inventory
public void AddItem(GameObject theItem) {

        /*
        Whatever collectable Luna just collided with
        is passed into this function and represented
        by the pseudonym theItem. Therefore, anything
        you want to do to the collectable, such as
        giving it a new position, can be done by
        manipulating theItem variable.
        */

} //end function
```

The AddItem() function accepts an argument of the type GameObject and gives it the pseudonym theItem. We know from our Collectable script that the object passed into this function is the latest collectable that Luna has collided with. Therefore, we can use this function to accomplish the first and second requirements of this challenge. The collectable, using the pseudonym `theItem`, can be added to our `List` via the `Add()` function. In addition, we can set the collectable's position to align it properly within the on-screen inventory.

From the hints included in this chapter and your previous coding experience, you should be able to achieve the remaining objectives of this challenge. See if you can put a working solution together before proceeding to the example solution.

▌ Example Solution: Keeping Track of Collectables in an Inventory

This challenge involved managing an on-screen inventory of Luna's collectables. As a reminder, the challenge requirements are listed:

1. Each object that the player collects must be stored in a `List`.

2. When an object is collected, it should be added to the `List`. It should also be positioned next to the previous item in the on-screen inventory.

3. When the player presses the T key, the last object in the on-screen inventory should be removed. It should also be removed from the `List`. If no objects exist, the key press should have no effect.

A pseudocode example of the logic behind the example solution is provided:

```
Declare and initialize inventory LIST
IF object collected, CALL AddItem()
IF T key pressed, CALL RemoveItem()

AddItem()
    • ADD item to inventory LIST
    • Set x position EQUAL TO -Screen.width / 2 + half item width
      + index position * inventory LIST COUNT - 1
    • Set y position EQUAL TO other objects in inventory
    • Set parent EQUAL TO inventory object in scene

RemoveItem()
    • IF inventory LIST COUNT IS GREATER THAN 0:
        o REMOVE item at inventory LIST COUNT - 1
        o DESTROY item
```

We will break down each requirement to examine how you could have solved this challenge by coding your CollectableInventory script. The first requirement notes that a `List` should be used to keep track of Luna's collectables. Therefore, we should declare and initialize a `List` in our code.

```
//excerpt from CollectableInventory script

//the stored inventory of collected objects
private List<GameObject> _inventory;
```

```
//init
void Start() {

        //initialize inventory
        _inventory = new List<GameObject>();

} //end function
```

We create a global `List` variable called `_inventory` to store our collect-ables. We specify the `GameObject` type for the `List`, since our collectables are of this type. Then, the `List` is initialized in the `Start()` function.

The second requirement states that a collected object needs to be added to our `List` and positioned within the on-screen inventory. Recall that upon detecting a collision between Luna and a collectable, the Collectable script sends an argument to the CollectableInventory script's `AddItem()` function. That argument represents the object that was just collected. Therefore, we can handle our second requirement inside the `AddItem()` function.

```
//excerpt from CollectableInventory script

//add an object to the inventory
//note: the Collectable script references this function; when
  collected, the collectable is passed into this function, so it
  can be added to the inventory
public void AddItem(GameObject theItem) {

        //add the item to the inventory
        _inventory.Add(theItem);

        //position the item in the inventory
        //creates a row of inventory items along the bottom of the
          screen

        //retrieve the current position
        Vector3 pos = theItem.transform.position;

        //retrieve the size
        Vector3 size = theItem.GetComponent<SpriteRenderer>().
          bounds.size;

        //set the x position inside the inventory
        //align the latest item at the end of the preceding items
        float xPos = (-0.5f * Screen.width / 100.0f) + 0.5f * size.x
                     + (_inventory.Count - 1) * size.x;

        //set the y position at the bottom of the screen
        float yPos = (-0.5f * Screen.height / 100.0f) + 0.5f
          * size.y;

        //update position values
        pos.x = xPos;
        pos.y = yPos;

        //set the updated position
        theItem.transform.position = pos;

        //add item to inventory GameObject in scene
        theItem.transform.parent = gameObject.transform;

} //end function
```

The AddItem() function identifies the collectable GameObject passed into it using the pseudonym theItem. It takes this collectable and adds it to the _inventory List with Add(). Next, the original position is stored, so it can be updated later. Meanwhile, the size is stored to make our code more readable. Then, the new x and y position calculations are made. The on-screen inventory in this example is placed at the lower-left-hand corner of the screen. Each collected object will line up in a row from left to right. Therefore, they all have the same y position, which is equal to the bottom edge of the screen plus half of the object's height (size.y). As we are accustomed to, using half of the object's height adjusts for its center origin point. However, each collectable object needs to have a different x position inside the inventory. Any time a new object is collected, we should account for how many objects are already in the inventory. To start, we take the left edge of the screen plus one half the object width (size.x), which gets our collectable precisely to the left edge of the screen. Next, we add the full width of the collectable multiplied by 1 less than the total Count of items in our _inventory List. This adjustment ensures that our collectables line up neatly beside one another on the screen. To see how this works, try drawing out the inventory and performing the x position calculation for each object (Figure 7.1).

The first object is placed flush to the left side of the screen. This is because _inventory only has a Count of 1. After 1 is subtracted from the Count, the x position adjustment equals 0. However, the second object gets offset by the width of one collectable. That's because one collectable is already present in the inventory. If we didn't make this adjustment, both collectables would be placed on top of each other at the lower left-hand corner of the screen. Yet, by offsetting the x position to account for the collectable that's already in the inventory, we get the objects to line up. As more collectables are added to the inventory, each one is placed at the end of the line. Furthermore, this calculation will work if collectables are removed from the inventory. The Count of our _inventory List always knows how many collectables are inside. Therefore, our x position calculation always finds exactly where to place the next collectable in the on-screen inventory. Once the x and y position values are calculated, they are used to update the position of the collectable. Last, the collectable's parent is set to the Inventory GameObject in the Unity scene. This ensures our collectables are neatly organized under a single parent.

The third requirement notes that a T key press should remove the last collectable from the inventory, provided such an object exists. We handle the key press in Update() and subsequently call the RemoveItem() function.

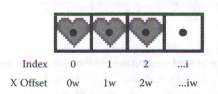

Index	0	1	2	...i
X Offset	0w	1w	2w	...iw

Figure 7.1 The x position offset for several collectable objects is depicted. In the example solution, every object begins from the left edge of the screen plus half of the object width (w). Subsequently, to line the objects up in a row, each is offset based on its index position in the _inventory List. For instance, the offset for the object at index position 2 would be 2w. Thus, regardless of the number of objects in the inventory, the latest one will always be added to the end of the line.

```
//excerpt from CollectableInventory script

//update
void Update() {

        //check for t key press
        if (Input.GetKeyDown(KeyCode.T)) {

                //remove item from inventory
                RemoveItem();

        } //end if

} //end function
```

The RemoveItem() function needs to eliminate the last collectable from our _inventory List, as well as remove it from the on-screen inventory. However, it should only do so when there are actually collectables inside the inventory. Here's one way the function could be structured:

```
//remove the most recent object from the inventory
public void RemoveItem() {

        //only remove if at least one item exists
        if (_inventory.Count > 0) {

                //store item
                GameObject lastItem = _inventory[_inventory.Count - 1];

                //remove the last item in the inventory
                _inventory.RemoveAt(_inventory.Count - 1);

                //destroy item
                Destroy(lastItem);

        } //end if

} //end function
```

Before doing anything else, RemoveItem() ensures that the Count of the _inventory List is greater than 0. Therefore, our code only proceeds if there is at least one collectable in the inventory. Afterwards, the function accesses the last collectable in the _inventory List and stores it in a GameObject variable named lastItem. Recall that objects inside Lists can be accessed using square brackets and an index positon. Meanwhile, Count returns the total number of objects in a List. Since our List is zero indexed, we can find the very last index position by taking Count - 1. That is how the last inventory collectable is retrieved in this example. Once the collectable is stored in a variable, we can safely remove it from our _inventory List. Here, the RemoveAt() function is used with an index position of Count - 1. Finally, to complete the task of removing the collectable from our on-screen inventory, we use the Destroy() function.

Summary

You have created an on-screen inventory for visualizing the objects that Luna collects throughout her journey. In addition, you coded a List to manage the addition and removal of objects in your inventory system. You can expand upon this functionality to introduce a variety of compelling features, such as equipment and consumable item systems, into your games. You have begun managing groups of objects effectively in your code and should be able to accomplish all of these objectives:

- Create an on-screen inventory system for a game character

- Store multiple objects simultaneously in an inventory

- Apply the C# using directive to access external namespaces

- Manage collections of objects using the C# List

- Utilize arguments that are passed into functions

- Access objects that are stored inside a C# List

- Add objects to and remove objects from a C# List

In the next challenge, you will continue building your knowledge of loops and groups of objects. This will require introducing a few friends to accompany Luna as she travels through the surface world.

References

Microsoft Corporation. 2015a. List<T> Class. http://msdn.microsoft.com/library/6sh2ey19.aspx (accessed February 26, 2015).

Microsoft Corporation. 2015b. namespace (C# Reference). http://msdn.microsoft.com/library/z2kcy19k.aspx (accessed February 26, 2015).

Microsoft Corporation. 2015c. new Operator (C# Reference). http://msdn.microsoft.com/library/fa0ab757.aspx (accessed February 26, 2015).

Microsoft Corporation. 2015d. System.Collections.Generic Namespace. http://msdn.microsoft.com/library/system.collections.generic.aspx (accessed February 26, 2015).

Microsoft Corporation. 2015e. using Directive (C# Reference). http://msdn.microsoft.com/library/sf0df423.aspx (accessed February 26, 2015).

8 A Party of Heroes

Luna will need some support to succeed in her journey through the surface world. She'll also have more fun if we provide her with a few friends. You may remember that we defined stats for dryad, dwarf, and orc characters back in Chapter 2. We also introduced the backstory of three characters, including Lily the dryad, Pink Beard the dwarf, and Larg the orc. In this challenge, you will add these heroes to the game world and allow them to join Luna on her journey. Along the way, you'll learn more about managing groups of objects and iterating through them with loops.

▮ Goals

By the end of this chapter, you will be able to apply these coding techniques:

- Create a group of heroes inside the game world

- Manage groups of objects using unidimensional arrays

- Retrieve groups of objects from a Unity scene

- Iterate through groups of objects using `foreach` loops

▮ Required Files

In this chapter, you will need to use the following files from the *Chapter_08 > Software* folder:

- *Challenge > Assets > Scenes > Map.unity* to run, modify, and test your solution

- *Challenge > Assets > Scripts > HeroGroup.cs* to code your solution to the challenge

- *Demo > Mac/PC > HeroGroup* to demonstrate how your completed solution should work

- *Solution > HeroGroup.cs* to compare your solution to the provided example solution

▮ Challenge: Managing a Group of Heroes

Open the Map scene in Unity. In the Scene window, you will see that Luna is surrounded by our three new heroes: Lily the dryad, Pink Beard the dwarf, and Larg the orc. You will place your code for this challenge in the HeroGroup script. Note that this script is attached to the Player GameObject in the Unity scene. Inside the script, you have been provided with several empty functions, including Start(), Update(), ToggleMember(), RemoveMember(), and CheckCollisions(). Everything else will be coded by you. To get an idea of how this script should be crafted, take a look at the requirements for the completed solution:

1. All heroes who are currently in the group should be stored in a variable. Use a storage method that allows objects to be added and removed as needed. Initialize this variable in Start().

2. The Update() function should check for two key presses. When the player presses E, call the ToggleMember() function. When the player presses R, call the RemoveMember() function.

3. The CheckCollisions() function should locate all of the remaining heroes on the map and store them. Next, it should use a loop to iterate through each hero and check for a collision with Luna. If a collision is detected between Luna and a hero, that hero's sprite should be added to the group and the corresponding GameObject should be removed from the map.

4. The ToggleMember() function should change the sprite of the Player GameObject to the next hero in the group. If the last group member is reached, the function should cycle back around to the first group member.

5. The `RemoveMember()` function should delete the currently shown hero from the group. Subsequently, it should switch the Player `GameObject` sprite to the next hero in the group. However, if only one hero is in the group, the `RemoveMember()` function should have no effect.

Remember to sort out the logic for your solution based on these requirements. You should be able to code the first two requirements based on your success in prior challenges. Therefore, the following hints will focus on the remaining three requirements, which involve managing your group of heroes.

▐ Hint: Unidimensional Arrays

A *unidimensional array* is an efficient method for storing objects that exist in nearly all computer languages, including C#. In some ways, an array is similar to the C# `List` that you are already familiar with. Like a `List`, an array is zero indexed and stores objects of a specific data type. However, the major difference is that a `List` has a variable length, whereas an array has a fixed length. Therefore, any time you initialize an array, you must specify exactly what its length will be. Thereafter, the array cannot be resized, added to, or removed from. While the objects inside the array can still be accessed and modified, the overall size of the array is fixed at its original length. Table 8.1 summarizes the similarities and differences between the C# `List` and array.

The major characteristic that differs between a `List` and an array is length. Therefore, we can apply a simple decision process to choose the best type of storage for our needs. In general, arrays are optimized for faster storage and retrieval by the computer. Thus, they are the better choice in most circumstances. However, an array requires a fixed length to be specified at creation. In some circumstances, we need to add and remove objects in real time. Hence, providing a fixed size up front may not be possible or practical. For these situations, a `List` is a better choice, because it is flexible enough to increase or decrease its length over time. To summarize, if you can specify a fixed length for your group of objects, using an array is optimal. Yet, if you cannot provide a fixed length or need the flexibility to change the size of your group over time, use a `List`.

With the basic characteristics of arrays covered, let's look at how they are implemented in code. To declare an array in C#, provide a data type, followed by square brackets, and a variable name.

```
//declare an array that stores integers
int[] intArray;

//declare an array that stores GameObjects
GameObject[] inventoryArray;
```

Table 8.1 Comparison of C# `List` and Array Features

Feature	List	Array
Indexing	Zero indexed	Zero indexed
Data type	Single, fixed	Single, fixed
Length	Variable	Fixed

After declaration, you can initialize an array by calling its constructor with the new keyword. You must provide an integer value that represents the size of the array inside square brackets.

```
//initialize an array that stores 5 integers
intArray = new int[5];

/*
Initialize an array that stores GameObjects.
The size is set to an integer variable that
represents the maximum number of inventory items.
*/
int maxItems = 3;

inventoryArray = new GameObject[maxItems];
```

Alternatively, you can initialize an array and assign values straightaway. To do this, provide a series of comma-separated values inside curly brackets. Here are a pair of examples:

```
/*
Use curly brackets with comma-separated values to
provide an array with values on initialization.
*/

//initialize an array with integer values
intArray = new int[] {1, 2, 3, 4, 5};

//initialize an array with specific GameObjects
inventoryArray = new GameObject[] {Water, Food, Potion};
```

You can access a specific object from an array using its index position. Type the array name, followed by square brackets that contain the index position for the object.

```
//access array objects by their index position

/*
Assume that intArray currently contains these
values: 1, 2, 3, 4, 5
*/

//access the integers in intArray by their index positions
//recall that the array is zero indexed
intArray[0]; //this would retrieve the value 1 from intArray
intArray[1]; //2
intArray[2]; //3
intArray[3]; //4
intArray[4]; //5

/*
Assume that inventoryArray currently contains these
GameObjects: Water, Food, Potion
*/
```

```
//access the GameObjects in inventoryArray by their index positions
inventoryArray[0]; //Water
inventoryArray[1]; //Food
inventoryArray[2]; //Potion
```

Since an array has a fixed length, it does not have convenient add and remove functions like a `List` does. However, you can directly set the value of any array object. Simply access the object by its index position and set it equal to a value. Whatever was previously stored at that position in the array will be replaced by the value that you provide. Consider these examples:

```
//set the value of an array object using its index position

/*
Assume that intArray currently contains these
values: 1, 2, 3, 4, 5
*/

//change the values in intArray
intArray[0] = 10;
intArray[2] = 9;
intArray[4] = 0;

/*
The modified intArray contains these
values: 10, 2, 9, 4, 0
*/

/*
Assume that inventoryArray currently contains these
GameObjects: Water, Food, Potion
*/

//change the GameObjects in inventoryArray
inventoryArray[0] = Potion;
inventoryArray[1] = Water;
inventoryArray[2] = inventoryArray[1];

/*
The modified inventoryArray contains these
GameObjects: Potion, Water, Water
*/
```

To access the overall size of array, use the `Length` property. This functions identically to the `Count` property of a `List`. Thus, `Length` returns the total number of objects in the array. Recall that this information can be useful for a variety of things, such as looping through arrays and validating index values.

```
/*
Use the Length property to retrieve the total
number of objects in an array.

Assume that intArray currently contains these
values: 1, 2, 3, 4, 5
*/
```

```
intArray.Length; //this would equal 5

/*
Assume that inventoryArray currently contains these
GameObjects: Water, Food, Potion
*/

inventoryArray.Length; //this would equal 3
```

That covers the basics of unidimensional arrays in C#. Along with `List`, the array gives you a second excellent way to manage groups of objects in your code. Remember to think about whether you can assign a fixed length or need a variable length when choosing between an array and a `List`. This challenge provides you with the opportunity to apply an array and a `List` to handle different parts of your solution. Give them both a try in your code.

■ Hint: Unity Tags for Multiple Objects

Previously, we used Unity's built-in `GameObject.FindWithTag()` function to retrieve a single object with a specific tag. This works well when only one object has a given tag, such as a player in a one-player game. However, we can also assign the same tag to many objects in our Unity scene. For example, we might have several collectables or obstacles in our game world that use the same tag. Fortunately, we can use the `GameObject.FindGameObjectsWithTag()` function to retrieve all of the objects in our Unity scene that share a given tag. The function is applied similar to `GameObject.FindWithTag()`, except that `GameObject.FindGameObjectsWithTag()` returns a unidimensional array that contains every matching `GameObject`. An example follows:

```
//find all GameObjects that share a common tag
//find all objects with the tag called "tagString"
GameObject.FindGameObjectsWithTag("tagString");
```

Revisit the third requirement of your current challenge, which describes the `CheckCollisions()` function. The initial step for this function involves retrieving all of the remaining heroes on the map. Thereafter, you can iterate through the heroes and check for collisions with the player. Find the hero objects inside the Hierarchy window of your Unity project. You will see that they all have been tagged with *Hero* in the Unity Inspector. Therefore, you can retrieve all of the heroes using the `GameObject.FindGameObjectsWithTag()` function along with the *Hero* tag. Since this function returns a unidimensional array, you will want to set up a variable to store that information in your code. Here is an example of how you might handle this step in your `CheckCollisions()` function:

```
/*
Retrieve all of the remaining heroes
from the map using the Hero tag
and GameObject.FindGameObjectsWithTag()
function. Store these heroes in a local
unidimensional array variable inside
the CheckCollisions() function.
*/

GameObject[] heroes = GameObject.FindGameObjectsWithTag("Hero");
```

▐█ Hint: `foreach` Loops

You already know how to apply `for` and `while` loops. Let's introduce a different kind of loop, called `foreach`. Similar to other kinds of loops, we can use `foreach` to iterate through a group of objects and efficiently execute code many times over. The structure of a `foreach` loop requires these parts: the `foreach` keyword, a data type, a variable name, the `in` keyword, and a group of objects to iterate through. An example of this basic structure follows:

```
foreach (datatype aVariableName in aGroupOfObjects) {

    /*
    Any code placed here will execute each time the loop runs.
    To modify an individual object in the group as its turn comes
    up in the loop, refer to it using the provided variable name.
    */

}
```

Following the `foreach` keyword are two parentheses. Inside these parentheses, the first item listed is a data type. This can be a primitive or composite data type. It should match the type of objects contained within the group that is being iterated through. For instance, if you want to iterate through an array of the data type `GameObject`, the data type in your `foreach` loop should also be `GameObject`. Next comes a variable name that generically identifies the objects inside the group. This mirrors how pseudonyms are used to refer to function arguments. You experienced this during the previous collectable inventory challenge. When a function receives an argument, no matter what the argument's original name was, it is referred to by the pseudonym thereafter. Similarly, no matter what the name of a given object is inside its group, the variable name provided in the `foreach` loop will act as a pseudonym. Thereafter, the code inside our loop can refer to the object by the pseudonym. This makes it efficient for us to write our code a single time and apply it to all of the objects in the group. After the variable name, the `in` keyword is listed. This statement accompanies `foreach` as part of the required keywords to execute this type of loop (Microsoft Corporation 2015). Lastly, the loop requires us to provide a group of objects to iterate through. For example, we might provide the name of a `List` or array stored in our script. Once the required elements are arranged, we place any code that should be executed inside the loop's brackets.

The great thing about `foreach` loops is that they provide us with a fast and easy way to perform operations on an entire group of objects. The loop will gradually step through every individual object in a group and apply any code we want. You can think of a `foreach` loop as saying, "For each individual object in the group of objects, do this." Therefore, this kind of loop is useful when you want to modify several individual objects in a group. Here is a related code sample:

```
/*
Assume you are iterating through a group with the GameObject data
type and want to set the parent of each GameObject. You could use
the following code.
*/
```

```
//iterate through each GameObject in goGroup
foreach (GameObject aGO in goGroup) {

    //set the parent of the current GameObject
    aGO.transform.parent = gameObject.transform;

}
```

In this example, aGO is the pseudonym used to refer to the GameObject currently being iterated through. Meanwhile, goGroup is a collection that contains several GameObject variables. Inside the loop, the parent of the current GameObject being iterated through is set. The loop will continue doing the same for every object inside goGroup. Hence, once the loop has finished, every object inside goGroup will have the same parent assigned to it.

Consider the foreach loop in terms of the third requirement for this challenge. This requirement states that a loop should be used to iterate through the remaining heroes on the map. You already stored these heroes in a unidimensional array at the beginning of your CheckCollsions() function. Although you could use a familiar loop to complete this task, like for or while, try applying a foreach loop instead. With the foreach loop, you can easily iterate through every hero in your array. Here is an example to get you started:

```
/*
Recall that you already found and stored
all of the heroes remaining on the map in
a unidimensional array named heroes.
*/

//iterate through each hero remaining on the map
foreach (GameObject aHero in heroes) {

    //check this hero for collisions
    //execute additional code as necessary

}
```

This loop sets the stage for you to iterate through each of the remaining heroes on the map. Subsequently, you can check them individually for collisions with Luna. If a collision is found, you can add that hero's sprite to your group and remove the original object from the map. That fulfills everything necessary for requirement 3.

Notably, requirements 4 (ToggleMember() function) and 5 (RemoveMember() function) need no special hints beyond what you already know about computer coding. Therefore, you should read over the challenge requirements carefully and see if you can implement them at this point. Compare your own solution to the provided demo to make sure you have everything covered. Once you're satisfied with your work, proceed to the example solution for this challenge.

▌ Example Solution: Managing a Group of Heroes

Besides learning about unidimensional arrays and foreach loops, you had to reapply a number of previously exercised coding skills to solve this challenge.

In the end, you have the ability to add heroes to a group and switch between them during play. To recap, here are the requirements for the challenge:

1. All heroes who are currently in the group should be stored in a variable. Use a storage method that allows objects to be added and removed as needed. Initialize this variable in `Start()`.

2. The `Update()` function should check for two key presses. When the player presses E, call the `ToggleMember()` function. When the player presses R, call the `RemoveMember()` function.

3. The `CheckCollisions()` function should locate all of the remaining heroes on the map and store them. Next, it should use a loop to iterate through each hero and check for a collision with Luna. If a collision is detected between Luna and a hero, that hero's sprite should be added to the group and the corresponding `GameObject` should be removed from the map.

4. The `ToggleMember()` function should change the sprite of the Player `GameObject` to the next hero in the group. If the last group member is reached, the function should cycle back around to the first group member.

5. The `RemoveMember()` function should delete the currently shown hero from the group. Subsequently, it should switch the Player `GameObject` sprite to the next hero in the group. However, if only one hero is in the group, the `RemoveMember()` function should have no effect.

The logic for the example solution is depicted in a process map (Figure 8.1). Recall that the solution opened by declaring and initialing the `_memberSprites` `List` to store the hero group (requirement 1). In addition, the `Update()`

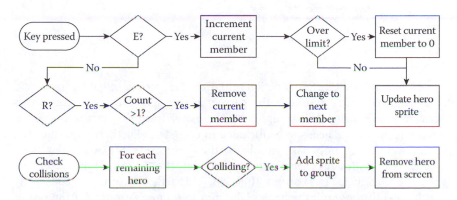

Figure 8.1 A process map illustrates the logic behind the example solution.

function checks for E and R key presses in order to call the `ToggleMember()` and `RemoveMember()` functions. The associated sample code follows:

```
//the member sprites
private List<Sprite> _memberSprites;

//index of current member selected in group
private int _currentMember;

//init
void Start() {

    //init List
    _memberSprites = new List<Sprite>();

    //add sprite of current player to List
    _memberSprites.Add(gameObject.GetComponent<SpriteRenderer>().
        sprite);

    //start at first member
    _currentMember = 0;

} //end function

//update
void Update() {

    //check collisions
    CheckCollisions();

    //check for e key press
    if (Input.GetKeyDown(KeyCode.E)) {

        //toggle member
        ToggleMember();

    } //end if

    //check for r key press
    if (Input.GetKeyDown(KeyCode.R)) {

        //remove member
        RemoveMember();

    } //end if

} //end function
```

Note that the `Start()` function initializes the `_memberSprites` List to store hero sprites and adds the current player sprite to the List. That's because Luna's sprite already represents the player from the start of the game. Therefore, her sprite needs to be included in the List. Furthermore, since the List begins with only a single object, the `_currentMember` index variable is set to 0. Besides checking for key presses, the `Update()` function also calls the `CheckCollisions()` function. This tells the script to constantly check for collisions with the heroes who may join Luna's group. For the rest of the solution, let's take a look at each of the three remaining functions in turn: CheckCollisions(), ToggleMember(), and RemoveMember(). We will start with CheckCollisions().

```
private void CheckCollisions() {

    //store remaining heroes in array
    //retrieve remaining heroes from scene
    GameObject[] heroes = GameObject.
        FindGameObjectsWithTag("Hero");

    //get player's current position
    Vector3 playerPos = gameObject.transform.position;

    //get player's size
    Vector3 playerSize = gameObject.
        GetComponent<SpriteRenderer>().bounds.size;

    //iterate through each hero on the map
    foreach (GameObject aHero in heroes) {

        //get hero position
        Vector3 heroPos = aHero.transform.position;

        //get hero size
        Vector3 heroSize = aHero.
            GetComponent<SpriteRenderer>().bounds.size;

        //set up collision flags
        bool isCollisionX = false;
        bool isCollisionY = false;

        //check x axis
        if (

            //player's right edge is past hero's left edge
            (playerPos.x + 0.5f * playerSize.x >= heroPos.x
                - 0.5f * heroSize.x)

            &&

            //player's left edge is past hero's right edge
            (playerPos.x - 0.5f * playerSize.x <= heroPos.x
                + 0.5f * heroSize.x)

        ) {

            //toggle flag
            isCollisionX = true;

        } //end if

        //check y axis
        if (

            //player's top edge is above hero's bottom edge
            (playerPos.y + 0.5f * playerSize.y >= heroPos.y
                - 0.5f * heroSize.y)

            &&
```

```
                //player's bottom edge is below hero's top edge
                (playerPos.y - 0.5f * playerSize.y <= heroPos.y
                    + 0.5f * heroSize.y)

        ) {

                //toggle flag
                isCollisionY = true;

        } //end if

        //if the objects overlap on both the x and y axes,
            there is a collision
        if (isCollisionX && isCollisionY) {

                Debug.Log("[HeroGroup] Player collision detected;
                    a new hero has joined your party!");

                //add the hero's sprite to the array
                _memberSprites.Add(aHero.GetComponent
                    <SpriteRenderer>().sprite);
                //remove the hero from the scene
                Destroy(aHero);

        } //end if

    } //end foreach

} //end function
```

To fulfill requirement 3, the CheckCollisions() function retrieves the remaining heroes on the map using GameObject.FindGameObjects-WithTag() and stores them in a local unidimensional array. Afterwards, the function iterates through each hero in turn with a foreach loop. Inside the loop, the code checks for AABB collisions, as we have done several times before. While the collision checks are identical to what we have used in the past, this example demonstrates a slightly different format. Here, two separate Boolean flags are used to detect the x and y axis collisions: isCollisionX and isCollisionY. When the positions of the player and the hero overlap on a given axis, its flag is set to true. If both flags are true at the end of the collision check, we are certain that a collision has occurred. That's because both x and y axis overlap are required to determine a two-dimensional (2D) collision. In the event that a collision occurs, the final section of the function is executed. There, the hero's sprite is added to our _memberSprites List for safekeeping and the original hero object is destroyed to remove it from the map. This concludes the CheckCollisions() function and requirement 3. Next comes the ToggleMember() function.

```
public void ToggleMember() {

        //increment current index
        _currentMember++;
```

```
//verify that index is within bounds and reset if necessary
if (_currentMember > _memberSprites.Count - 1) {

    //reset to first member
    _currentMember = 0;

} //end if

//update the renderer based on the current index
gameObject.GetComponent<SpriteRenderer>().sprite
    = _memberSprites[_currentMember];

} //end function
```

For requirement 4, the `ToggleMember()` function begins by incrementing the `_currentMember` index variable. Recall that this variable keeps track of which hero sprite in our `_memberSprites` List is currently displayed. By incrementing the index, it is setting the stage to switch to the next character sprite. However, it must verify that the index value is valid by comparing it to the highest index in the `_memberSprites` List, which is `_memberSprites.Count – 1`. Should the index value be out of range, it resets the `_currentMember` variable back to 0. This has the effect of returning to the first sprite, thus looping back around to the start of the `_memberSprites` List. Lastly, the `ToggleMember()` function must physically change the sprite shown on the screen. It does so by accessing the `SpriteRenderer` component of the Player `GameObject` and setting its `sprite` equal to the `_currentMember` selected from the `_memberSprites` List. Hence, with the `ToggleMember()` function, players are able to switch through the group of heroes in sequence and display their sprites on screen. The final function in this solution is `RemoveMember()`.

```
public void RemoveMember() {

    //only remove if more than one member exists
    if (_memberSprites.Count > 1) {

        //remove member from group
        _memberSprites.RemoveAt(_currentMember);

        //offset index value
        /*
        Index Notes
        Since an object was removed from the List, the
        next index value is one lower than before. Thus,
        we offset the index by -1 before incrementing it
        again in ToggleMember().
        */
        _currentMember--;

        //toggle member
        ToggleMember();

    } //end if

} //end function
```

To satisfy requirement 5, the RemoveMember() function verifies that more than one hero is in the group. It does so by checking that the Count of the _memberSprites List is greater than 1. If not, we prevent the player from deleting the one and only remaining character sprite. However, if there are multiple heroes in the group, the code proceeds to remove the currently selected hero from _memberSprites using the RemoveAt() function. Subsequently, it decrements the _currentMember index variable and calls the ToggleMember() function to swap the on-screen sprite to the next hero in the _memberSprites List.

Note that the decrement of _currentMember is a necessary step to ensure that our code accurately switches to the next hero in line. After a member is removed from the group, the remaining heroes in the List will have index positions that are 1 less than before. Imagine a neat row of heroes lined up. Remove the second, which leaves a gap between the members of the group. Slide the last two heroes over to fill the gap (Figure 8.2). In doing so, you have moved the third hero into the slot the second had previously occupied and the fourth into the slot of the third.

This is similar to what happens when you remove an object from a List. Objects that come after the removed item will have their index values reduced by 1 as they fill in the gap. This is why we must reduce the _currentMember value by 1 after removing a hero from _memberSprites. That way, when _currentMember is later incremented in the ToggleMember() function, it will reflect the proper index position of the next hero in line. With all of the requirements met, you have succeeded in passing this challenge. Have fun finding friends to accompany Luna.

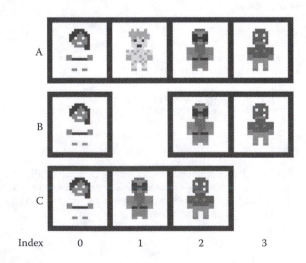

Figure 8.2 (A) A group of four heroes is shown. (B) The second hero is removed. (C) The remaining heroes slide over to fill the vacated space. This demonstrates how the index values of a List are updated when an object is removed.

Summary

Not only have you created an entire party of heroes to accompany Luna on her journey, but you have also learned to manage groups of objects with the unidimensional array and `List`. Meanwhile, `foreach` loops join `while` and `for` loops in your arsenal of techniques to iterate through groups of objects. With these methods in hand, your coding skills continue to grow.

- Create a group of heroes inside the game world

- Manage groups of objects using unidimensional arrays

- Retrieve groups of objects from a Unity scene

- Iterate through groups of objects using `foreach` loops

With an entire party of heroes in our game world and lots of things to collect, let's focus on sprucing up the map itself. In the upcoming challenge, you will generate a unique map from several different tile designs.

Reference

Microsoft Corporation. 2015. foreach, in (C# Reference). http://msdn.microsoft.com/library/ttw7t8t6.aspx (accessed March 3, 2015).

9 Generating a Tile Map

Luna is surrounded by a number of collectable objects and friendly heroes in the surface world. However, the world map of our game has remained a bit drab throughout the journey to date. Let's change that. In this challenge, you will implement a tile map to create a unique and visually pleasing world for our game. A tile map is a game development technique that has been used to create countless classic games, including *Super Mario Bros.* and *The Legend of Zelda*, among many others. Knowing how to utilize tile maps effectively will serve you well in your future two-dimensional (2D) game development.

Goals

By the end of this chapter, you will be able to apply these coding techniques:

- Generate a map from a collection of tiles
- Store information in multidimensional arrays
- Perform complex iteration using nested loops
- Populate multidimensional arrays using nested loops

▌ Required Files

In this chapter, you will need to use the following files from the *Chapter_09 > Software* folder:

- *Challenge > Assets > Scenes > Map.unity* to run, modify, and test your solution

- *Challenge > Assets > Scripts > RandomMap.cs* to code your solution to the challenge

- *Demo > Mac/PC > RandomMap* to demonstrate how your completed solution should work

- *Solution ⋅> RandomMap.cs* to compare your solution to the provided example solution

▌ Challenge: Generating a Tile Map

Your primary responsibility for this challenge is to randomly generate a world map using a set of prefab tiles. Without looking ahead to the Unity project or code, try to describe a logical solution based on the following requirements. Due to the visual nature of this challenge, it may be especially helpful for you to draw out your ideas on paper.

1. Your RandomMap script should calculate the total number of rows and columns in the map based on the current screen size and the size of the tiles being used. It should use these values to initialize a multidimensional array of integers that represents the tile map.

2. The CreateMap() function should use nested loops to populate the map array with random index values drawn from the array of possible tiles.

3. The DisplayMap() function should use nested loops to iterate through the map array. Based on the index values stored in the array, this function should clone, position, and parent the corresponding prefabs from the tile array.

With your initial logic established, open the Map scene in Unity and the RandomMap script in your code editor. In the Unity Hierarchy window, look for the BgMap GameObject, which can be found inside the Background. In the Inspector, you will see that BgMap has the RandomMap script attached. Additionally, four tile prefabs have been defined in the Inspector. These represent the four different background tiles that you will use to generate your map. You can view the individual tiles themselves in your *Assets > Prefabs* folder.

Switch to the RandomMap script. This is where you will code your solution to this challenge. You have been provided with a unidimensional array named `tilePrefabs`. This array contains the background tiles that you will use to generate your map. Beyond that, you have been provided with empty `Start()`, `CreateMap()`, and `DisplayMap()` functions. Everything else in this challenge will be coded by you. You are already familiar with cloning prefabs in Unity from the Chapter 6 challenge. Therefore, the upcoming hints will focus on helping you turn multidimensional arrays and nested loops into a functional tile map for your game.

Hint: Tile Maps in Games

A tile map is a convenient way to organize a 2D game world and conserve art assets. The rectangular row and column structure of a tile map makes it easy to position objects. In addition, a tile map requires relatively few images, but is able to produce a wide variety of game worlds. Further, these features make designing levels efficient. Lastly, a tile map approach is suitable for many different types of games. For example, it can be applied to games seen from a top-down, isometric, or side perspective. Moreover, it can be used to make games that focus on action, exploration, or solving puzzles. The potential applications for a tile map are practically endless. Therefore, once you master the tile map technique, you will be able to apply it to many future games that you want to create.

Let's explore the fundamentals of how a tile map works. Imagine that the entire map is one large rectangle, like a piece of paper. Draw a series of evenly spaced vertical and horizontal lines across the paper and you will form a grid of squares (Figure 9.1). Each individual square on your paper is like a tile.

The tiles are the foundation of a tile map. A tile is a single unit of the map, like one square in a grid. When many tiles are arranged together, an entire map is formed. Note that the tiles are evenly sized and spaced. That is because each tile is a square and has the same dimensions as every other tile. Typically, game tiles are defined in pixels (px) at even powers of 2 to support efficient computer processing. For example, common tile sizes are 16×16 px (2^4), 32×32 px (2^5), and 64×64 px (2^6). Indeed, all of the tiles used in this book are 64×64 px. Other sizes can be used. When choosing a tile size for future projects, keep in mind that the primary goal is to reuse small, easy-to-process tiles to create large, diverse game worlds. Thus, the effectiveness of the tile map approach is maximized.

If you look inside the *Assets > Textures* folder of your Unity project, you will see that the provided *Grass* tiles have been imported as one large image and sliced into individual 64×64 px tiles (Figure 9.2).

This is a common technique for producing art in tile map games. Art asset production and management is beyond the scope of this book, so these kinds of things have been set up for you. Nevertheless,

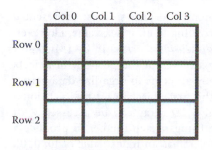

Figure 9.1 A tile map is formed from a grid of spaces laid out into three rows and four columns.

Figure 9.2 A single image containing all of the background tiles was imported into Unity. It was later sliced into several individual tiles.

feel free to further explore these aspects of Unity at your leisure and to incorporate your own art into the projects. Continuing, if you look in the *Assets > Prefabs* folder, you will see that the map tiles have been saved with the GameObject data type. This is what allows us to assign the tile prefabs to the RandomMap script and subsequently clone them to produce our map. Figure 9.3 depicts an example world map that can be produced from the tiles provided in this project. Additional information has been overlaid to conceptualize the structure of the tile map.

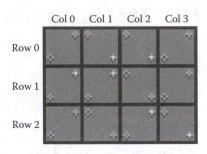

Figure 9.3 An example randomly generated tile map is shown. The overlay highlights how the map is made up of rows and columns of individual tiles.

As you can see, the rectangular shape of the tile map can be represented as a table with rows and columns. Horizontally, the rows flow from top to bottom. Vertically, the columns flow from left to right. With a table-like grid of rows and columns, we can think of our tile map as a coordinate system. For instance, the tile at the top-left corner of the map is located at position (0, 0), whereas the tile at the bottom-right corner is located at position (2, 3). By conceptualizing our tile map as a coordinate grid system, we are able to represent it effectively in computer code. This is where multidimensional arrays come into play.

▌ Hint: Multidimensional Arrays

Thus far, you have practiced using unidimensional arrays. These represent a single group of objects that are ordered according to an index value. However, we also have the capability to utilize *multidimensional arrays* in C# (Microsoft Corporation 2015). Multidimensional arrays represent the position of objects using two or more index values. Hence, they allow us to organize data across multiple dimensions. For example, while the first object in a unidimensional array is found at index 0, the first item in a 2D array can be accessed with the indices [0, 0]. Meanwhile, we can take things a step further to produce a three-dimensional (3D) array whose first object has an index value of [0, 0, 0]. Moreover, there are other types of multidimensional arrays as well, including *jagged* arrays, which are composed of several arrays stored inside a parent array. With all of these multidimensional arrays to choose from, we have many options for structuring data in our game world. The primary features of these multidimensional arrays are summarized in Table 9.1.

When it comes to producing a rectangular tile map to fill our screen, a 2D array is the optimal choice. Therefore, we will focus on implementing a 2D array for the current challenge. You can think of a 2D array as a table of rows and columns. The rows run vertically across the table, starting from 0 at the top and moving downward. The columns run horizontally across the table from left to right, with 0 starting at the left. Therefore, the first value in a 2D array can be found at the index position [0, 0]. Meanwhile, the last value in the 2D array can be accessed at [maximum row value, maximum column value]. Table 9.2 depicts the rows and columns of a 2D array structure.

Notice that the row value comes first and the column comes second when accessing a value in a 2D array. This may seem counterintuitive, because we usually think of coordinates for graphs, tables, or spreadsheets in (x, y) or (column, row) format. However, the notation is reversed when accessing the values inside a 2D array. The first value defines which row we want to access. Then, the second value defines which column to access. This is an important point to keep in mind when accessing values from a 2D array. Suppose that the example array were filled with Boolean values (Table 9.3). Can you determine what values would be retrieved at the index positions of [0, 0], [1, 2], and [2, 0]?

You should have retrieved the following values: true at [0, 0], false at [1, 2], and true at [2, 0]. Review the previous sections, as well as Tables 9.2 and 9.3, until you are comfortable with the structure of 2D arrays.

Table 9.1 Multidimensional Array Types

Type	Indices	Initialization[a]	Access	Structure
2D	2	*type*[,] array2D	array2D[0, 0]	A table of rows and columns
3D	3	*type*[, ,] array3D	array3D[0, 0, 0]	A cube of length, width, and height
Jagged	2	*type*[][] arrayJag	arrayJag[0][0]	An array with other arrays inside

[a] Replace *type* with any valid data type.

Table 9.2 4 × 3 2D Array Structure with Index Positions Shown

	Col. 0	Col. 1	Col. 2
Row 0	[0, 0]	[0, 1]	[0, 2]
Row 1	[1, 0]	[1, 1]	[1, 2]
Row 2	[2, 0]	[2, 1]	[2, 2]
Row 3	[3, 0]	[3, 1]	[3, 2]

Table 9.3 4 × 3 2D Array of Booleans

True	True	False
False	True	False
True	True	True
False	False	False

With an understanding of how 2D arrays are structured, let's look at their implementation in code. The principles are quite similar to those of unidimensional arrays, with a few minor changes to account for the added dimension. You can declare a 2D array with a data type, square brackets, a comma to separate the two dimensions, and a variable name.

```
//declare a 2D array of Booleans
bool[,] bool2d;

//declare a 2D array of integers
int[,] int2d;
```

Like unidimensional arrays, 2D arrays have a fixed length. Since a 2D array has two dimensions, we must initialize the array with both the total number of rows and the total columns. Following the new keyword, we place these values inside the square brackets of the 2D array.

```
//initialize a 2D array of Booleans
//with 5 rows and 2 columns
bool2d = new bool[5, 2];

//declare a 2D array of integers
//with 12 rows and 16 columns
int2d = new int[12, 16];
```

To access an object inside a 2D array, follow the array name with square brackets that contain the object's 2D index position. The value of the object will be returned.

```
/*
Assume that we have an integer array
named int2d with 3 rows, 3 columns,
and the following values.

[3] [8] [1]
[9] [2] [7]
[4] [6] [5]

//access the integers in int2d by their index positions
//recall that the array is zero indexed
int2d[0, 0]; //this would retrieve the value 3
int2d[0, 1]; //8
int2d[0, 2]; //1
int2d[1, 0]; //9
int2d[1, 1]; //2
int2d[1, 2]; //7
int2d[2, 0]; //4
int2d[2, 1]; //6
int2d[2, 2]; //5
```

Values in 2D arrays are set similar to their unidimensional counterparts. We must only remember to include a two-part index value. Otherwise, the process of stating the array name, including an index within square brackets, and setting the expression equal to a value is identical.

```
/*
Assume that we have an integer array
named int2d with 3 rows, 3 columns,
and the following values.

[3] [8] [1]
[9] [2] [7]
[4] [6] [5]

//change the values in the array
int2d[0, 0] = 7;
int2d[1, 2] = 6;
int2d[2, 1] = 3;

/*
After the modifications, int2d
Contains these values.
*/

[7] [8] [1]
[9] [2] [6]
[4] [3] [5]
```

Much like other arrays, the length of the 2D array can be accessed with the Length property. Notably, the Length of an array is not modified by how many dimensions it has. Instead, the Length of an array always reflects the total number of objects it contains. Hence, no matter how many index values we use to refer to the position of an object, it still counts as a single object in the array. Therefore, the Length of an array always refers to the total quantity of objects it stores. Conveniently, for a 2D array, the Length will always match the number of rows multiplied by the number of columns.

```
/*
Assume that we have an integer array
named int2d with 3 rows, 3 columns,
and the following values.

[3] [8] [1]
[9] [2] [7]
[4] [6] [5]
*/

//retrieve the length of the array
int2d.Length; //this would equal 9
```

That covers the fundamentals of 2D arrays. Hopefully, you are comfortable enough to proceed with a specific application of 2D arrays to the current challenge. If not, review the prior topics in this hint and try experimenting with a few 2D arrays in your own code. When you are ready, proceed to learn how to set up a 2D array for use in this challenge.

The first requirement in this challenge can be satisfied by establishing a 2D array to represent the tile map for our game world. To determine the size of the array's rows and columns, we can use the screen height and width, as well as the tile size.

```
//excerpt from RandomMap script

//default size of tiles, in pixels
public int tileSize;

//number of map rows
private int _numRow;

//number of map columns
private int _numCol;

//map array
private int[,] _mapArray;

//array for holding tile prefabs
//defined in Unity Inspector
public GameObject[] tilePrefabs;

//init
void Start() {

    //determine map properties based on screen size
    _numCol = Screen.width / tileSize;
    _numRow = Screen.height / tileSize;

    //initialize map array
    _mapArray = new int[_numRow, _numCol];

} //end function
```

For convenience, we declare a `public tileSize` variable to represent the dimensions of our tiles, in pixels. Since it is public, it can easily be set from the Unity Inspector. In this book, all of the tiles are 64 × 64 px, so a value of 64 should be set. However, should you want to reuse this script in the future or experiment with your own tiles, you could easily do so by changing the value of `tileSize` in the Unity Inspector. Next, we declare two integers, `_numRow` and `_numCol`, to represent the number of rows and columns in the map. Also, we declare a 2D array called `_mapArray` to represent our tile map. Recall that the `tilePrefabs` unidimensional array was provided for us and contains the tile prefabs that will eventually be displayed in our game world. Meanwhile, `_mapArray` represents the raw data structure behind our world map. It will ultimately store randomized index values from the `tilePrefabs` array (see requirement 2), which are integers. Therefore, our `_mapArray` is declared as a 2D array of integers. Indeed, a 2D array of integers is the best choice in this circumstance and many others when it comes to producing tile maps for games. This is because integers can represent many different tiles using simple identification numbers, such as the values 0 through 9.

Continuing, we proceed to initialize our variables inside the `Start()` function. The number of rows and columns is calculated based on the current screen size and the tile size. This ensures that our map fills the entire screen, so long as we play the game at a resolution that is evenly divisible by

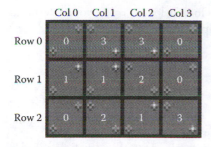

	Col 0	Col 1	Col 2	Col 3
Row 0	0	3	3	0
Row 1	1	1	2	0
Row 2	0	2	1	3

Figure 9.4 A randomly generated tile map is shown. The overlay depicts the 2D array of integers that represents the underlying structure of the tile map.

the tile size. Lastly, we initialize our 2D array using the calculated number of rows and columns. This code should give you a head start on setting up your own script and accomplishing requirement 1.

Before moving on, take a moment to visualize what your completed game world will look like in terms of its underlying 2D array structure (Figure 9.4). This should help you conceptualize the world you are working to create through your code.

▮ Hint: Nested Loops

At this point, your 2D map array is ready to store information about the game world. This is where a new looping technique will prove most useful. You are already quite familiar with a variety of loops, including for, foreach, and while. A normal loop is wonderful for iterating through a single group of objects, producing a consecutive list of values, or executing a code segment over and over. However, there are times when we want to produce multiple, distinct values or iterate through objects in multidimensional arrays. In these circumstances, a single loop is not enough. However, we can use nested loops to traverse multiple iterations simultaneously. Nesting involves placing one loop inside another. Therefore, if we write a normal loop, then place another loop inside of it, we have produced nested loops. Here is an example of a nested for loop:

```
//outer loop
for (int i = 0; i < 3; i++) {

        //inner loop
        for (int j = 5; j > 0; j--) {

                //print the current iteration values
                Debug.Log("Iteration values (i, j) = (" + i + ","
                + j + ")");

        } //end inner loop

} //end outer loop
```

As you can see, we begin by writing a standard loop, which we can refer to as the *outer loop*. To produce nested loops, we position a second, *inner loop* within the brackets of the outer loop. Normally, we use i as our iteration variable for loops. However, since the outer loop has used i already, we proceed to designate j for the inner loop. This reflects common coding practice for naming iteration variables inside nested loops. Note that the code within the inner loop prints a message that contains the current value of the iteration variables. Step through the sample code again. See if you can determine what values are printed from start to finish in these nested loops. Take a look below to verify your interpretation. You can also write the loop into a script and test it for yourself.

```
//outer loop
for (int i = 0; i < 3; i++) {

        //inner loop
        for (int j = 5; j > 0; j--) {

                //print the current iteration values
                Debug.Log("Iteration values (i, j) = (" + i + ","
                    + j + ")");

        } //end inner loop

} //end outer loop

/*
These nested loops would print the
following values from start to
finish. Recall that the values are
printed in (i, j) format. Thus, the
value of the outer loop is printed
first, followed by the inner loop.
*/

(0,5) //outer loop begins first iteration, inner loop begins
(0,4)
(0,3)
(0,2)
(0,1) //inner loop ends all iterations
(1,5) //outer loop begins second iteration
(1,4)
(1,3)
(1,2)
(1,1) //inner loop ends all iterations
(2,5) //outer loop begins third iteration
(2,4)
(2,3)
(2,2)
(2,1) //inner loop ends, outer loop ends
```

Recall that all code in a script is executed from top to bottom, left to right. Therefore, the outer loop is entered first with a value of 0. Next, the inner loop is reached. Thus, the code of the inner loop will proceed until the entire loop is completed. Only after the inner loop is completely finished will we begin the subsequent iteration of the outer loop. Thus, when the outer loop begins, it yields a value of 0. Afterwards, the inner loop yields values of 5, 4, 3, 2, and 1 before it finishes. Only then do we come back around to the start of the outer loop. That is, the outer loop completes a single iteration only after the inner loop has completed all of its iterations. At that point, the cycle continues until the entire nested loop process has finished.

Although it is common to use two nested for loops, be aware that other options are available. Any of the other loop types can be nested inside one another. You can also mix and match types if you desire. Furthermore, you could even nest more than two loops inside one another. Yet, while there are many possibilities for nested loops, you will most often only need to nest two loops together. Beyond that, your code becomes unwieldy and you would likely prefer an alternative solution. Nevertheless, keep nested loops in mind when solving problems through your computer code. As you will come to see, nested loops are especially useful for iterating through and populating multidimensional arrays.

▌ Hint: Nested Loops with Multidimensional Arrays

Nested loops and multidimensional arrays go hand in hand. Why? Recall that multidimensional arrays, such as our 2D tile map array, require multiple index values to access their objects. Furthermore, when we create nested loops, both the outer loop and the inner loop utilize iteration variables. Therefore, the iteration variable values from our nested loops can be used to represent the index positions in our 2D array. By iterating through the index positions of our 2D array, we can assign which tile prefabs will appear at which positions in our tile map. This is precisely what we need to do to fulfill the second requirement for this challenge. Our `CreateMap()` function should take random index values from the `tilePrefabs` array, which represent different map tiles, and slot them into the index positions of our `_mapArray`. Thus, our map array will contain a randomly generated numerical representation of our world map. This code sample provides one possible implementation for the `CreateMap()` function.

```
//randomly generate numeric map representation based on tiles
private void CreateMap() {

        //fill the map array with random tiles from prefab array
        //iterate through map columns (x)
        for (int col = 0; col < _numCol; col++) {

                //iterate through map rows (y)
                for (int row = 0; row < _numRow; row++) {

                        //get a random tile from prefab array
                        //random index value based on array size
                        int randIndex = Random.Range(0, tilePrefabs.
                          Length);

                        //store the tile's index value in the map array
                        _mapArray[row, col] = randIndex;

                } //end inner for

        } //end outer for

} //end function
```

We can accomplish our task with just a few lines of code, but it is important to understand exactly what is happening inside the `CreateMap()` function. We begin with a nested loop. The outer loop iterates through all of the columns in the map, starting from 0 and counting upward. The inner loop similarly iterates through the rows from 0 onward. Think back to the structure of our 2D array, whose [0, 0] index begins in the upper left-hand corner. Our outer loop enters the first column on the left side, then the inner loop fills every row in that column moving downward. After every row in the first column is filled, our outer loop moves one column to the right and the inner loop once again fills every row from top to bottom. You should be able to picture this process in your mind. Imagine that our 2D array begins as an empty table of rows and columns. When our nested loop begins, the space in the upper-left corner is filled, followed by every space beneath it. Once the bottom space is filled, we step to the right one column and fill it from top to bottom. Subsequently, we take another step to the right and continue to fill each column in sequence from top to bottom. Thus, once our nested loops are complete, the entire table is filled. This process is visualized in Figure 9.5.

What values are we filling our 2D array with? Inside our nested loop, we use Unity's `Random.Range()` function to select a random index value from our `tilePrefabs` array. Each index value represents a different tile that we will use to generate our map. All of the tiles are stored in the `tilePrefabs` array, so we can refer to each one uniquely by its index value. Once we randomly calculate a tile's index value, we put it into our map array. Remember that 2D arrays are accessed by row first, then column. Hence, we take the row value from the inner loop and the column value from the outer loop to identify the current index position in our map array. We set that index position in our map array equal to the random tile value we previously calculated. This process repeats until our nested loops have iterated through every row and column to assign a random tile at each map position. Thus, when the entire `CreateMap()` function is finished, we have a randomly generated 2D array of integers. Each integer value represents an index position from the `tilePrefabs` array. Hence, at each position in the map array, we identified a tile prefab `GameObject` that will ultimately be displayed in our game. A sample visualization of a world map at this stage is provided in Table 9.4.

The only step remaining in this challenge is to complete the third requirement by writing the `DisplayMap()` function. You already know how to instantiate the prefabs that represent our map tiles. So, all you need to do is iterate through the entire numerical 2D map array that you just created and instantiate the appropriate tile prefab stored at each map position. You will also want to position each tile in a way that represents the rectangular structure of our world map and provide all tiles with a common parent. Once you have completed the `DisplayMap()` function, you should be able to run your code and see the world map come to life!

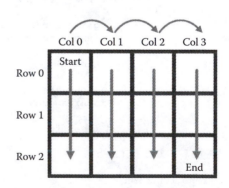

Figure 9.5 A nested `for` loop fills our 2D array starting from the top-left corner. Once the first column is entered, every row below it is filled. Next, the second column is entered and every row below it is filled. This process continues until every position in the array is filled, ending with the bottom-right corner.

Table 9.4 World Map as 2D Array of Integers
Representing Index Positions from Prefab Array

	Col. 0	Col. 1	Col. 2
Row 0	1	3	1
Row 1	0	3	0
Row 2	0	0	2
Row 3	3	1	2

▋ Example Solution: Generating a Tile Map

To review, let's take another look at the requirements for this challenge:

1. Your RandomMap script should calculate the total number of rows and columns in the map based on the current screen size and the size of the tiles being used. It should use these values to initialize a multidimensional array of integers that represents the tile map.

2. The `CreateMap()` function should use nested loops to populate the map array with random index values drawn from the array of possible tiles.

3. The `DisplayMap()` function should use nested loops to iterate through the map array. Based on the index values stored in the array, this function should clone, position, and parent the corresponding prefabs from the tile array.

Sample logic for this challenge is provided in the following pseudocode:

```
Declare int map array, number of rows, number of columns

Start()
```
- Number of columns = screen width / tile size
- Number of rows = screen height / tile size
- Initialize int map array with [number of rows, number of columns]
- CALL CreateMap()
- CALL DisplayMap()

```
CreateMap()
Outer FOR colCounter = 0 IS LESS THAN number of columns, each
iteration:
```
- Inner FOR rowCounter = 0 IS LESS THAN number of rows, each iteration:
    1. Generate random index value between 0 and tilePrefabs. Length
    2. Set map array[rowCounter, colCounter] EQUAL TO random index value

```
DisplayMap()
Outer FOR colCounter = 0 IS LESS THAN number of columns, each
iteration:
    • Inner FOR rowCounter = 0 IS LESS THAN number of rows, each
      iteration:
        1. Instantiate tile at tilePrefabs[mapArray[rowCounter,
           colCounter]]
        2. Set tile's x position EQUAL TO the column value times the
           tile size, offset for the center origin and converted to
           world units
        3. Set tile's y position EQUAL TO the row value times the
           tile size, offset for the center origin and converted to
           world units
        4. Set tile's position based on calculated values
        5. Set tile's parent EQUAL TO map object in scene
```

We'll break down the example solution according to each requirement. The first requirement involves setting up our RandomMap script to handle its major responsibilities of generating and displaying the tile map. We begin by declaring a few variables.

```
//excerpt from RandomMap script

//default size of tiles, in pixels
public int tileSize;

//pixels to world units conversion for Unity Assets
public int pixelsToUnits;

//number of map rows
private int _numRow;

//number of map columns
private int _numCol;

//map array
private int[,] _mapArray;

//array for holding tile prefabs
//defined in Unity Inspector
public GameObject[] tilePrefabs;
```

For convenience, we declare public `tileSize` and `pixelsToUnits` variables. That way, these variables can be set to appropriate values in the Unity Inspector. In this book, all of the tiles are 64 × 64 px, so a value of 64 should be applied. In addition, we use the default Unity setting of 100 to convert the pixels of our images into world units. However, you may want to use this script with different settings in the future and could easily do so by changing these values in the Unity Inspector. Furthermore, we declare variables to store the number of rows and columns for our map. Lastly, we declare a 2D array of integers to represent our tile map. These variables are initialized in the `Start()` function. Recall that the `tilePrefabs` array was already provided and stores the different tiles that will later compose our map.

```
void Start() {

    //determine map properties based on screen size
    _numCol = Screen.width / tileSize;
    _numRow = Screen.height / tileSize;

    //initialize map array
    _mapArray = new int[_numRow, _numCol];

    //generate map array
    CreateMap();

    //display tiles from map array
    DisplayMap();

} //end function
```

To calculate the number of columns for our tile map, we divide the total screen width by the tile size. Similarly, to calculate the number of rows, we divide the screen height by the tile size. Ideally, our game should be played at a resolution evenly divisible by the tile size to ensure that our map fills the entire screen. With our 64 × 64 px tiles, a suggested screen resolution is 1024 × 768 px, which equates to 16 columns and 12 rows. After calculating the number of columns and rows, we use these values to initialize the fixed size of our 2D map array. Lastly, we call the CreateMap() function, followed by the DisplayMap() function, which leads us into our subsequent requirements. Our task for the second requirement was to code the CreateMap() function, such that our array is populated with random prefab tiles. Here's how it can be done:

```
private void CreateMap() {

    //fill the map array with random tiles from prefab array
    //iterate through map columns (x)
    for (int col = 0; col < _numCol; col++) {

        //iterate through map rows (y)
        for (int row = 0; row < _numRow; row++) {

            //get a random tile from prefab array
            //random index value based on array size
            int randIndex = Random.Range(0, tilePrefabs.
              Length);

            //store the tile's index value in the map array
            _mapArray[row, col] = randIndex;

        } //end inner for

    } //end outer for

} //end function
```

Inside CreateMap(), we apply a nested for loop to iterate through the columns and rows of our 2D map array. In each iteration of the loop, we use

Random.Range() to draw a random index value from our tilePrefabs array. Then, we identify the index position for our map array by taking the row value from the inner loop and the column value from the outer loop. We set that index position in our map array equal to the value randomly drawn from the tilePrefabs array. When the process is complete, we have filled our entire 2D array with random integer values that represent our different map tiles. For the third, and final requirement, we need to display our tiles on screen.

```
private void DisplayMap() {

        //loop through the map array
        //iterate through map columns (x)
        for (int col = 0; col < _numCol; col++) {

                //iterate through map rows (y)
                for (int row = 0; row < _numRow; row++) {

                        //clone prefab tile based on value stored in map
                            array
                        GameObject displayTile = (GameObject)
                            Instantiate(tilePrefabs[_mapArray[row, col]]);

                        //calculate tile position
                        //x position
                        float xPos = (float)(col * tileSize - Screen.
                            width / 2 + tileSize / 2) / pixelsToUnits;

                        //y position
                        float yPos = (float)(Screen.height / 2 - row
                            * tileSize - tileSize / 2) / pixelsToUnits;

                        //z position
                        //maintain z position of parent object
                        float zPos = gameObject.transform.position.z;

                        //set position
                        displayTile.transform.position = new
                            Vector3(xPos, yPos, zPos);

                        //add the tile to the map game object in Unity
                            scene
                        //set parent
                        displayTile.transform.parent = gameObject.
                            transform;

                } //end inner for

        } //end outer for

} //end function
```

In the DisplayMap() function, we once again utilize nested for loops to traverse our 2D map array. However, this time around, we retrieve the index values stored in our 2D array and use them to instantiate tile prefabs. While we apply our familiar Unity `Instantiate()` function, notice the bolded syntax used to determine which tile should be cloned.

```
//clone prefab tile based on value stored in map array
GameObject displayTile =
    (GameObject)Instantiate(tilePrefabs[_mapArray[row, col]]);
```

Inside the `Instantiate()` function, we are accessing a `GameObject` from the `tilePrefabs` array. To retrieve that object, we must provide an index value. Recall that our 2D map array has stored an integer that represents each tile's prefab. Therefore, we access the tile prefab value stored at the current index position in our 2D map array. The current index position is determined by the row and column iteration variables of our nested loops. For instance, in the first iteration of our nested loops, we would arrive at an index position of [0, 0] in our map array. When we retrieve the value stored at [0, 0] in our 2D map array, we might find it to be 2. Thus, the value of 2 is passed to the `tilePrefabs` array, which returns the associated tile prefab. That prefab is cloned using the `Instantiate()` function. In this manner, each iteration of our nested loops produces another cloned tile based on the information stored in our 2D map array.

Once our tiles have been cloned, we must position them visually in the rectangular shape of our map. To do so, we convert the tile map's column and row coordinates into Unity world coordinates and apply them to the cloned tile's position.

```
//excerpt from DisplayMap() function

//calculate tile position
//x position
float xPos = (float)(col * tileSize - Screen.width / 2
    + tileSize / 2) / pixelsToUnits;

//y position
float yPos = (float)(Screen.height / 2 - row * tileSize
    - tileSize / 2) / pixelsToUnits;

//z position
//maintain z position of parent object
float zPos = gameObject.transform.position.z;

//set position
displayTile.transform.position = new Vector3(xPos, yPos, zPos);
```

To better understand how the position is calculated, refer back to the visualization of our tile map's rows and columns in Figure 9.3. The x position is calculated using the current column value from our nested loops, the tile size, and the screen width. The formula first multiplies the column by the tile size. This shifts the position of the tile to the appropriate column in our map. Next, we subtract half the width of the screen. Recall that the origin of the Unity world is in the center of the screen, but our 2D map array is a rectangle that has a top-left origin point. Thus, it is necessary to subtract half of the screen width to maintain our map's origin point relative to the Unity world coordinates. Afterwards, the half tile size is added to the x position. This compensates for the fact that our tile prefabs have a center origin point. This adjustment lines our tiles up perfectly within the column structure of our map. The calculation for the y position is similar, with the exception that the current row value from our nested loops and the screen height are used in place of the column value and screen width. For the z position, we simply retain the same value as our parent GameObject. See if you can reason through these calculations for yourself. Drawing a picture will help you to understand how the positioning formulas line up the tiles within our rectangular map structure.

Notice that the formulas for our x and y positions both have a float cast before them. That's because Unity's Vector3 position requires float values to be specified, while our tile map uses integers to represent the column and row coordinates. By adding a float cast, we ensure that our integer calculations are converted into the proper data type. With the converted world coordinates in hand, we set the position of the cloned tile equal to a Vector3 composed of our x, y, and z position variables.

```
//excerpt from DisplayMap() function

//set position
displayTile.transform.position = new Vector3(xPos, yPos, zPos);
```

The final step to complete our DisplayMap() function is to set the parent of our cloned tiles to a common object. In this case, we utilize the BgMap object in our scene, which this script is attached to. Assigning a parent is especially important in this case, because our map is going to be made of many tiles. Using a common parent keeps our Hierarchy window clean and allows us to manage all of our tiles via a common parent, should the need arise.

```
//excerpt from DisplayMap() function

//add the tile to the map game object in Unity scene
//set parent
displayTile.transform.parent = gameObject.transform;
```

With CreateMap() and DisplayMap() completed, all three requirements have been met. You have extensively applied 2D arrays and nested loops in this challenge. Your RandomMap script can now generate beautiful, unique maps for Luna to explore in the game world. Run your project several times over to see the magic happen before your eyes.

Summary

You have livened up the game world for Luna and her friends with a randomly generated map. We will continue to build upon the tile map structure that you coded in this challenge. By exploring the applications of a tile map structure in our game, you will gain additional experience with this valuable game development technique. Surely, you will find many future opportunities to apply tile maps in 2D games. At this point, you should be comfortable completing these coding tasks:

- Generate a map from a collection of tiles

- Store information in multidimensional arrays

- Perform complex iteration using nested loops

- Populate multidimensional arrays using nested loops

The application of our tile map doesn't have to end at the background layer of a map. We can also apply the convenient and orderly tile structure to other areas of our game world. In the upcoming challenge, you will spawn objects at positions on the tile map.

Reference

Microsoft Corporation. 2015. Multidimensional Arrays (C# Programming Guide). http://msdn.microsoft.com/library/2yd9wwz4.aspx (accessed March 6, 2015).

10 Spawning Objects on a Tile Map

Previously, we spawned collectables randomly using Unity world coordinates. Now that we've implemented a nice tile map structure for our game world, we should revisit the concept of spawning objects. Instead of placing objects at arbitrary coordinates in the game world, we can choose to fill the positions of our tile map. By utilizing our tile map structure to position spawned objects, we can take greater control over our game world and set the stage for managing many different objects on our map. To begin this process, we will write a script to spawn objects at random positions on our tile map.

▌ Goals

By the end of this chapter, you will be able to apply these coding techniques:

- Spawn multiple objects on a tile map

- Ensure that spawned objects do not overlap on a tile map

- Write custom functions

- Create functions that return information

- Make functions that utilize arguments

■ Required Files

In this chapter, you will need to use the following files from the *Chapter_10 > Software* folder:

- *Challenge > Assets > Scenes > Map.unity* to run, modify, and test your solution

- *Challenge > Assets > Scripts > MapSpawn.cs* to code your solution to the challenge

- *Demo > Mac/PC > MapSpawn* to demonstrate how your completed solution should work

- *Solution > MapSpawn.cs* to compare your solution to the provided example solution

■ Challenge: Spawning Objects on a Tile Map

This is your biggest challenge yet. Open the Map scene in Unity. Building from the previous challenge, you have been provided with a complete RandomMap script that will generate the background layer for the game world. Thus, your focus in this challenge will be on the MapSpawn script that generates a layer of objects on top of your background map. Open the MapSpawn script in your code editor. You have been provided with a single variable, named `tilePrefab`, which represents the tile that you will spawn.

```
//tile prefab defined in Unity inspector
public GameObject tilePrefab;
```

In your Unity project's Hierarchy window, find the Collectables `GameObject` inside the Middleground. In the Inspector, you can see that the MapSpawn script has been attached to the Collectables `GameObject`. Furthermore, the Collectable prefab from the *Assets > Prefabs* folder has been assigned to the MapSpawn's `tilePrefab` variable (Figure 10.1). Thus, your MapSpawn script has stored the Collectable prefab in a variable named `tilePrefab`.

This is all you are provided with to get your MapSpawn script started. Other than that, you will need to write all of the code necessary to spawn the Collectable prefab at random positions on the tile map. Unlike previous challenges, you are not provided with any functions. That's because you will be learning to write your own functions in this challenge. In fact, from this point forward, you will be coding nearly everything required to complete challenges. Remember to sort out the logic behind your solution before proceeding to implement your code and review the hints. Drawing may be especially helpful for reasoning out how to position the spawned tiles on your map. The requirements for this challenge are listed:

1. Your MapSpawn script should clone a specified number of tile prefabs. These spawns should be placed at randomly generated positions on the tile map. All spawns should share a common parent `GameObject`.

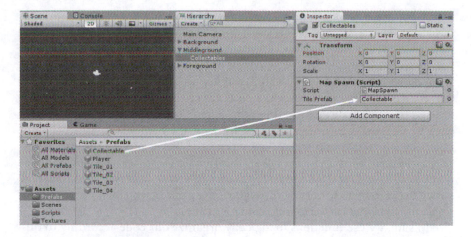

Figure 10.1 The Collectable prefab has been assigned to the MapSpawn script's `tilePrefab` variable.

2. Your script should ensure that no spawns overlap one another on the tile map. However, you must also ensure that the total number of specified tiles is spawned before the script is complete. Hence, you cannot merely skip tiles with duplicate positions, but must find a way to ensure that all tiles are spawned at unique positions.

3. You will write your own functions for the MapSpawn script. Make sure to experiment with different types of functions. Write at least one function that returns a value. In addition, write at least one function that accepts arguments.

Hint: Functions

Essentially, a function is a block of code that can be executed on demand. Although you have not written your own functions up to this point, you have been writing code for functions all along. For instance, in the previous challenge, you wrote all of the code for the `CreateMap()` and `DisplayMap()` functions. Note that those two functions have distinct purposes. One generates the mathematical representation of a tile map as a two-dimensional (2D) array of integers, while the other takes care of visualizing tile prefabs on screen. This division of responsibilities is one of the key features of functions. That is, we use functions to break our code into small, readable portions with specific responsibilities. Technically speaking, we could put the entire code for a game into a single function. However, the code would be unbearably long and complicated. We would have a very difficult time adding new features or fixing bugs if all of our code were placed in one giant function. Instead, we choose to make many functions that accomplish smaller, more specific tasks. This helps to make our code easier to understand, maintain, and reuse.

Another major benefit of functions is that they save us from rewriting the same code over and over. When we write a function, we can call it time and time again. A function can be called simply by typing its name with parentheses. Any time a function is called, all of the code inside of it will execute. If we didn't have the ability to call functions, we would have to rewrite all of that code every time we needed it. Hence, functions are helpful when we need to reuse the same code multiple times throughout our game. For example, think back to the challenge where you kept track of the heroes who joined Luna's group in the HeroGroup script. Every time the player presses the E key, the ToggleMember() function is called. This function switches which hero is currently visible on screen. Since the player can add several heroes to the group and switch between them frequently throughout the game, it pays off for us to write a single function that can be reused numerous times.

In sum, we use functions to logically organize our code according to different responsibilities and to efficiently reuse the same code throughout our software. Thus, when creating your own functions, you should look for opportunities to separate code to accomplish distinct tasks. For example, code that handles keyboard input might be separated from code that handles moving an object around the screen. You should also look for opportunities to write reusable code through functions. For instance, if a player can collide with many objects at any moment during the game, it makes sense to create a function that checks for collisions.

Now that you're familiar with the reasoning behind functions, let's look at how you can write them yourself. In their most basic form, functions need an access level, return type, and name, followed by parentheses and curly brackets. Inside the brackets, we place the code that will execute when the function is called.

```
//basic function structure
//replace ACCESS with an access level, like private or public
//replace RTYPE with a return type or void if nothing is returned
//replace FunctionName with any valid name of your choice
ACCESS RTYPE FunctionName() {

    /*
    Any code that needs to execute
    when the function is called
    should be placed within the
    curly brackets.
    */
}
```

In many ways, writing functions is similar to creating variables. We start with an access level. Like variables, most of the time, we can use private, since our functions do not need to be accessed outside of the immediate script in which they are created. However, we could also use public if a function needs to be called from another script. Alternatively, there are less common access levels that serve special purposes. Next comes the return type. For the most basic functions, there is no information returned. Therefore, the void keyword is used to indicate that no data are returned from the function. Additional options for return values will be covered in an upcoming hint. Then, we must give our function a valid name, similar to how we name variables. Following the function name is a pair of parentheses and curly brackets. Again, the code that belongs to the function goes inside the curly brackets. With these pieces in place, we have formed a basic function structure. To further demonstrate this structure, reexamine some of the functions that you used in prior challenges.

```
/*
The following functions belong to scripts
that you worked on in previous challenges.
Each function utilizes a basic structure
no return type or arguments. The code inside
each function has been removed to help you
focus on the foundational structure of
functions. Once you write the structure of a
function, you can put a wide variety of code
inside its curly brackets.
*/

//from UserInvis.cs, Chapter 4
//check invisibility states
private void CheckInvis() {

    //function code here

}

//from Collectable.cs, Chapter 5
//check collisions
private void CheckCollisions() {

    //function code here

}

//from HeroGroup.cs, Chapter 8
//remove group member
private void RemoveMember() {

    //function code here

}

//from RandomMap.cs, Chapter 9
//randomly generate numeric map representation based on tiles
private void CreateMap() {

    //function code here

}

/*
A function can be called by typing
its name, followed by parentheses.
Each of the previous example
functions can be called, like so.
*/
```

```
//call each function
CheckInvis();
CheckCollisions();
RemoveMember();
CreateMap();
```

■ Hint: Functions with Return Values

In our basic function structure, we apply a return type of void to indicate that no information is returned. Expanding on this concept, it is important to note that we have the option to return information back to the caller of any function. To do so, we should replace void with a specific data type to be returned. This data type can be primitive or composite. For example, to return an integer from a function, we would specify int between the access level and the function name. In the same way, we could also return a composite data type, like a GameObject or SpriteRenderer. See the following code samples that specify different return types for functions. The return types have been bolded.

```
//example return functions
//return a bool that indicates whether the
//player is currently colliding with anything
private bool CheckCollisions() {

    //function code here

}

//return a GameObject that represents a cloned prefab
private GameObject ClonePrefab() {

    //function code here

}
```

Besides identifying a data type to return, the key feature of a return function is that it provides information back to the source that called it. In other words, this type of function *returns* information. Specifically, the final duty of the function is to provide information of the specified return type. Once this information is returned, the function ends immediately. No code should be written in a function after the information is returned, because that code will never be executed. Therefore, providing information is always the last thing that a return function does. In order to return information, a function must use the return keyword (Microsoft Corporation 2015c). Following the return keyword comes the information to be returned. This information can take the form of a value, such as the number 1, or a variable, such as a GameObject that represents a character in the game world. Take a look at our expanded sample functions, which now return information. The return code has been bolded.

```
//example return functions
//return a bool that indicates whether the
//player is currently colliding with anything
```

```
private bool CheckCollisions() {

    /*
    In the body of this function, code would
    be included to check the player for
    collisions and return the appropriate
    value of true or false.
    */

    //check collision
    if (/*collision detection code goes here*/) {

        //return true to indicate collision
        return true;

    }

    //otherwise
    else {

        //return false to indicate no collision
        return false;

    }
}

//return a GameObject that represents a cloned prefab
private GameObject ClonePrefab() {

    //set up a local variable to store the cloned prefab
    GameObject clone;

    /*
    In the body of this function, code would
    be included to instantiate a prefab clone.
    Subsequently, that clone could be returned.
    */

    //return the cloned prefab
    return clone;

}
```

Once information is returned, it gets sent back to the source that called the function in the first place. Typically, we want to store this information. Thus, it is common to set up a variable to *catch* the information provided by a return function. Indeed, you have already done this many times, although you have not yet written your own custom return functions. For instance, every time you call Unity's Instantiate() function to clone a prefab, an object is returned back to you. Previously, we stored the information returned by the Instantiate() function in a GameObject variable and proceeded to position it thereafter. This process is similar to executing a pass in basketball. One player throws the ball, like a return function that provides information, and the receiving player catches the ball, like a variable stores information. Once the information is stored in a variable, it may be further utilized in our code. Another option is to use the information right away, perhaps as part of a conditional statement. Let's examine how the information in our example return functions could be used.

```
//use the information returned by
//CheckCollisions() in an if statement
if (CheckCollisions() == true) {

    /*
    If the value returned by the
    CheckCollisions() function is
    true, the code placed here will
    be executed.
    */

}

//store the information returned by
//ClonePrefab() in a GameObject
GameObject exampleClone = ClonePrefab();

/*
After executing the above code, we would
have a cloned prefab saved in a variable
called exampleClone. Subsequently, we
could further manipulate this GameObject
in our code. For example, we could set
the position of the clone.
*/
```

That covers the fundamentals of return functions. Do not hesitate to apply return functions in your solution to this challenge and in your future game development. Return functions are especially useful when you need to perform calculations and provide information back to the caller. Return functions are unique in that they always give information back when called. Yet, return functions become even more powerful when they are integrated with arguments, which is our next topic of discussion.

■ Hint: Functions with Arguments

The remaining fundamental aspect of functions is that they can accept arguments. An argument represents information that is provided to a function. That information can take the form of a primitive or composite data type. A function that receives an argument can utilize it in its code. You have already practiced calling many functions that accept arguments. The first time you used an argument was in the Destroy() function for the Collectable challenge in Chapter 5. Recall that you must pass an object into the Destroy() function to remove it from the game, as in Destroy(collectable). In addition, you have seen functions that accept multiple arguments. For example, whenever you use Random.Range(), you must provide a minimum and a maximum value, such as Random.Range(0, 5). The 0 and 5 in this example are arguments, which the Random.Range() function uses to calculate a random number. Look back to the code you wrote for previous challenges and you will see many more examples of where you have provided arguments to functions.

At this point, you want to write your own functions that accept arguments. Once again, we can build from the basic function structure that was introduced earlier. Instead of leaving the parentheses of our function empty, we can define an argument by providing a data type and pseudonym. That pseudonym can be any valid variable name.

```
//example argument functions

//check a given GameObject for collisions
private void CheckCollisions(GameObject theGameObject) {

    /*
    The function code could refer to the argument
    passed into it under the pseudonym of theGameObject.
    Note that the pseudonym can be any valid variable
    name and is defined by you when you write a function.
    */

}

//add a bonus score to the player
private void AddBonusScore(int theBonusAmount) {

    /*
    In the body of this function, we could receive
    the argument under the pseudonym of theBonusAmount
    and add it to the player's score.
    */

}
```

Recall our discussion of pseudonyms from the Collectable Inventory challenge in Chapter 7. When we give a pseudonym to an argument, it acts as a generic name that represents the information passed into the function. Thus, the pseudonym can be used to refer to the provided information in the function code, regardless of what the argument's original variable name or value was. This allows us to write a function that can utilize any argument that gets passed in, so long as it is of the appropriate data type. In this sample code, we see examples of single and multiple argument functions. Note that multiple arguments can be added to a function by putting a comma between them. You can define any number of arguments for a function this way, as shown:

```
//example multiple argument functions

//create a tile map, given the number of rows and columns
private void CreateTileMapWithSize(int theNumRow, int theNumCol) {

    /*
    This function would use the theNumRow and
    theNumCol arguments to initialize a 2D
    map array.
    */

}

//spawn an object at a specific position
private void SpawnAtPos(GameObject theSpawn, Vector3 thePos) {
```

```
/*
This function would clone theSpawn GameObject
and then set its x and y position based on the
values stored in thePos Vector3 argument.
*/

}
```

To reiterate, when you call a function that accepts arguments, you must pass in information that matches the data type of the arguments in the function definition. Here are a few examples:

```
//calling argument functions

//check collisions for the a GameObject variable named Player
CheckCollisions(Player);

//add a bonus of 100 points to the player's score
AddBonusScore(100);

//create a tile map with 5 rows and 3 columns
CreateTileMapWithSize(5, 3);

//spawn a GameObject variable named Collectable
//at a given position
SpawnAtPos(Collectable, new Vector3(0, 0, 0));
```

Another important distinction to make is how an argument is passed into the function. Certain arguments are *passed by value* (Microsoft Corporation 2015b), while others are *passed by reference* (Microsoft Corporation 2015a). When an argument is passed by value, its literal value is provided to the function, distinct from anything already stored in the computer's memory. For example, suppose you create an integer, name it valueInt, and assign it a value of 4. If you pass valueInt as an argument into a function, that function receives a value of 4, but not the valueInt variable itself. Hence, if the function were to modify the argument it received, the original valueInt variable would remain unchanged. By contrast, when an argument is passed by reference, the function is pointed to the same space in the computer's memory where the data are stored. Thus, if the function modifies the argument, the original variable will be modified as well. For instance, when you pass a GameObject into the Destroy() function, the actual object that you passed in is removed from the game world. Think back to primitive and composite data types for an easy way to identify whether an argument is passed by value or reference. At the fundamental level, primitive data types are passed by value, whereas composite data types are passed by reference. Thus, when you pass an argument in the form of a bool, int, float, or double, the function receives a value only. Yet, when you pass an argument in the form of a string, List, GameObject, or any other composite data type, the function references the original object itself. It is important to be aware of whether you are or are not modifying objects that are passed into functions, as this will have different implications for how information flows through your code. So long as you are aware of how values are passed, you will be in a good position to maintain

10. Spawning Objects on a Tile Map

control and consistency throughout your code. In the following code sample, the difference between passing arguments by value and reference is demonstrated:

```
//primitive data types are passed by value
//thus, the original data passed in is not modified
//create an integer
int aValue = 5;

//print the value
Debug.Log(aValue); //5

//pass the integer into a function
PassValue(aValue);

//define the function
private void PassValue(int theValue) {

    //add 1 to the value
    theValue++;

    //print the value
    Debug.Log(theValue); //6

}

//print the value again
Debug.Log(aValue); //still 5

//composite data types are passed by reference
//thus, the original data and argument are the same
//assume we set the position of the attached GameObject
gameObject.transform.position = new Vector3(0, 0, 0);

//print the position
Debug.Log(gameObject.transform.position); //0, 0, 0

//pass the object into a function
PassReference(gameObject);

//define the function
private void PassReference(GameObject theGameObject) {

    //set the position
    theGameObject.transform.position = new Vector3(1, 1, 1);

    //print the position
    Debug.Log(theGameObject); //1, 1, 1

}

//print the position
Debug.Log(gameObject.transform.position); //now also 1, 1, 1
```

On a final note for functions, be aware that standard, return, and argument functions are not mutually exclusive. Thus, they can be mixed and matched at will. For example, it is perfectly fine to have both a return value and several arguments in a single function. The capability of functions to accept, calculate, and return information provides you with a tremendous amount of flexibility in how you solve computer problems. Be creative and effective in using functions to organize your code. Examples of functions that return values and accept arguments are provided for reference:

```
//example mixed return and argument functions

//create and return a tile map, given the number of rows and
    columns
private int[,] CreateTileMapWithSize(int theNumRow, int theNumCol) {

    //initialize the array
    int[,] mapArray = new int[theNumRow, theNumCol];

    //return the array
    return mapArray;

}

//add a bonus score to the player and return the updated score
private int AddBonusScore(int theCurrentScore, int theBonusAmount) {

    //increment the current score with the bonus amount
    theCurrentScore += theBonusAmount;

    //return the updated score
    return theCurrentScore;

}
```

Your true challenge in this chapter is to explore how to write functions effectively. Most of the details in the requirements involve tasks you are already familiar with. Specifically, you are well practiced in cloning prefabs and generating random positions. Using techniques for managing groups of objects, you can accomplish the task of ensuring no spawns overlap one another. Thus, the unique part of this challenge is that you are going to invent functions of your own to accomplish these goals. Be creative and come up with a solution that is truly your own. Then, proceed to compare and contrast your work with the provided example solution.

▮ Example Solution: Spawning Objects on a Tile Map

Naturally, since you organized your own code and wrote your own functions for this challenge, your solution will likely differ from the example. Nevertheless, it is useful to review your own code in contrast to that written by others. Often, you will gain unexpected insights into the different ways a problem can be solved. As a reminder, the complete challenge requirements are listed:

1. Your MapSpawn script should clone a specified number of tile prefabs. These spawns should be placed at randomly generated positions on the tile map. All spawns should share a common parent GameObject.

2. Your script should ensure that no spawns overlap one another on the tile map. However, you must also ensure that the total number of specified tiles is spawned before the script is complete. Hence, you cannot merely skip tiles with duplicate positions, but must find a way to ensure that all tiles are spawned at unique positions.

3. You will write your own functions for the MapSpawn script. Make sure to experiment with different types of functions. Write at least one function that returns a value. In addition, write at least one function that accepts arguments.

Meanwhile, Figure 10.2 conveys the logic behind the sample solution.

As with most problems that can be solved using computers, it is helpful to break this challenge down into pieces. Let's start by setting up some variables to store the necessary information.

```
//tile size, in pixels
public int tileSize;

//pixels to Unity world units conversion
public int pixelsToUnits;

//number of tiles to spawn
public int numTiles;

//tile prefab defined in Unity inspector
public GameObject tilePrefab;
```

We include our familiar tile size and pixels to units variables for making calculations based on the tile map structure. In addition, we declare an integer, called numTiles, to specify the number of objects to spawn. Each of these three variables is public and can be set via the Unity Inspector.

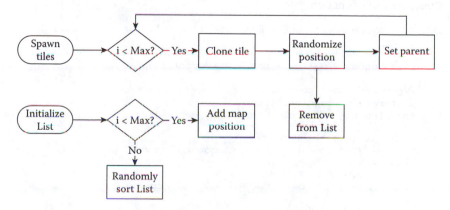

Figure 10.2 A process map illustrates the logic behind the example solution. A List storing all potential map positions is created and randomly sorted. Based on the specified number of tiles to spawn, each tile is cloned, retrieves a unique map position from the List, and is given a parent.

Lastly, the `tilePrefab` variable, which was provided at the start of the challenge, stores the prefab associated with this script. The overall flow of the MapSpawn script's responsibilities is managed in the `Start()` function.

```
void Start() {

    //determine map properties based on screen size
    int numCol = Screen.width / tileSize;
    int numRow = Screen.height / tileSize;

    //create open positions collection
    List<Vector2> openPos = CreatePos(numCol, numRow);

    //randomize order of open positions
    RandSortPos(openPos);

    //check that valid number of tiles is specified
    //if more tiles have been specified than are open
    if (numTiles > openPos.Count) {

        //restrict to number of open positions
        numTiles = openPos.Count;

    } //end if

    //store collection of cloned tiles
    GameObject[] spawnTiles = CloneTiles(tilePrefab, numTiles);

    //spawn tiles at random positions
    SpawnTilesAtRandPos(spawnTiles, openPos, tileSize,
        pixelsToUnits);

} //end function
```

We begin by calculating the number of rows and columns for the tile map based on the current screen dimensions and tile size. A `List` of `Vector2` variables named `openPos` is created to ensure that no spawned tiles overlap. To accomplish this, every possible map position is stored in the `List` by the `CreatePos()` function.

```
private List<Vector2> CreatePos(int theNumCol, int theNumRow) {

    //create collection to store open positions
    List<Vector2> allPos = new List<Vector2>();

    //populate open positions
    //iterate through columns
    for (int col = 0; col < theNumCol; col++) {

        //iterate through rows
        for (int row = 0; row < theNumRow; row++) {

            //store position
            Vector2 pos = new Vector2(col, row);

            //add position
            allPos.Add(pos);

        } //end inner for

    } //end outer for
```

```
        //return open positions
        return allPos;

} //end function
```

This is an example of a function that accepts multiple arguments and returns information. To prepare the return type, a local `List` variable named `allPos` is initialized. Following, we use nested loops to add every tile map position to the `List` in the form of `Vector2` variables. Once the nested loops are complete, all map positions have been added to the `List`, which is returned back to the caller of the function. Note that our `Start()` function set up the `openPos` `List` to catch the information returned by the `CreatePos()` function. Hence, `openPos` now contains all of the possible tile map positions.

```
//excerpt from Start() function

//create open positions collection
openPos = CreatePos(numCol, numRow);
```

Once all of the map positions are stored in a `List`, the next thing we want to do is randomize their order. This will help us to ensure that no tiles overlap one another on the map. Whenever we need to position a tile, we retrieve it from the randomized `List`. After the position is used, we remove it from the `List`. Therefore, our system ensures that we always get a random position and that no positions are ever used more than once. To make this work, we randomize the order of the open map positions by calling the `RandSortPos()` function.

```
private void RandSortPos(List<Vector2> thePositions) {

    //start counter at last item in collection
    int indexCounter = thePositions.Count;

    //loop through items
    while (indexCounter > 1) {

        //decrement counter
        indexCounter--;

        //store a copy of the original value
        Vector2 original = new Vector2(thePositions[indexCounter].x,
            thePositions[indexCounter].y);

        //calculate random index value
        int randIndex = Random.Range(0, indexCounter);

        //swap the original value for the random
        thePositions[indexCounter] = thePositions[randIndex];

        //swap the random value for the original
        thePositions[randIndex] = original;

    } //end while

} //end function
```

This function accepts a single argument that represents the List to sort. In our case, it is the openPos List. Subsequently, the positions are randomly shuffled within the List. The shuffling is accomplished using a while loop and Sattolo's sorting algorithm (Wilson 2005). We set up a counter that is equal to the number of items inside the List. The while loop continues so long as the counter is greater than 1. Inside the loop, the counter is immediately decremented. The counter is used to draw the last item from the List and store it in a local variable named original. Next, Random.Range() is used to calculate an index value between 0 and 1 less than the value of the counter. Hence, every position in the List that precedes original is eligible to be selected. Then, a swap is performed. The List item at the same index as the counter is set equal to the List item at the random index. Immediately after, the List item at the random index is set equal to the position stored in original. Effectively, this means that the last item in the List trades places with another, randomly selected, item in the List. Sattolo's algorithm helps us to loop through our entire List a single time, performing these random swaps over and over. Once the loop is complete, we have a nicely shuffled List. Thus, instead of openPos storing the positions (0, 0) at index 0, (0, 1) at index 1, (0, 2) at index 2, and so on, in sequential order, the positions are randomly shuffled. See Figure 10.3 for a visual depiction of the shuffling process.

At this point, our MapSpawn script has created and randomized a List of possible spawn positions. Moving along in the Start() function, we make a simple check to ensure that a valid number of tiles has been defined in the Unity Inspector.

```
//excerpt from Start() function

//check that valid number of tiles is specified
//if more tiles have been specified than are open
```

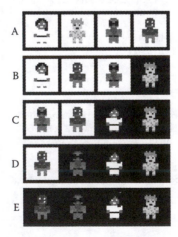

Figure 10.3 The diagram depicts how our List is shuffled. At each step, the last person is swapped randomly with one of the preceding people. The darkened squares represent finalized positions. Starting at A, Larg is swapped with Lily to yield B. In B, Pink Beard is swapped with Luna to yield C. Finally, in C, Pink Beard is swapped with Larg to yield D. The final outcome is shown in E.

```
if (numTiles > openPos.Count) {

        //restrict to number of open positions
        numTiles = openPos.Count;

} //end if
```

As you can see, we check whether more tiles have been asked to spawn than open positions exist on our map. To ensure such a mistake does not disrupt the function of our program and produce errors, we cap the maximum number of spawns to the total number of open positions. From here, we can at last focus on spawning our tiles. In Start(), a GameObject array named spawnTiles is set equal to the CloneTiles() function.

```
private GameObject[] CloneTiles(GameObject thePrefab, int
   theNumClones) {

    //store clones in array
    GameObject[] cloneTiles = new GameObject[theNumClones];

    //populate cloned tiles array
    for (int i = 0; i < theNumClones; i++) {

        //clone prefab tile
        GameObject cloneTile = (GameObject)Instantiate(thePrefab);

        //add the tile to the map game object in Unity scene
        //set parent
        cloneTile.transform.parent = gameObject.transform;

        //add to clone array
        cloneTiles[i] = cloneTile;

    } //end for

    //return clone array
    return cloneTiles;

} //end function
```

The CloneTiles() function is intended only to handle the cloning and parenting of prefabs, but not their positioning. It accepts a GameObject that represents the tile prefab and an integer that indicates the number of copies to be cloned. It starts by initializing a GameObject array with a size equal to the total number of tiles that need to be cloned. A loop is created to run one time for each of these tiles. Inside the loop, each tile is cloned from a prefab, parented, and added to the array. At the end of this process, the entire array of cloned tiles is returned. Thus, our spawnTiles array contains all of the tiles that need to be positioned on the map. The final step is to randomly position these tiles. This is accomplished using the SpawnTilesAtRandPos() function, which accepts a GameObject array to position, a List of available map positions, the tile size, and the pixels to units conversion. For us, the spawn-Tiles array contains every tile awaiting a position, while the openPos List stores the available map positions. Meanwhile, our tileSize and `pixelsToUnits` variables contain the remaining information. Therefore, we pass `spawnTiles`, `openPos`, `tileSize`, and `pixelsToUnits` as arguments into the `SpawnTilesAtRandPos()` function.

```
private void SpawnTilesAtRandPos(GameObject[] theTiles, List<Vector2>
    theOpenPos, int theTileSize, int thePixelsToUnits) {

    //loop through tiles
    foreach (GameObject aTile in theTiles) {

        //select the next open map position
        float randCol = theOpenPos[0].x;
        float randRow = theOpenPos[0].y;

        //remove the used position
        theOpenPos.RemoveAt(0);

        //calculate the position in world units
        //x position
        float xPos = (randCol * theTileSize - Screen.width / 2
            + theTileSize / 2) / thePixelsToUnits;

        //y position
        float yPos = (Screen.height / 2 - randRow * theTileSize
            - theTileSize / 2) / thePixelsToUnits;

        //z position
        float zPos = gameObject.transform.position.z;

        //set tile position
        aTile.transform.position = new Vector3(xPos, yPos, zPos);

    } //end foreach

} //end function
```

The `SpawnTilesAtRandPos()` function loops through each `GameObject` in the provided array argument. The column and row coordinates from the first position in the `List` of open positions are stored in `float` variables. Remember how we shuffled the `List` earlier? This makes it convenient for us to take a random position whenever we need it by simply asking for the first item. Afterwards, the position is removed from the `List` using `RemoveAt()`. This prevents it from ever being used again and ensures that our spawns do not overlap one another on the map. Following, the map position taken from the `List` is converted into Unity world coordinates. The position of the current tile is set equal to a `Vector3` formed by the Unity world coordinates. This completes a single iteration of the loop. In total, the loop will step through each spawn tile, remove an open map position from the `List`, and set the tile's position. Once complete, all of the tiles have been positioned.

To summarize, the MapSpawn script starts by populating a `List` with all of the possible positions on the tile map in the `CreatePos()` function. Next, it randomly shuffles the order of those map positions using the `RandSortPos()`. Based on the number of tiles specified in the Unity Inspector, it clones and parents the tiles in `CloneTiles()`. Lastly, the tiles are positioned, while ensuring they never overlap, in the `SpawnTilesAtRandPos()` function.

As noted earlier, your solution likely differs from the example, which is fine. For a challenge of this complexity and with very little code provided up front, we would expect people to come up with a wide variety of solutions. The important factors for your success in this challenge are that you learned how to organize your code using functions and how to spawn objects on a tile map. Many more opportunities will come for you to utilize functions, so this is only the beginning.

Summary

Writing your own functions is a big step in your growth as a coder. You have the power to organize your code and solve problems in an infinite variety of ways. You have also expanded the capacity of your tile map to handle the spawning of objects. This means that you can add all kinds of things to your game world, like characters, collectables, and obstacles. Having completed this challenge, you should be able to perform all of these coding tasks:

- Spawn multiple objects on a tile map

- Ensure that spawned objects do not overlap on a tile map

- Write custom functions

- Create functions that return information

- Make functions that utilize arguments

The complexity of our project, and our game world, continues to increase. As we add more features to our game, we need to think about how they will be organized. Therefore, our next challenge will involve managing the generation of an entire game map, along with all of the objects that may be placed upon it.

References

Microsoft Corporation. 2015a. Passing Reference-Type Parameters (C# Programming Guide). https://msdn.microsoft.com/library/s6938f28.aspx (accessed March 11, 2015).

Microsoft Corporation. 2015b. Passing Value-Type Parameters (C# Programming Guide). http://msdn.microsoft.com/library/9t0za5es.aspx (accessed March 11, 2015).

Microsoft Corporation. 2015c. return (C# Reference). http://msdn.microsoft.com/library/1h3swy84.aspx (accessed March 11, 2015).

Wilson, M. 2005. Overview of Sattolo's algorithm. In *Algorithms Seminar 2002–2004*, ed. F. Chyzak, 105–108. France: INRIA.

11 Level Generation

In the preceding challenge, we created a MapSpawn script to handle spawning objects on our tile map. While the script is nicely composed to spawn a single object without any overlapping positions, our game levels likely want to include many different objects. For instance, we may want to add things like heroes, collectables, obstacles, doors, and so on, to our map. Fortunately, our MapSpawn script works with any type of tile prefab. Therefore, we can add a new MapSpawn for each type of object we want to spawn. Unfortunately, our various MapSpawn scripts are completely independent and unaware of one another. Hence, they cannot coordinate to ensure that their tiles do not overlap, among other things. Thus, it is time to think about how we will organize all of the individual pieces that compose our map. In this challenge, we will introduce a script that is responsible for managing all of the spawned objects in our game world.

▌▌ Goals

By the end of this chapter, you will be able to apply these coding techniques:

- Design unique game levels with just a few scripts

- Manage all objects spawned on a tile map

- Apply the principles of coupling and cohesion

- Refactor code to enhance organization

Required Files

In this chapter, you will need to use the following files from the *Chapter_11 > Software* folder:

- *Challenge > Assets > Scenes > Map.unity* to run, modify, and test your solution

- *Challenge > Assets > Scripts > MapManager.cs, MapSpawn.cs, RandomMap.cs*, and *UserMove.cs* to code your solution to the challenge

- *Demo > Mac/PC > MapManager* to demonstrate how your completed solution should work

- *Solution > MapManager.cs, MapSpawn.cs, RandomMap.cs*, and *UserMove.cs* to compare your solution to the provided example solution

Challenge: Generating the Map Scene

Open the Map scene for this challenge in Unity and look to the Hierarchy window. A MapGenerator GameObject has been created and has a MapGenerator script attached to it (Figure 11.1).

This is the primary script that you will edit for this challenge. Currently, it is empty, so it will be your responsibility to use it effectively to achieve the goals of this challenge. Meanwhile, under the Background GameObject, you will find the BgMap GameObject, which contains our RandomMap script (Figure 11.2). As always, RandomMap is used to create the tile map background for our game world.

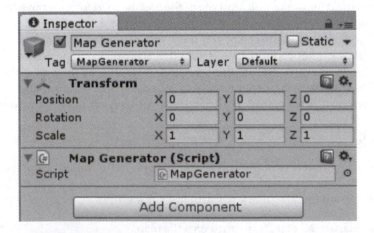

Figure 11.1 A MapGenerator GameObject and the associated MapGenerator script have been provided in the Unity project.

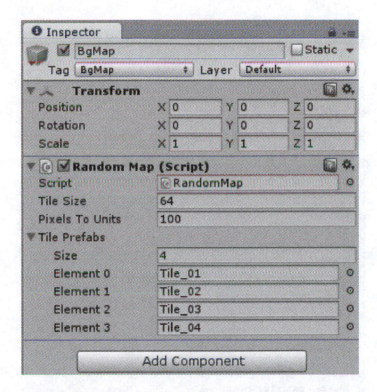

Figure 11.2 A BgMap GameObject and the associated RandomMap script have been provided in the Unity project.

In the Foreground, you will find the familiar Player GameObject, which we have used throughout the challenges. Meanwhile, the Middleground contains the Collectables GameObject and Stairs GameObject (Figure 11.3). Both of these have MapSpawn scripts attached to them and are used to spawn different types of tiles on our map.

Hence, unlike the last chapter, where we spawned only one type of object on our map, we are now spawning multiple types of objects. Indeed, this is the very reason why we are in need of the MapGenerator script. The basic concept behind this challenge is to gain better control of how the game world is created, while also making our scripts independent of one another. Instead of having all of our scripts run their respective Start() functions as soon as the game is launched, we will use the MapGenerator to tell each script what it should do and when. As our game world becomes more complex, it becomes necessary to have better control over its creation. At the same time, we want to maintain independence between our scripts, such as RandomMap and MapSpawn, so they can be easily reused in future projects. This challenge entails implementing a few fundamental computer science approaches, which will be explored in the hints.

The requirements for this challenge follow. Consider working on one requirement at a time and testing to make sure it works, before proceeding to another. This will help you to focus in on your solution and put it together piece by piece.

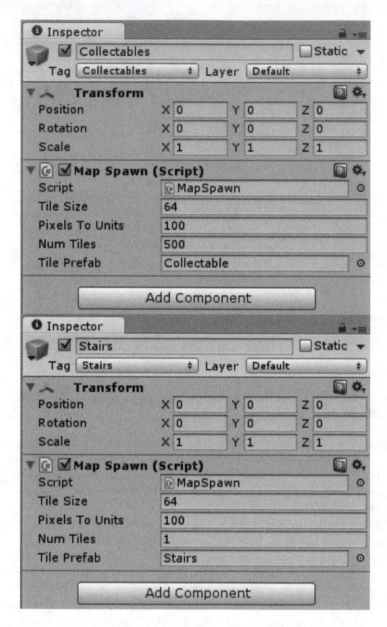

Figure 11.3 Inside the Middleground GameObject are the Collectables GameObject and Stairs GameObject. Both have MapSpawn scripts associated with them.

Also note that this challenge will require you to edit several scripts, in addition to writing the MapGenerator, such as RandomMap, MapSpawn, and UserMove. Furthermore, every aforementioned GameObject, including BgMap, Collectables, Stairs, and Player, has a tag assigned to it in the Unity Inspector window. This will make it easy for you to access them inside your MapGenerator script using Unity's `FindWithTag()` function. Since much of this challenge involves reorganizing your code and defining the responsibilities for each script, it may be useful to visualize your logic as a diagram of the relationships between your scripts.

1. The MapGenerator script should manage the creation and display of the background layer of the tile map. It should control when the RandomMap script executes its code and provide it with any necessary information.

2. The MapGenerator script should manage the creation and display of the Middleground layer of the tile map. It should control when all MapSpawn scripts execute their code and provide them with any necessary information. The MapGenerator script should also ensure that no tiles in this layer of the map overlap one another.

3. The MapGenerator script should include a function to spawn the Player `GameObject` at a specified row and column position on the tile map. For example, the Player `GameObject` could be spawned at (0, 0) when a level is created.

▐ Hint: Coupling and Cohesion

The term *coupling* refers to how interrelated different aspects of our code are. In other words, coupling measures how dependent our scripts are upon one another. If our scripts refer to one another often and rely on many other scripts to perform their responsibilities, they are tightly coupled. On the other hand, if our scripts can perform their tasks without relying on any other scripts, they are loosely coupled. Generally speaking, it is desirable for our scripts to be loosely coupled. By keeping our scripts independent of one another, we create code that is easier to understand, maintain, and reuse. For instance, if we clearly establish the responsibilities of RandomMap without referencing code stored in other scripts, it will be easy to understand that RandomMap handles the creation of a tile map just by looking at it. Similarly, should we need to make a change to RandomMap, no other scripts will be affected since they are independent of one another. Furthermore, if our RandomMap script is entirely independent of other scripts, it can be readily applied to future projects that require a tile map. Hence, keeping our scripts loosely coupled and independent of one another brings us several benefits.

An accompanying coding term, known as *cohesion*, refers to how closely our different pieces of code relate to one another. Think in terms of our scripts once again. If all of the code contained within a script strongly supports the responsibilities of that script, we have high cohesion. In contrast, if we combine many unrelated features into a single script or otherwise put divergent pieces of code together, we have low cohesion. Generally, we want our scripts to have high cohesion. Similar to loose coupling, high cohesion helps us create code that is easy to understand, maintain, and reuse. For example, inside the RandomMap script, we wrote functions that create and display a tile map. We could also have placed several other features in that script, such as those found in our UserMove script. However, it wouldn't make much sense for our RandomMap script, whose job is to handle the creation of a tile map structure, to also move our character around the screen. Instead, we opt to make each script responsible for its own tasks and only include highly related code that supports the achievement of those tasks. Hence, our RandomMap script focuses on creating a tile map structure. Our MapSpawn script focuses on cloning, positioning, and displaying a given prefab atop the tile map. Our UserMove script focuses on handling user input to move a character. By separating the responsibilities of our scripts and only including relevant code in each individual script, we are able to achieve loose coupling and high cohesion at the same time.

The Unity game engine that we are working with in all of our challenges is designed to support loose coupling and high cohesion. Unity has a *component-based* structure. That is, the objects in the game engine are formed by attaching small, distinct pieces of functionality to them. These pieces are known as *components*. Unity provides us with the GameObject, which has a wide variety of components that can be added to it. Some components that we have already seen include Transform, SpriteRenderer, and scripts.

As an example, look to the Player GameObject in the Map scene for the current challenge. You will see that it has Transform, SpriteRenderer, and UserMove script components attached (Figure 11.4). The Transform gives Luna a position, the SpriteRenderer makes her visible on the screen, and the UserMove script allows us to control her with the keyboard. All of these are

Figure 11.4 In the Unity scene, Luna is represented by the Player GameObject. This GameObject has Transform, SpriteRenderer, and script components.

necessary elements for the Player `GameObject` in our game. Indeed, all of them relate closely to the same objective of creating a functional character in our game world. Yet, at the same time, each component handles its own unique responsibilities that are distinct from the others. Therefore, our Player `GameObject` and its components have loose coupling and high cohesion. These characteristics are naturally supported by the design of the Unity game engine. By using the power of the Unity engine, we can achieve loosely coupled and highly cohesive code in our game development.

▌▌ Hint: Refactoring for Better Management

Although we gain some important benefits through loose coupling and high cohesion, there are some drawbacks as well. When all of our scripts are independent of each other, they perform their responsibilities without any awareness of the other scripts. Without any kind of communication between our scripts, we have little control over the kind of game world we create. Imagine that we add several different MapSpawn scripts to our Unity scene. Each script will randomly spawn a different object on our map, such as stairs, heroes, or collectables. Since each MapSpawn script is independent of the others, there is no way for the scripts to ensure that their tiles do not overlap one another. Each script will merely spawn its own tile at random positions without any knowledge of the other scripts. Therefore, it is quite likely that the spawns will overlap one another, which is an undesirable outcome in our game design.

One solution to the lack of control that comes along with loose coupling and high cohesion is to *refactor* our code using a manager script. Refactoring refers to the process of reorganizing our code to change its structure, but without changing its overall functionality. One approach is to have an entity that handles the control of and communication between several independent scripts. In our current challenge, we are introducing a MapGenerator script to manage the creation of our entire map scene. The MapGenerator is responsible for telling RandomMap to create the background tile map, all of the MapSpawn scripts to spawn their objects on top of the tile map, and the Player `GameObject` where to be positioned when the scene is loaded. Additionally, the MapGenerator will ensure that none of the spawned tiles overlap one another. In the end, each of our scripts will remain independent and benefit from loose coupling and high cohesion. However, the MapGenerator script will be an exception, because it is aware of each script's responsibilities and passes any necessary information to them.

To incorporate the MapGenerator effectively into our game project, we will need to do a bit of refactoring in our scripts. We want to put in the effort to make our scripts completely independent from one another. Simultaneously, we want to design our MapGenerator script to control all of the independent scripts, such that we can create our game world effectively. To begin, it may be helpful to sort out the logic behind what each script in our project should be responsible for. Think about what responsibilities should belong to the MapGenerator and what responsibilities should belong to the independent scripts: RandomMap, MapSpawn, and UserMove. Table 11.1 portrays one way that the responsibilities between the scripts could be divided.

Table 11.1 Script Responsibilities

MapGenerator	RandomMap	MapSpawn	UserMove
Tells other scripts when to execute	Generates 2D array to represent the tile map	Clones a specified number of tile prefabs	Checks for user input
Stores information common to all map scripts	Displays background layer of tile map from a set of prefabs	Randomly positions tiles on the map	Moves the player based on user input
Passes other scripts information as needed			
Keeps track of where objects are spawned to ensure none overlap			

Based on how you plan to divide the responsibilities between your scripts, you should proceed to implement your solution. Remember our goals of creating scripts that are loosely coupled and highly cohesive. Also recall that our manager is the glue that holds all of our independent scripts together and allows us to control the creation of our map. Note that this challenge involves refactoring portions of the code in several scripts, as well as writing the MapManager from scratch. Feel free to explore the scripts and modify anything necessary to execute your solution. Along the way, keep the requirements in mind as a guide for how your solution should ultimately function. Focus on one requirement at a time and implement your solution piece by piece.

▊ Example Solution: Generating the Map Scene

Recall that the overall objective of this challenge is to gain more detailed control over the design of our tile map. This requires us to refactor our code to maximize the effectiveness of our MapGenerator script, while rendering our RandomMap and MapSpawn scripts loosely coupled and highly cohesive. Let's revisit the challenge requirements:

1. The MapGenerator script should manage the creation and display of the background layer of the tile map. It should control when the RandomMap script executes its code and provide it with any necessary information.

2. The MapGenerator script should manage the creation and display of the Middleground layer of the tile map. It should control when all MapSpawn scripts execute their code and provide them with any necessary information. The MapGenerator script should also ensure that no tiles in this layer of the map overlap one another.

3. The MapGenerator script should include a function to spawn the Player GameObject at a specified row and column position on the tile map. For example, the Player GameObject could be spawned at (0, 0) when a level is created.

Figure 11.5 provides a visual diagram of the relationships between the MapGenerator and the associated scripts in the example solution.

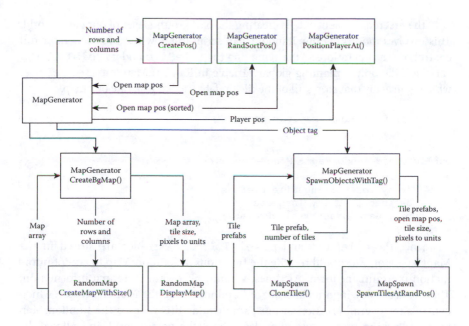

Figure 11.5 The relationships between the MapGenerator and associated scripts in the example solution are portrayed. Notice the flow of information into and out of the MapGenerator and its functions. The functions in the RandomMap and MapSpawn scripts can receive and return information, but they never communicate directly with one another. Instead, all information flows through the MapGenerator.

To review the example solution, we will break down the script responsibilities and requirements step by step. Two of the MapManager's responsibilities from Table 11.1 involve storing information and passing it to the other scripts as needed. You may have noticed that we previously stored the `tileSize` and `pixelsToUnits` conversion as variables in both our RandomMap and MapSpawn scripts. It is not ideal for us to duplicate this information in both scripts, especially since we have a MapGenerator to handle such things. Therefore, we will move our `tileSize` and `pixelsToUnits` variables to our MapGenerator script. At the same time, we will remove these variables from the RandomMap and MapSpawn scripts. That way, the information is stored a single time in a single place. Thus, we simplify our code and make it more efficient. When other scripts need this information, it will be the MapGenerator's job to pass it along.

```
//excerpt from MapGenerator script

//class definition
public class MapGenerator: MonoBehaviour {

    //default size of tiles, in pixels
    public int tileSize;

    //pixels to Unity world units conversion
    public int pixelsToUnits;
```

The first requirement entails creating the background layer of our game world. This involves modifying our RandomMap script to allow the MapGenerator full control over its operations. After removing the `tileSize` and `pixelsToUnits` variables, the only remaining global variable in RandomMap is `tilePrefabs`, which is an array that stores all of the tile prefabs used to generate our map.

```
//excerpt from RandomMap script

//class definition
public class RandomMap : MonoBehaviour {

    //array for holding tile prefabs
    //defined in Unity Inspector
    public GameObject[] tilePrefabs;
```

Since the `tileSize` and `pixelsToUnits` variables are stored in the MapGenerator, we should rewrite the functions in RandomMap to accept information in argument form. At times, we may also want to return information. Thus, data are flowing into and out of RandomMap to the MapGenerator, which controls the overall creation of our game world. This relieves the RandomMap script of having to store its own data about the game world and allows the MapGenerator to take control. In the previous challenge, our RandomMap script had two functions: one to create the tile map's data structure and one to display the tile map in our scene. Again, we will use two functions to maintain these qualities. However, the way we pass information into and out of these functions will change. Let's consider how to create the tile map's data structure first. We will use a function called `CreateMapWithSize()`. This function is very similar to the `CreateMap()` function that we wrote in Chapter 9's challenge. The differences are in bold.

```
//generate tile map with given size and return it
public int[,] CreateMapWithSize(int theNumCol, int theNumRow) {

    //initialize map array
    int[,] mapArray = new int[theNumRow, theNumCol];

    //fill the map array with random tiles from prefab array
    //iterate through map columns (x)
    for (int col = 0; col < theNumCol; col++) {

        //iterate through map rows (y)
        for (int row = 0; row < _numRow; row++) {

            //get a random tile from prefab array
            //random index value based on array size
            int randIndex = Random.Range(0, tilePrefabs.Length);

            //store the tile's index value in the map array
            mapArray[row, col] = randIndex;

        } //end inner for

    } //end outer for
```

```
    //return map array
    return mapArray;

} //end function
```

As you can see, this function accepts a number of rows and columns as arguments to determine the size of the tile map two-dimensional (2D) array. This information will be provided by the MapGenerator, so RandomMap doesn't need to worry about it. Instead of storing a global 2D array to represent the tile map, a local mapArray variable is created inside the function. Using our familiar nested loops, the array is populated with random index values that represent the tile prefabs. Afterwards, the local mapArray is returned by the function. This array is ultimately passed back to the MapGenerator. Hence, we have accomplished our task of passing information from the MapGenerator to RandomMap and back to the MapGenerator. Essentially, this makes the RandomMap script entirely independent and relieved from having to store permanent information about our game world. All of the lasting information is handled by the MapGenerator instead. The other major responsibility of RandomMap is to display the tile map in the scene. Again, we have a function similar to Chapter 9's DisplayMap(), except that our updated function receives additional arguments, which are provided by the MapGenerator.

```
//display the tiles
public void DisplayMap(int[,] theMapArray, int theTileSize, int
    thePixelsToUnits) {

    //retrieve array size
    int numRow = theMapArray.GetLength(0);
    int numCol = theMapArray.GetLength(1);

    //loop through the map array
    //iterate through map columns (x)
    for (int col = numCol - 1; col > -1; col--) {

        //iterate through map rows (y)
        for (int row = numRow - 1; row > -1; row--) {

            //clone prefab tile based on value stored in map array
            GameObject displayTile = (GameObject)Instantiate
                (tilePrefabs[theMapArray[row, col]]);

            //calculate tile position
            //x position
            float xPos = (float)(col * theTileSize - Screen.width / 2
                + theTileSize / 2) / thePixelsToUnits;

            //y position
            float yPos = (float)(Screen.height / 2 - row
                * theTileSize - theTileSize / 2) / thePixelsToUnits;

            //z position
            //maintain z position of parent object
            float zPos = gameObject.transform.position.z;

            //set position
            displayTile.transform.position = new Vector3(xPos,
                yPos, zPos);
```

```
        //add the tile to the map game object in Unity scene
        //set parent
        displayTile.transform.parent = gameObject.transform;

    } //end inner for

  } //end outer for

} //end function
```

Rather than leveraging global variables stored in RandomMap, our `DisplayMap()` function now accepts arguments for the 2D tile map array, tile size, and pixels to units conversion. It gets the number of rows and columns from the map array argument and uses them to iterate through all of the tiles. For each tile, a prefab is cloned, positioned, and parented, as we have done many times before. Notably, this function is almost identical to our previous one, with the exception that it utilizes arguments passed to it from the MapGenerator instead of variables stored within the RandomMap script itself. That covers the refactoring of our RandomMap script. Let's return to the MapGenerator to see exactly how it creates the background layer of our tile map. Inside the `Start()` function, you will see that the MapGenerator calls its own `CreateBgMap()` function.

```
//excerpt from MapGenerator script

//create background map
private void CreateBgMap() {

        //get map object from scene
        RandomMap bgMap = GameObject.FindWithTag("BgMap").
          GetComponent<RandomMap>();

        //determine map properties based on screen size
        int numCol = Screen.width / tileSize;
        int numRow = Screen.height / tileSize;

        //generate map array
        int[,] middleMap = bgMap.createMapWithSize(numCol, numRow);

        //display tiles
        bgMap.displayMap(middleMap, tileSize, pixelsToUnits);

} //end function
```

To begin, `CreateBgMap()` finds the RandomMap script in the Unity scene by its tag. Next, it calculates the number of rows and columns for the tile map using the current screen size and tile size. This information is passed into the RandomMap's `CreateMapWithSize()` function. A 2D array representing the tile map is returned and stored in the `middleMap` variable. Last, the tile map array, tile size, and pixels to units conversion are passed into the RandomMap's `DisplayMap()` function. Thus, the background layer of our tile map has been generated and displayed. Notice how the MapGenerator script was in total control of this process. Meanwhile, the RandomMap script merely received information, performed calculations, and returned information back to the MapGenerator.

This is precisely what we wanted to happen. At this point, we have achieved the first requirement for this challenge, so our next step is to handle the spawning of objects atop our tile map.

Take a look at the MapSpawn script and we'll discuss how it can be refactored to work effectively with our MapGenerator. The script is based on our Chapter 10 challenge, but it has been modified. Similar to RandomMap, MapSpawn no longer stores the `tileSize` or `pixelsToUnits` variables. However, it retains two key variables.

```
//excerpt from MapSpawn script

//class definition
public class MapSpawn : MonoBehaviour {

    //number of tiles to spawn
    public int numTiles;

    //tile prefab defined in Unity Inspector
    public GameObject tilePrefab;
```

Both variables are defined in the Unity Inspector for the script. As before, the `numTiles` variable specifies how many clones the script will make and `tilePrefab` defines which tile prefab the script will spawn. Recall that our previous MapSpawn script stored all of the open tile map positions and kept track of which were still available for spawning. This is now the responsibility of the MapGenerator, so the associated variables and functions have been removed from MapSpawn. The MapGenerator can keep track of any number of MapSpawn scripts, so the responsibility of avoiding overlap is better served by the MapGenerator. Thus, our MapSpawn script is left with two functions: `CloneTiles()` and `SpawnTilesAtRandPos()`. Both of these functions are already prepared to receive information from the MapGenerator and do not need to be refactored further. Therefore, we should return to the MapGenerator and examine how it handles the MapSpawn scripts. To keep track of all possible spawn positions in the Middleground layer of the map, the MapGenerator declares a `List` of `Vector2` variables named `_middleOpenPos`.

```
//excerpt from MapGenerator script

//default size of tiles, in pixels
public int tileSize;

//pixels to Unity world units conversion
public int pixelsToUnits;

//available positions in middleground layer
private List<Vector2> _middleOpenPos;
```

Previously, our MapSpawn script contained a `List` of the available map positions, which was populated and shuffled using functions named `CreatePos()` and `RandSortPos()`. However, now that our MapGenerator is responsible for these duties, the functions have been placed there and removed from MapSpawn.

Inside Start(), the MapGenerator initializes the _middleOpenPos List, populates it with every open position in our tile map, and then randomizes the order of the List.

```
//excerpt from MapGenerator script

void Start() {

    //determine map size based on screen/tile size
    int numCol = Screen.width / tileSize;
    int numRow = Screen.height / tileSize;

    //populate middleground with open positions
    _middleOpenPos = CreatePos(numCol, numRow);

    //randomize order of open positions
    RandSortPos(_middleOpenPos);
```

The MapGenerator's CreatePos() and RandSortPos() functions are identical to those in the MapSpawn script from the Chapter 10 challenge. Yet, the MapGenerator stores the _middleOpenPos List of available positions in a global variable. Therefore, it can keep track of all objects spawned on the map and ensure they don't overlap. In contrast, each of our MapSpawn scripts is independent and unaware of any other scripts. Thus, we gain the benefit of better control over our spawned objects by refactoring this code to appear in the MapGenerator.

The MapGenerator uses tags to handle the spawning of objects in the Middleground layer of the tile map. For instance, we have GameObject variables in our Unity scene tagged *Stairs* and *Collectables*. These objects have MapSpawn scripts attached to them, which indicate the quantity and type of prefab to spawn on the tile map. A custom function named SpawnObjectsWithTag() is written in the MapGenerator script to handle the execution of any MapSpawn script according to the tag of its associated GameObject.

```
//excerpt from MapGenerator script

//spawn objects associated with a specific tag
private void SpawnObjectsWithTag(string theTag) {

    //retrieve game object associated with tag
    GameObject parentObject = GameObject.FindWithTag(theTag);

    //verify that object exists in scene
    if (parentObject != null) {

        //retrieve spawn script
        MapSpawn spawnScript = parentObject.
          GetComponent<MapSpawn>();

        //if more tiles have been specified than are open
        if (spawnScript.numTiles > _middleOpenPos.Count) {
```

```
        //restrict to number of available tiles
        spawnScript.numTiles = _middleOpenPos.Count;

    } //end if

    //clone tiles
    GameObject[] spawnTiles = spawnScript.CloneTiles(spawnScript.
        tilePrefab, spawnScript.numTiles);

    //spawn tile at random position
    spawnScript.SpawnTilesAtRandPos(spawnTiles, _middleOpenPos,
        tileSize, pixelsToUnits);

    } //end if

} //end function
```

The SpawnObjectsWithTag() function receives a string argument that represents a tag in our Unity scene. It uses the argument in tandem with the FindWithTag() function to store a local variable that represents the associated GameObject.

```
//excerpt from MapGenerator script
//from SpawnObjectsWithTag() function

//retrieve game object associated with tag
GameObject parentObject = GameObject.FindWithTag(theTag);
```

A conditional statement verifies that the object exists before proceeding. Otherwise, there's a risk we would attempt to manipulate an object that doesn't exist, which would produce an error. Assuming the object is valid, its MapSpawn script is retrieved with GetComponent() and stored locally as spawnScript.

```
//excerpt from MapGenerator script
//from SpawnObjectsWithTag() function

//verify that object exists in scene
if (parentObject != null) {

    //retrieve spawn script
    MapSpawn spawnScript = parentObject.GetComponent<MapSpawn>();
```

Another if statement checks whether the script's specified number of spawns is greater than the total number of available map positions in the Middleground layer. If the original number is less, it will be used. Otherwise, the number of tiles is set to the total number available instead. It wouldn't make sense to allow more tiles to be spawned than there are empty positions, since some tiles would overlap.

```
//excerpt from MapGenerator script
//from SpawnObjectsWithTag() function

//if more tiles have been specified than are open
if (spawnScript.numTiles > _middleOpenPos.Count) {
```

```
            //restrict to number of available tiles
            spawnScript.numTiles = _middleOpenPos.Count;

} //end if
```

Following, a local `GameObject` array of named `spawnTiles` is created by calling the MapSpawn script's `CloneTiles()` function. Lastly, the MapGenerator calls the MapSpawn's `SpawnTilesAtRandPos()` function.

```
//excerpt from MapGenerator script
//from SpawnObjectsWithTag() function

//clone tiles
GameObject[] spawnTiles = spawnScript.CloneTiles(spawnScript.
    tilePrefab, spawnScript.numTiles);

//spawn tile at random position
spawnScript.SpawnTilesAtRandPos(spawnTiles, _middleOpenPos,
    tileSize, pixelsToUnits);
```

The MapGenerator passes the tile size, pixels to units conversion, array of cloned tile prefabs, and `List` of available positions as arguments. These pieces of information ensure that the MapSpawn script performs its duties in accordance with the level being generated by the MapGenerator. For instance, providing the tile array and open position `List` ensures no tiles overlap, while the tile size and pixels to units values ensure the positions are calculated according to the size of our tile map.

That completes the `SpawnObjectsWithTag()` function. The nice thing about this function is that it can handle any type of tile prefab, so long as it is tagged in our Unity scene and associated with a MapSpawn script. Therefore, no matter how many different objects we want to include in our game world, this single function can handle them all. It only takes a simple function call by the MapGenerator to execute `SpawnObjectsWithTag()` for each object we want to place on our map. On that note, in the MapGenerator's `Start()` function, the `SpawnObjectsWithTag()` function is used to spawn stairs and collectables.

```
//excerpt from MapManager script
//from Start() function

//stairs
SpawnObjectsWithTag("Stairs");

//collectables
SpawnObjectsWithTag("Collectables");
```

Thus, the MapGenerator controls how the MapSpawn scripts spawn various objects on the tile map. It also keeps track of which positions are available to prevent any overlap. With these tasks complete, we have successfully achieved the second challenge requirement.

All that remains is the third requirement, which entails positioning the player on the tile map. A public `Vector2` variable, named `playerPos`, is included in the MapGenerator. This will control where the player is spawned when the level is created. By making the variable public, the player's starting position can be set in the Unity Inspector window.

```
//excerpt from MapManager script

//default size of tiles, in pixels
public int tileSize;

//pixels to Unity world units conversion
public int pixelsToUnits;

//position for player when map is loaded
public Vector2 playerPos;

//available positions in middleground layer
private List<Vector2> _middleOpenPos;
```

Inside the MapGenerator's `Start()` function, the `PositionPlayerAt()` function is called and the `playerPos` variable is passed in. Note that the player is spawned before the stairs, which are spawned before the collectables. Since we have limited map spaces, it is important to spawn the most important objects before less important ones. Without a player, we have no game. Therefore, it must be the top priority and come first in the code that spawns objects on our map.

```
//excerpt from MapManager script
//from Start() function

//position player
PositionPlayerAt(playerPos);

//stairs
SpawnObjectsWithTag("Stairs");

//collectables
SpawnObjectsWithTag("Collectables");
```

Let's take a look at the `PositionPlayerAt()` function, which handles the positioning of the Player `GameObject` when our level loads.

```
//excerpt from MapGenerator script

private void PositionPlayerAt(Vector2 thePos) {

    //get player game object from scene
    GameObject player = GameObject.FindWithTag("Player");

    //calculate player position in world units
    //x position
    float xPos = thePos.x * player.GetComponent<SpriteRenderer>().
        bounds.size.x - 0.5f * Screen.width / pixelsToUnits + 0.5f
        * player.GetComponent<SpriteRenderer>().bounds.size.x;

    //y position
    float yPos = 0.5f * Screen.height / pixelsToUnits - thePos.y
        * player.GetComponent<SpriteRenderer>().bounds.size.y - 0.5f
        * player.GetComponent<SpriteRenderer>().bounds.size.y;
```

```
//store position
Vector3 playerPos = new Vector3(xPos, yPos, zPos);

//set position
player.transform.position = playerPos;

//exclude player pos
//prevents immediate collision when loading scene
_middleOpenPos.Remove(thePos);

} //end function
```

The `PositionPlayerAt()` function receives a `Vector2` argument representing the column and row coordinates where the player should be spawned. It searches for the Player `GameObject` in the Unity scene by tag and stores it in a local variable.

```
//excerpt from MapGenerator script
//from PositionPlayerAt() function

//get player game object from scene
GameObject player = GameObject.FindWithTag("Player");
```

Next, the `Vector2` x and y values are converted into Unity world coordinates. The z coordinate for the player is retained. Then, the calculated world position is stored in a `Vector3` variable. The `position` variable of the Player `GameObject` is set equal to the calculated `Vector3` position.

```
//excerpt from MapGenerator script
//from PositionPlayerAt() function

//calculate player position in world units
//x position
float xPos = thePos.x * player.GetComponent<SpriteRenderer>().
   bounds.size.x - 0.5f * Screen.width / pixelsToUnits + 0.5f
   * player.GetComponent<SpriteRenderer>().bounds.size.x;

//y position
float yPos = 0.5f * Screen.height / pixelsToUnits - thePos.y
   * player.GetComponent<SpriteRenderer>().bounds.size.y - 0.5f
   * player.GetComponent<SpriteRenderer>().bounds.size.y;

//store position
Vector3 playerPos = new Vector3(xPos, yPos, zPos);

//set position
player.transform.position = playerPos;
```

Lastly, the player's tile map position is removed from the MapGenerator's `List` of available positions. This prevents another tile from being spawned right on top of the player when the level is created.

```
//excerpt from MapGenerator script
//from PositionPlayerAt() function
```

```
//exclude player pos
//prevents immediate collision when loading scene
_middleOpenPos.Remove(thePos);
```

Having added our function to spawn the player when the level is generated, we have successfully completed the third and final requirement for this challenge. Be sure to review the entire example MapGenerator script and make sure you understand it before proceeding further. It is also a good idea to go back and revise your own solution to fulfill any missing requirements, fix bugs, or enhance its features.

Summary

In this challenge, you worked to enhance the generation of levels for your game world. You refactored your code to improve its coupling and cohesion. The MapGenerator you coded provides an easy way to create a wide variety of levels. If you want to add new objects to your map, simply add MapSpawn scripts to your Unity scene and call them in the MapGenerator's SpawnObjectsWithTag() function. Having taken control of the creation of your game levels, you should be capable of these coding tasks:

- Design unique game levels with just a few scripts

- Manage all objects spawned on a tile map

- Apply the principles of coupling and cohesion

- Refactor code to enhance organization

You have implemented a tile map and level generation system that can produce many unique maps quickly and easily. Thus, it is time for us to expand beyond a single scene in our Unity project and consider how to add many different levels to our game. In the upcoming challenge, you will implement a system to handle switching between levels.

12 Game State Management

One of the fundamental components of game development is state management. Often, a single entity, known as a *game state manager*, is used to handle such responsibilities. The state manager keeps track of things like what scene the game is in and whether the game has been won or lost. It is responsible for switching between scenes, like the title screen, menus, and levels. It also manages starting, stopping, and resetting the gameplay. Currently, your game world has many objects that can be configured to produce a variety of levels. In this challenge, you will create a state manager to handle switching between the different levels in your game world.

▌ Goals

By the end of this chapter, you will be able to apply these coding techniques:

- Code a game state manager to handle switching between different levels
- Implement the singleton design pattern
- Manage the timing of instantiation and persistence of objects in Unity
- Load different scenes in Unity
- Utilize Unity's physics engine for two-dimensional (2D) collisions

▐▌ Required Files

In this chapter, you will need to use the following files from the *Chapter_12 > Software* folder:

- *Challenge > Assets > Scenes > Map.unity* and *Dungeon.unity* to run, modify, and test your solution

- *Challenge > Assets > Scripts > StateManager.cs*, *MapManager.cs*, and *UserMove.cs* to code your solution to the challenge

- *Demo > Mac/PC > StateManager* to demonstrate how your completed solution should work

- *Solution > StateManager.cs*, *MapManager.cs*, and *UserMove.cs* to compare your solution to the provided example solution

▐▌ Challenge: Managing the Game State

Notably, this is the first project in which you have multiple scenes. One is called Map and one is called Dungeon. The Map scene mirrors what we have been working on all along. The only addition to this is the Stairs GameObject inside the Middleground GameObject. As you can see in the Inspector window for the Stairs, a MapSpawn script has been configured to spawn a single StairsDown prefab (Figure 12.1). Also note that the Stairs GameObject has been given a tag of *Stairs*.

If you play the scene immediately, you will see a map generated that is similar to that in the previous challenge, except that a staircase is also included (Figure 12.2).

At this time, double-click on the Dungeon scene inside the Project window's *Assets > Scenes* folder (Figure 12.3). This will open the Dungeon scene in the Unity editor. Any time you want to switch between scenes in Unity, just double-click

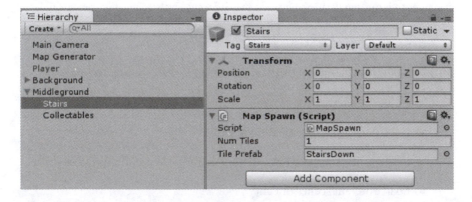

Figure 12.1 A Stairs GameObject with a MapSpawn script has been included in the Map scene.

---

12. Game State Management

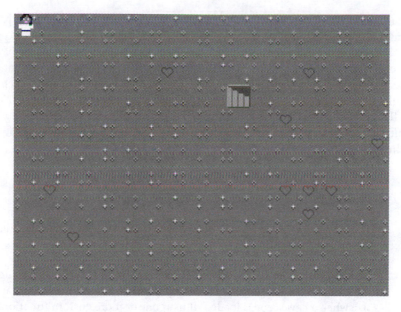

Figure 12.2 If you run the Map scene, you will see a familiar, randomly generated game world with the addition of a set of stairs.

on the associated scene. Always remember to save the scene you are working on before switching to another scene.

The Dungeon scene is nearly identical to the Map scene. One exception is that a cool set of dungeon floor tiles are being used to generate the background tile map. You can view the individual tiles in the Project window's *Assets > Prefabs* folder (Figure 12.4).

The other exception is that no Player GameObject is included in the Dungeon scene. This is because our game only has a single player. Therefore, we will reuse the player from our Map scene in the Dungeon scene, rather than duplicating it. Otherwise, the Dungeon scene, like the Map scene, uses a RandomMap script to generate background tiles and MapSpawn scripts to spawn collectable objects and stairs.

Switch back to your Map scene. It is recommended that you treat the Map scene as your default workspace for this challenge and do most of your

Figure 12.3 To open a scene in the Unity editor, navigate to the *Assets > Scenes* folder and double-click on the scene you would like to open.

Figure 12.4 A set of dungeon floor tiles has been included in the Unity project.

testing there. As you gradually build out your solution, you will launch the game from the Map scene and allow Luna to explore various levels of the Dungeon scene.

To accomplish the goals of this challenge, you will code the entirety of the StateManager script, as well as modify other scripts as necessary. Recall that the objective of your state manager is to allow a single entity to handle the switching of all scenes in the game. With this in mind, here are the requirements for this challenge. In addition to sorting out the logic behind how you will approach your solution, make sure to leverage the hints in this chapter, since several advanced coding concepts are introduced.

1. The StateManager script implements a singleton instance of the state manager.

2. The state manager is never destroyed as scenes are switched. Similarly, the player is never destroyed.

3. The state manager is responsible for controlling all scene switching in the game. It is also responsible for updating the camera's orthographic size when a new scene is loaded. It uses one or more custom functions to accomplish these tasks.

4. The UserMove script checks for collisions between the player and the stairs in each scene. Upon collision, a command is issued to the state manager to switch scenes.

▌ Hint: Singleton Design Pattern

The first requirement for this challenge entails setting up your state manager as a singleton instance, so let's discuss what it means to do so. In coding, a *design pattern* is a common approach to solving a problem. It has been tried, tested, and shown to generally apply in many contexts. There are many different design patterns available to us. For this challenge, we will implement a design pattern known as the *singleton*. In order to be a singleton, there must be only one instance, or copy, of a given *class*. You can think of a class as a customized combination of variables and functions created for a specific purpose (Microsoft Corporation 2015a). For example, the scripts you have been working on throughout this book are all examples of classes. You'll even notice that the `class` keyword appears near the top of every one of our scripts. In the singleton design pattern, one instance of a class will be created and never duplicated thereafter. Since we only require a single object to manage the scenes in our game, and because we wouldn't want several objects interfering with one another on this critical responsibility, our state manager is an excellent candidate for the singleton design pattern. Let's consider how the singleton design pattern can be implemented in the context of our StateManager class.

```
public class StateManager:MonoBehaviour {

    //singleton instance
    private static StateManager _Instance;
```

```
//singleton accessor
//access StateManager.Instance from other classes
public static StateManager Instance {

    //create instance via getter
    get {

        //check for existing instance
        //if no instance
        if (_Instance == null) {

            //create game object
            GameObject StateManagerObj = new GameObject();
            StateManagerObj.name = "State Manager";

            //create instance
            _Instance = StateManagerObj.
                AddComponent<StateManager>();

        } //end if

        //return the instance
        return _Instance;

    } //end get

} //end accessor

} //end class
```

There is quite a bit happening in this intriguing code sample, so let's break it down piece by piece. The first thing we do in our StateManager script is set up a `private` variable with a data type of `StateManager` and a name of `_Instance`.

```
//excerpt from StateManager script

//singleton instance
private static StateManager _Instance;
```

As required by the singleton design pattern, this represents the one and only instance of our StateManager class. Also notice the `static` keyword, which we are using for the first time. Whenever we make something static, we are saying that it belongs to a class itself, rather than any particular instance of the class (Microsoft Corporation 2015a). In practical terms, a `static` variable or function is identical across all instances of a class. Normally, we can create multiple instances of our classes and then set their variables or call their functions independently. For example, we can configure one MapSpawn script to spawn collectables and another to spawn stairs. However, this is not the case when using the `static` keyword. No matter how many copies of a class there are, a `static` variable or function will be identical across all of them.

After declaring a private, static instance of the StateManager class, we handle its creation through a getter accessor function. Quite some time ago, in the

Chapter 4 challenge, we used `get` and `set` accessors to modify the access levels of our variables. As a reminder, here is a code snippet:

```
//create a getter and setter
//define a public version of a variable with a data type and name
public dataType publicVarName {

    //create a getter with the get keyword
    //the return keyword is followed by the private variable
    get { return _privateVarName; }

    //create a setter with the set keyword
    //set the private variable equal to the value keyword
    set { _privateVarName = value; }

}
```

At that time, it was noted that custom features can be added to accessor functions. Our singleton design pattern adds a number of specialized features to what is otherwise a simple getter. To start, the accessor variable is defined.

```
//excerpt from StateManager script

//singleton accessor
//access StateManager.Instance from other classes
public static StateManager Instance {

} //end accessor
```

A `public` variable of the type `StateManager` and name `Instance` is established. Note once again that the `static` keyword is used. This means that the `Instance` variable belongs to the StateManager class. Therefore, no matter where it is accessed in our code, it will always refer to the same singleton instance. Conveniently, we can refer to our state manager instance from anywhere in our game's code by typing `StateManager.Instance`. This allows us to send the state manager commands, such as triggering the scene to be changed. Subsequently, we can add the typical getter code to our accessor definition.

```
//singleton accessor
//access StateManager.Instance from other classes
public static StateManager Instance {

    //standard getter
    get {

            //return the instance
            return _Instance;

    } //end get

} //end accessor
```

This is the standard getter code we are familiar with. Whenever an external script might try to access `StateManager.Instance`, the `private` `_Instance` variable would be returned. However, to fulfill the singleton design pattern, we want to add custom code to our getter that controls how it is created.

```
//singleton accessor
//access StateManager.Instance from other classes
public static StateManager Instance {

    //create instance via getter
    get {

        //check for existing instance
        //if no instance
        if (_Instance == null) {

            //create game object
            GameObject StateManagerObj = new GameObject();
            StateManagerObj.name = "State Manager";

            //create instance
            _Instance = StateManagerObj.
                AddComponent<StateManager>();

        } //end if

        //return the instance
        return _Instance;

    } //end get

} //end accessor
```

Recall that we never want to duplicate a singleton. Therefore, when another script tries to get our singleton instance, we first check whether it is null. If it is not null, the instance that already exists is simply returned. Hence, once the instance is created, it is never duplicated. On the contrary, if our singleton instance happens to be null, we need to create it. Therefore, we create a new empty GameObject named StateManagerObj. Next, we set its name property to "State Manager". This process is the code equivalent of creating a new GameObject in the Unity editor and changing its name in the Hierarchy window. Lastly, to identify our singleton instance, we add a StateManager script to StateManagerObj and set the _Instance variable equal to it. At this point, we have created the one and only copy of our singleton instance. If any other script attempts to access StateManager.Instance, we will simply return the _Instance variable that has already been defined. To summarize, we have created a script with a single state manager instance that can be accessed throughout all of our code. If another script tries to access the state manager, but no instance exists yet, it is automatically created. Yet, if the instance already exists, it is simply returned, so no duplication occurs. This completes the singleton design pattern and the first challenge requirement.

In the end, we have implemented a sophisticated singleton design pattern for our state manager. Reread this section as many times as you need. Work through the code line by line to make sure you understand everything that is happening. The wonderful thing about this implementation is that you can apply it any time you need to create a singleton. In game development, singletons are useful for a variety of purposes, including state, audio, animation, and score managers. Thus, you can expect to utilize the singleton design pattern many times in your future as a game developer.

▌ Hint: The Unity `Awake()` and `DontDestroyOnLoad()` Functions

We have made consistent use of Unity's built-in functions to help control the flow of information throughout our code. Recall that `Update()` helps us manage our game loop by running every frame throughout the duration of a scene. Meanwhile, we have used `Start()` to accomplish one-time actions at the beginning of our scripts, such as initializing variables. Let's introduce another Unity function that helps us control the order in which our code is executed: `Awake()`.

The `Awake()` function is called a single time when a script is loaded (Unity Technologies n.d.g). It is similar to `Start()`, because it is executed only one time. However, `Awake()` is always executed before `Start()`. Thus, we can use `Awake()` and `Start()` together to gain deeper control over the order in which our code is executed. An example of the basic `Awake()` function structure is provided:

```
//Unity's Awake() function
//use to set up references and other critical code
//executes before Start(), just as a script is loaded
void Awake() {

    //place code here

}
```

Suppose we have two scripts. If one script's code is placed in `Awake()` and the other's is placed in `Start()`, we can be confident that the code in `Awake()` will be executed first. This subtle tuning of our code's execution is useful for managing the flow of information throughout our game. For instance, `Awake()` is commonly used to prepare references to the various objects in our game, such as with `GameObject.FindWithTag()`. Subsequently, `Start()` can safely be used to reference these objects, as well as initialize variables. Should we handle these items out of order, we would certainly run into errors, like null object references. As always, it is important to be aware of how our code operates and to take as much control over it as we can. Dividing responsibilities between `Awake()` and `Start()` helps us to manage our code better.

In this challenge, the second requirement entails ensuring that our state manager and player are never destroyed. Normally, whenever Unity loads a new scene, it destroys everything in the previous scene. This includes every `GameObject`, script, and other component. However, Unity provides us with a simple way to flag an object so it does not get destroyed. The `DontDestroyOnLoad()` function receives an object as an argument and ensures that the object persists throughout all of the scenes in our game (Unity Technologies n.d.h).

Thereafter, it is our own responsibility to destroy the object at a later time. Commonly, the `DontDestroyOnLoad()` function is used in tandem with the C# `this` keyword. Simply put, the `this` keyword refers to the specific instance of an object at hand (Microsoft Corporation 2015b). For example, if we call `this` from inside a script, we are referring to that script itself. Combining these together, we arrive at a universal way to ensure an object does not get destroyed when switching scenes in Unity.

```
//Unity's DontDestroyOnLoad() function
//use to ensure an object is not destroyed when switching scenes
//this keyword refers to the script itself
DontDestroyOnLoad(this);
```

As an example, let's consider how to make sure our state manager is not destroyed when switching scenes. Naturally, our singleton state manager instance needs to survive throughout the duration of our game, since it is responsible for switching scenes. Inside our StateManager script, we can utilize the `Awake()` function to call `DontDestroyOnLoad()` right when our script is loaded. By placing this code in `Awake()`, we can be certain no other in-game activities will occur beforehand that might destroy or otherwise interfere with our script.

```
//excerpt from StateManager script

//awake
void Awake() {

    //prevent this script from being destroyed
    //when application switches scenes
    DontDestroyOnLoad(this);

} //end function
```

With that simple combination of `Awake()` and `DontDestroyOnLoad()`, we can be confident that our state manager will persist throughout the game without being destroyed automatically as scenes are changed. We have also fulfilled the second requirement for this challenge.

In addition, see if you can apply this same code to your Player `GameObject`. Think about it. The player is something that needs to persist throughout the entire game, no matter how many different scenes we load. In which script could you incorporate an `Awake()` and `DontDestroyOnLoad()` to ensure that the Player `GameObject` sticks around throughout the game?

▌ Hint: The Unity `Application.LoadLevel()` Function

The primary responsibility of the state manager is to switch between the scenes in our game. The third challenge requirement specifically addresses this point. Fortunately, Unity provides a convenient built-in function for switching scenes. The `Application.LoadLevel()` function accepts an argument that represents a scene and subsequently loads that scene (Unity Technologies n.d.a). The argument can be in the form of a `string` that represents the scene's name, such as "Map" or "Dungeon", or an index value that matches the scenes found in the *File > Build Settings ...* menu. For clarity, it is better to use the scene name, since it makes your code easier to interpret. A scene can be loaded by name in this manner:

```
//load a scene by name
//use Application.LoadLevel() with a string that represents the
    scene's name
//the scene name should match the name of the scene file in the
    Assets folder
//load a scene named theSceneName
Application.LoadLevel("theSceneName");
```

For better organization, the `Application.LoadLevel()` function should always be called from inside your state manager, rather than in various other scripts throughout your program. However, certain events in other areas of your game, such as the player colliding with the stairs, may trigger your state manager to switch scenes. Therefore, it would be useful if your state manager had a custom function for switching to the appropriate scene at the appropriate time. That way, other scripts could notify the state manager when the scene needs to be changed and provide the appropriate information in the form of an argument. Based on your prior coding knowledge, you should be able to write a custom function to handle this task. Give it a try.

A secondary responsibility for the state manager, also noted in the third challenge requirement, is to update the camera's orthographic size when a scene is loaded. At heart, Unity is a three-dimensional (3D) game engine. However, we are able to use it as if it is a 2D game engine. This is made possible through *orthographic projection*. Essentially, orthographic projection uses a camera to make a 3D world appear as if it is 2D. This is accomplished by perfectly aligning the camera to be orthogonal (perpendicular) to the plane in which our game is created. Imagine that our 2D game world is drawn on one wall in a typical, rectangular room. If we focus a camera directly at that wall only, we can create the illusion that the entire space is 2D, even though it is truly a much larger, 3D space. When we use Unity in 2D mode, this is basically what happens.

You may have noticed that every Unity scene has a Main Camera `GameObject`. Indeed, this camera is necessary for us to visualize our scene and create the 2D effect. If you look at the Inspector window for a camera in a scene, you will see that it has a `Projection` dropbox in which the `Orthographic` option is set, as well as a `Size` field (Figure 12.5). The `Size` field determines how large the viewport is for our camera, and thus how much of our game world is visible when the game is played.

In the case of our current game, we always want to show the entire game world, regardless of what resolution the game will be played at. Therefore, we need to update the main camera every time a new scene is loaded. This will override the default size of the camera in the Unity editor and replace it with an appropriate size according to the current screen resolution. Since our state

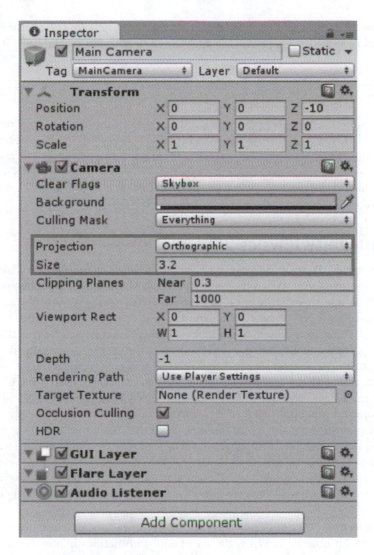

Figure 12.5 When using Unity in 2D mode, the main camera is set up for orthographic projection. Its size determines how large the camera's view is.

manager is responsible for all scene switching, it makes sense for it to handle updating the camera's orthographic size. To set the main camera's orthographic size, we need to access the `Camera.main.orthographicsize` property (Unity Technologies n.d.c). As it turns out, the proper orthographic camera size, regardless of the screen resolution, is one-half the screen height. Naturally, this value would be in pixels. For instance, with a 1024 × 768 px resolution, our height of 768 px would be halved to yield 384 px. However, since the main camera measures its orthographic size in Unity world units, the pixel value must additionally be divided by our pixels to units ratio. As you may recall, the default conversion ratio in Unity, which we have maintained throughout our work, is 100 px per

1 world unit. Putting it all together, here is the code you can use to ensure your camera in any scene is updated to match the current screen resolution:

```
//update camera orthographic size
//equals one half the screen height in Unity world units
Camera.main.orthographicSize = 0.5f * Screen.height / 100.0f;
```

However, a couple of points remain for you to fulfill this challenge requirement. First, you should write a custom function inside your StateManager script that can handle updating the camera's orthographic size whenever it is asked to do so. Second, you need to call this function whenever a new scene is loaded. Think about when and where in your game's code that it would be most appropriate to do so.

▌ Hint: Unity Physics 2D Collisions

The fourth challenge requirement recommends checking for player collisions in the UserMove script. When the player collides with the stairs, the state manager should be told to switch scenes. In previous challenges, you went through the painstaking process of conceptualizing and coding collisions by hand. You're a stronger coder for going through that process and have earned skills that you can apply to many different games. However, in the case of Unity game development, there is a simpler way to handle collision detection. Unity has a built-in physics engine that is quite powerful, yet easy to use. If you keep using Unity to make games, you will most likely leverage the physics engine to speed up your development process. Therefore, it is worthwhile for us to practice applying the physics engine from this point forward. Note that the Unity physics engine is quite robust and able to support advanced systems. You may go on to create physics-based games, like *Angry Birds* or *Portal*, using this engine. However, for the purposes of this book, we will focus on applying the physics engine to replicate the Axis-Aligned Bounding Box (AABB) collisions we previously coded by hand.

Detecting physics 2D collisions in Unity requires certain components to be added to our objects, as well as the use of built-in functions in our scripts. Since we want our physics components to apply to all copies of our objects, we will work in the *Assets > Prefabs* folder for the following steps. Recall that applying a change to a prefab updates every copy of that prefab throughout our scenes. In our game, the Player GameObject is present throughout the entire game, controlled by the player, and collides with many other objects, such as stairs, heroes, and collectables. Therefore, it makes sense to use our Player GameObject as the primary source of collision detection.

Click on the Player prefab. We need to add two components: a Rigidbody2D and a BoxCollider2D. In the Inspector window, add a Rigidbody2D component by clicking on the *Add Component* button, followed by *Physics 2D > Rigidbody 2D*. The Rigidbody2D component makes our player visible to Unity's physics engine (Unity Technologies n.d.i). We only need to add a Rigidbody2D component to one of the objects involved in a collision. Note that several fine-tuned physics options are made available to the `Rigidbody2D` component. For our purposes, the defaults are suitable, with the exception of the `Gravity Scale` property. Our game doesn't have gravity, and we don't want our objects to unexpectedly fall off of the screen due to gravitational force. Setting the `Gravity Scale` property to 0 prevents any unintended effects. Afterwards, add a `BoxCollider2D` component to the Player prefab by clicking on the *Add Component* button, followed by *Physics 2D > Box Collider 2D*. The `BoxCollider2D` component represents an axis-aligned bounding box (Unity Technologies n.d.b). In the past, you manually calculated the bounding boxes of objects, including their top, bottom, left, and right edges. Conveniently, the `BoxCollider2D` component automatically provides our player with a bounding box that matches the size of its sprite. If you like, you may adjust the size and position of the bounding box to fine-tune the collision detection. Just like in our manual calculations, this bounding box will be used by the physics engine to determine whether our player is colliding in 2D space. The fully configured `RigidBody2D` and `BoxCollider2D` components for our Player prefab are shown in Figure 12.6.

With the physics engine components successfully applied to our Player prefab, we will move on to the StairsDown prefab. Since our player is the primary collision object and contains a `Rigidbody2D` component, we do not need to add one to StairsDown. However, StairsDown does need a `BoxCollider2D` component, so add one now by clicking on the *Add Component* button and selecting *Physics 2D > Box Collider 2D*. In addition, click on the `Is Trigger` checkbox in the StairsDown `BoxCollider2D` component. This marks the collision with StairsDown as one that triggers something to happen in the game. Generally, it is good to use triggers for one-time collisions that immediately cause something to happen in the game. For our game, colliding with the stairs promptly causes the game to switch scenes, which is a good example of triggered behavior. The fully configured `BoxCollider2D` component for the StairsDown prefab is shown in Figure 12.7.

With the physics engine prepared to detect collisions between our player and stairs, only one step remains. We will use Unity's built-in physics functions to manage the player's collisions. Since we marked our StairsDown collision as a trigger, we have access to three of Unity's collision functions. The `OnTriggerEnter2D()` function is called the moment a collision is registered between two objects (Unity Technologies n.d.d). In contrast, `OnTriggerExit2D()` is called the moment two objects that are colliding cease to collide (Unity Technologies n.d.e). Meanwhile, `OnTriggerStay2D()` is called each frame that two objects continue to collide with one another (Unity Technologies n.d.f). As you can see, these three functions give us quite a bit of flexibility in managing how objects collide and what events are triggered as a result.

Our UserMove script is responsible for moving the Player `GameObject`. Therefore, it is appropriate to place our collision checking code in that script. The moment our player collides with the stairs, we want to trigger the state manager to switch scenes. Thus, it would be best to utilize the `OnTriggerEnter2D()` function. Let's look at how this function can be applied in code.

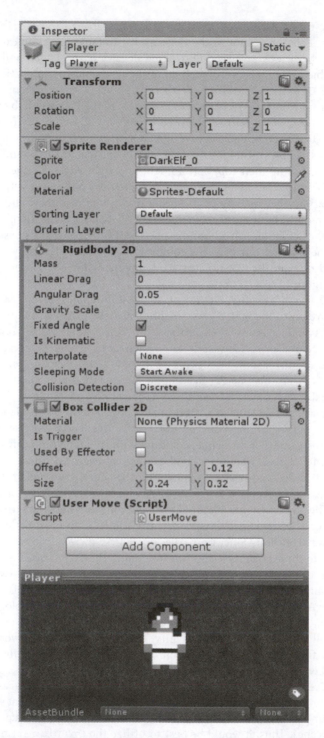

Figure 12.6 The Player prefab is shown with `RigidBody2D` and `BoxCollider2D` components configured for AABB collisions.

12. Game State Management

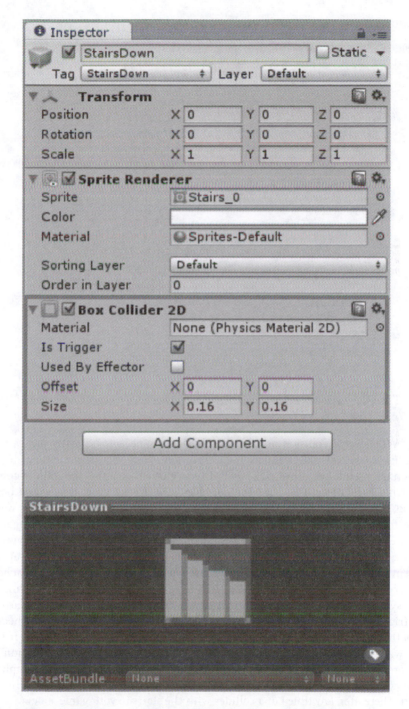

Figure 12.7 The StairsDown prefab is shown with a `BoxCollider2D` component configured for triggered collisions.

```
//excerpt from UserMove script

//check collisions
//called immediately when a collision is detected
void OnTriggerEnter2D(Collider2D theCollider) {

    //disable collider
    theCollider.enabled = false;

    //retrieve the tag for the collider's game object
    string tag = theCollider.gameObject.tag;

    //check the tag
    switch (tag) {

        //stairs
        case "StairsDown":

            //tell the state manager to switch scenes

            break;

        //default
        case default:

            Debug.Log("[UserMove] Collision ignored");

            break;

    } //end switch

} //end function
```

Whenever a collision occurs, the physics engine automatically passes the OnTriggerEnter2D() function an argument. Here, that argument has been given the pseudonym theCollider. This argument contains the collider component of the object that has been collided with. In our case, that would be a BoxCollider2D component, but it works for other types of colliders as well. The first thing we do is disable the collider by setting its enabled property to false. This is because we only want the collision to trigger a single event. If we didn't disable the collider, it might trigger multiple events over subsequent frames. Following, from the collider argument, we access the attached GameObject and its tag via theCollider.gameObject.tag. Using Unity's tag system, we can sort out the exact object that was collided with and use it to trigger the proper events in our game. For instance, the sample code checks whether the collision was made with an object tagged "StairsDown". If so, we want to tell the state manager to switch scenes. Otherwise, the collision is ignored. To fulfill the fourth challenge requirement, you only need to complete this collision code by calling to your custom state manager scene switching function. Thereafter, any time Luna collides with the stairs in your game, a new scene will be loaded. That gets you pretty close to having a whole game put together!

This brief example shows how fast and easy it is to take advantage of Unity's physics engine to handle AABB collisions. In fact, you can handle all of the collisions in our game using this method. If you're feeling gutsy, try adding physics collisions to the Collectable prefab and incorporating it into your `OnTriggerEnter2D()` function. After you have implemented all of the challenge requirements in your own way, proceed to review the example solution.

◼ Example Solution: Managing the Game State

You have learned some important new coding techniques throughout this challenge. The example solution will be broken down according to the challenge requirement:

1. The StateManager script implements a singleton instance of the state manager.

2. The state manager is never destroyed as scenes are switched. Similarly, the player is never destroyed.

3. The state manager is responsible for controlling all scene switching in the game. It is also responsible for updating the camera's orthographic size when a new scene is loaded. It uses one or more custom functions to accomplish these tasks.

4. The UserMove script checks for collisions between the player and the stairs in each scene. Upon collision, a command is issued to the state manager to switch scenes.

The following pseudocode describes the implementation of the StateManager script in the example solution:

```
Declare PRIVATE STATIC _Instance

PUBLIC STATIC Instance getter {

        IF _Instance IS NULL:
            • Create new GameObject
            • Add StateManager script to GameObject
            • Set _Instance EQUAL TO StateManager script

        Return _Instance

}

Awake()
    • DontDestroyOnLoad(this)

SwitchSceneTo()
    • Receive string with scene name
    • Pass string to Application.LoadLevel()

UpdateCamSize()
    • Receive int screen height and int pixels to units conversion
    • Set main camera orthographic size EQUAL TO 0.5f * screen height /
      pixels to units
```

The first challenge requirement entails implementing the state manager according to the singleton design pattern. This is discussed in detail in the *Hint: Singleton Design Pattern* section. Hence, only the code and a brief summary are reiterated here.

```
//excerpt from StateManager script

//singleton instance
private static StateManager _Instance;

//singleton accessor
//access StateManager.Instance from other classes
public static StateManager Instance {

    //create instance via getter
    get {

        //check for existing instance
        //if no instance
        if (_Instance == null) {

            //create game object
            GameObject StateManagerObj = new GameObject();
            StateManagerObj.name = "State Manager";

            //create instance
            _Instance = StateManagerObj.
                AddComponent<StateManager>();

        } //end if

        //return the instance
        return _Instance;

    } //end get

} //end accessor
```

Inside the StateManager script, a private, static variable of the StateManager type is defined and named _Instance. This represents the one and only instance of the StateManager class that will exist throughout our game. A custom, public getter function is defined under the name Instance. This allows other scripts to access the state manager instance using StateManager.Instance. The getter checks whether the private _Instance variable has been defined. If so, it is returned to the caller. However, if no instance yet exists, a new GameObject is created, named, and equipped with a StateManager script. Then, the _Instance is set equal to the newly created StateManager script. Thereafter, the instance is defined and will be returned when requested by another script.

The second requirement dictates that our state manager and player should never be destroyed. Normally, Unity destroys everything in the existing scene before loading another. However, using a combination of Awake() and DontDestroyOnLoad(), we can tell Unity that we want certain objects to stick around instead of being destroyed. The code is identical for both our state manager and our player. Therefore, make sure the following code appears in your StateManager script and your UserMove script:

```
//excerpt from both StateManager script and UserMove script

//awake
void Awake() {

    //prevent this script from being destroyed
    // when application switches scenes
    DontDestroyOnLoad(this);

} //end function
```

The third requirement concerns the state manager's responsibilities to change scenes and keep the camera's orthographic size updated. This is a good opportunity to write some custom functions into our StateManager script. One will be used to manage the switching of scenes.

```
//excerpt from StateManager script

//switch scene by name
public void SwitchSceneTo(string theScene) {

    //load next scene
    Application.LoadLevel("theScene");

} //end function
```

The custom `SwitchSceneTo()` function accepts a `string` argument containing the name of the scene that should be loaded. It then passes the scene name to the `Application.LoadLevel()` function. Conveniently, this allows any other script to command our StateManager to switch scenes by calling `StateManager.Instance.SwitchSceneTo()` and providing the name of the desired scene as an argument. Another custom function is used to update the camera's orthographic size.

```
//excerpt from StateManager script

//update camera size
//based on screen resolution and pixels to units conversion
public void UpdateCamSize(int theScreenHeight, int
    thePixelsToUnits) {

    //update camera orthographic size
    Camera.main.orthographicSize = 0.5f * theScreenHeight /
        thePixelsToUnits;

} //end function
```

The `UpdateCamSize()` function accepts two integers as arguments. One represents the screen height, while the other holds the Unity pixels to units conversion ratio. Given these values, the function calculates and sets the appropriate orthographic camera size for the scene. Remember that we want to update the camera size every time a scene is loaded. Therefore, the `UpdateCamSize()` function must be called in our code at the appropriate time. One way to accomplish this is to add the following line to the `Start()` function in your MapGenerator script:

```
//excerpt from MapGenerator script
//Start() function

//update camera size
StateManager.Instance.UpdateCamSize(Screen.height,
    pixelsToUnits);
```

The MapGenerator is a useful place to call our `UpdateCamSize()` function, because every one of our game levels uses this script. Therefore, every time a new level is created, the camera size will be updated.

The fourth, and final, requirement for this challenge involves adding physics engine collisions to the Player `GameObject` and managing them via the UserMove script. Recall that the Player prefab must have `Rigidbody2D` and `BoxCollider2D` components attached. Meanwhile, to detect collisions with the StairsDown prefab, we add a `BoxCollider2D` to it and check the `IsTrigger` box. Subsequently, we can take advantage of Unity's built-in `OnTriggerEnter2D()` function inside our UserMove script.

```
//excerpt from UserMove script

//check collisions
//called immediately when a collision is detected
void OnTriggerEnter2D(Collider2D theCollider) {

        //disable collider
        theCollider.enabled = false;

        //retrieve the tag for the collider's game object
        string tag = theCollider.gameObject.tag;

        //check the tag
        switch (tag) {

                //stairs
                case "StairsDown":

                        //tell the state manager to switch scenes
                        StateManager.Instance.SwitchSceneTo("Dungeon");

                        break;

                //default
                case default:

                        Debug.Log("[UserMove] Collision ignored");

                        break;

        } //end switch

} //end function
```

When Unity's physics engine detects a collision, this function receives the associated collider and immediately disables it. It then retrieves the tag associated with the collider's `GameObject`. Using a `switch` statement, the tag is checked against our possible collision objects. Right now, we are only concerned with the *StairsDown* tag. We could, of course, add other collisions to the game by incorporating more tags into the `switch` statement. If the collision is indeed with the StairsDown object, then a command is issued to the state manager to switch scenes: `StateManager.Instance.SwitchSceneTo("Dungeon")`. This means that any time Luna collides with the stairs during play, a new Dungeon scene will be loaded. Thus, she can endlessly explore the depths of the dungeon! Test it out and see for yourself. That brings us to the end of this important challenge. Congratulations on making it this far.

Summary

You have successfully implemented a state manager that allows you to switch between different levels in your game world. Being able to code this fundamental game component will serve you well in future projects. Excitingly, your game now utilizes its level generation system to great effect. Every time Luna completes a dungeon level by reaching the stairs, a brand new one is generated for her to explore. Thus, your state manager enables an endless number of levels to appear in your game. Furthermore, the singleton design pattern is applicable to many other objects in game development, such as audio, animation, and score managers. At this point, you should be confident applying the following techniques:

- Code a game state manager to handle switching between different levels

- Implement the singleton design pattern

- Manage the timing of instantiation and persistence of objects in Unity

- Load different scenes in Unity

- Utilize Unity's physics engine for 2D collisions

Your game is nearly complete. Luna can explore the world, interact with heroes, and collect objects. You can generate an endless number of unique levels and travel between them. However, there are just a few more things that need to be done. In the next challenge, you will focus on bringing together the necessary pieces to round out the gameplay.

References

Microsoft Corporation. 2015a. Classes (C# Programming Guide). http://msdn.microsoft. com/library/x9afc042.aspx (accessed March 22, 2015).

Microsoft Corporation. 2015b. this (C# Reference). http://msdn.microsoft.com/library/ dk1507sz.aspx (accessed March 22, 2015).

Unity Technologies. n.d.a. Application.LoadLevel. http://docs.unity3d.com/ScriptReference/ Application.LoadLevel.html (accessed March 22, 2015).

Unity Technologies. n.d.b. BoxCollider2D. http://docs.unity3d.com/ScriptReference/ BoxCollider2D.html (accessed March 22, 2015).

Unity Technologies. n.d.c. Camera.orthographicSize. http://docs.unity3d.com/ ScriptReference/Camera-orthographicSize.html (accessed March 22, 2015).

Unity Technologies. n.d.d. Collider2D.OnTriggerEnter2D(Collider2D). http://docs.unity3d. com/ScriptReference/Collider2D.OnTriggerEnter2D.html (accessed March 22, 2015).

Unity Technologies. n.d.e. Collider2D.OnTriggerExit2D(Collider2D). http://docs.unity3d. com/ScriptReference/Collider2D.OnTriggerExit2D.html (accessed March 22, 2015).

Unity Technologies. n.d.f. Collider2D.OnTriggerStay2D(Collider2D). http://docs.unity3d. com/ScriptReference/Collider2D.OnTriggerStay2D.html (accessed March 22, 2015).

Unity Technologies. n.d.g. MonoBehaviour.Awake. http://docs.unity3d.com/ ScriptReference/MonoBehaviour.Awake.html (accessed March 22, 2015).

Unity Technologies. n.d.h. Object.DontDestroyOnLoad. http://docs.unity3d.com/ ScriptReference/Object.DontDestroyOnLoad.html (accessed March 22, 2015).

Unity Technologies. n.d.i. RigidBody2D. http://docs.unity3d.com/ScriptReference/ Rigidbody2D.html (accessed March 22, 2015).

13 Gameplay

Throughout this book, you have implemented a variety of game features. Soon, you will be applying your knowledge to code your own games, as well as studying more advanced topics. A good way to wrap up the current project is to pull together your previous solutions into a playable game. In this challenge, you will apply what you have learned to put Luna into a living, breathing game world. We'll add the other heroes and collectable objects back into our levels. Additionally, we'll create new computer-controlled obstacles to challenge Luna on her journey. All the while, the state manager will keep track of the win and loss conditions. By the time you complete this challenge, you'll be able to play your own game, which is something to be proud of.

▌ Goals

By the end of this chapter, you will be able to apply these coding techniques:

- Create autonomous moving objects using artificial intelligence (AI)

- Manage win and loss states in real time

- Track data, such as scoring, throughout the game

- Compile several features, including characters, collectables, and obstacles, into a playable game

Required Files

In this chapter, you will need to use the following files from the *Chapter_13 > Software* folder:

- *Challenge > Assets > Scenes > Map.unity* and *Dungeon.unity* to run, modify, and test your solution

- *Challenge > Assets > Scripts > AIMove.cs, StateManager.cs, MapGenerator.cs,* and *UserMove.cs* to code your solution to the challenge

- *Demo > Mac/PC > StateManager* to demonstrate how your completed solution should work

- *Solution > AIMove.cs, StateManager.cs, MapGenerator.cs,* and *UserMove.cs* to compare your solution to the provided example solution

Challenge: Bringing the Gameplay Together

This challenge will focus on bringing together the final pieces necessary to have a playable game. Essentially, that means you will need to add more collisions, obstacles, and interactions. You will use these features to craft a functional game system that can be won or lost by a player. Let's start by reviewing the Unity project provided for this challenge.

Two scripts that you previously worked on have been added back into the project with slight modifications. In the Map scene, the Inventory GameObject has the CollectableInventory script attached to it. You worked on this script in Chapter 7. It has been modified to contain a maximum number of objects. This lets us define how many collectables Luna can carry at once. It also has a setting to define the scale of the objects in the inventory. This helps to distinguish them from objects that are in the level and prevent the inventory from obstructing the player's view of the map. Both of these variables can be set from the Unity Inspector. In addition, the Inventory uses DontDestroyOnLoad() inside its Awake() function to make sure it doesn't get destroyed when a new level is loaded. The user input controls from the original version of this script have been removed. Lastly, the original version relied upon a Collectable script that was attached to each collectable object. However, the Collectable script is no longer necessary. Instead, the *Collectable* tag has been applied to every collectable object in the game (see the Collectable prefab in the *Assets > Prefabs* folder). Meanwhile, our UserMove script checks the player's collisions by tag. Hence, UserMove can pass the appropriate information to the CollectableInventory script when the player collides with a collectable. Make sure to review the Inventory GameObject and CollectableInventory script to make sure you understand these parts of the project.

Also in the Map scene, find the Player GameObject. Note that a HeroGroup script has been added. This script has been simplified from the version you created in Chapter 8. The user controls, collision checks, and ability to remove members have been deleted. These activities are handled in other areas of our code or are no longer necessary. Meanwhile, the `memberSprites` `List` has been made public. This will allow the UserMove script to add the appropriate hero to the group when it detects a collision. The remaining features in HeroGroup remain unchanged from the previous version. Review the HeroGroup script and make sure you understand all of its code.

Take a look at the *Assets* > *Prefabs* folder. Three prefabs have been created to represent the heroes in our game: Dryad, Dwarf, and Orc. They have been tagged with *Dryad*, *Dwarf*, and *Orc*, respectively. Each of these objects has a `SpriteRenderer` component to display its image and a `BoxCollider2D` component for collision detection (Figure 13.1). Thus, you can detect when Luna collides with these heroes inside your UserMove script and trigger the appropriate actions in your code.

Furthermore, note that five additional prefabs have been added to represent drakes. These are cleverly named *Drake_01, Drake_02, Drake_03, Drake_04*, and *Drake_05*. A drake is like a small dragon. In Luna's journey upon the surface world, drakes are going to be mischievous little creatures that get in the way. They will fly all over the dungeon. Luna will be challenged to avoid them while she seeks to save her friends. The drake prefabs have all been generically tagged as *Drake*. That is because they are not unique characters. The only difference between them is their color, and many of them can potentially be spawned in our levels. Like our heroes, the drake prefabs have `SpriteRenderer` and `BoxCollider2D` components (Figure 13.2). Thus, you can incorporate drake collisions into your UserMove script and trigger the appropriate events in your game.

Go to the Dungeon scene. Notice that two objects have been added to the Middleground. The Heroes `GameObject` contains children objects representing each of our heroes (Figure 13.3). Each has a MapSpawn script attached. Inside the MapSpawn script, the appropriate hero prefab has been assigned to the `tilePrefab` variable in the Unity Inspector. With these objects set up in the Unity scene, you can spawn your heroes by incorporating them into the code of your MapGenerator script.

Similarly, a Drakes object has been created in the Dungeon scene. It has five children objects, each with a tag, MapSpawn script, and associated prefab (Figure 13.4). Therefore, you can also incorporate drakes into your MapGenerator code to spawn them inside your game levels.

Now that you are familiar with the layout of the Unity project, let's move on to the objectives of this challenge. Everything necessary to bring the gameplay together is summarized in these requirements:

1. The AIMove script defines how drakes move around the screen.

   a. For example, the drakes may move in patterns around the screen to obstruct Luna's movement through the level.

2. The StateManager script keeps track of the game's score and win–loss state. It includes a function to reset the game once it ends.

   a. For instance, the number of levels completed and the number of heroes added to the party could be scored.

Figure 13.1 Dryad, Dwarf, and Orc prefabs have been added to the *Assets > Prefabs* folder. Each has the *Hero* tag, SpriteRenderer component, and BoxCollider2D component. As an example, the Dryad prefab is shown.

13. Gameplay

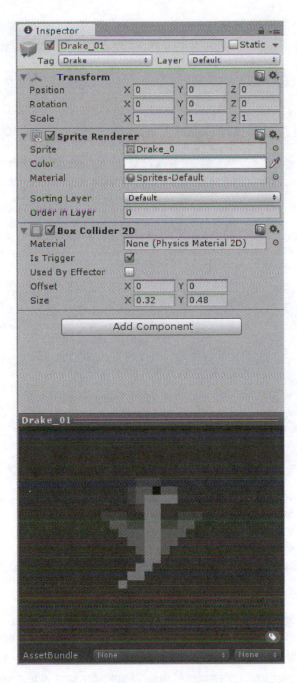

Figure 13.2 Five drake prefabs have been added to the *Assets* > *Prefabs* folder. Each has the *Drake* tag, `SpriteRenderer` component, and `BoxCollider2D` component. An example drake prefab is shown.

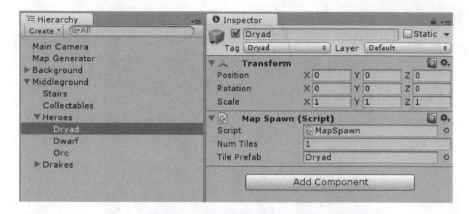

Figure 13.3 Inside the Middleground GameObject of the Dungeon scene, a Heroes GameObject has been added. It contains children objects with MapSpawn scripts for each of the heroes. As an example, the dryad is shown.

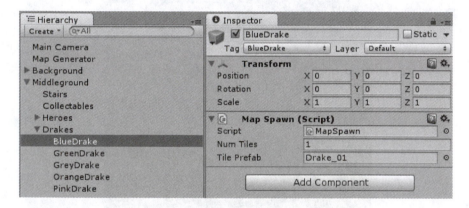

Figure 13.4 Inside the Middleground GameObject of the Dungeon scene, a Drakes GameObject has been added. It contains children objects with MapSpawn scripts for each of the drakes. An example drake is shown.

    b. For example, the game may be won when all heroes are added to the party, while it may be lost when the player collides with a drake, but has no inventory items remaining.

    c. Note that the reset function should restore all relevant variables and objects to their initial states, so the game can played again from the start.

3. The UserMove script uses Unity's 2D physics engine to detect collisions between the collectables, heroes, and drakes. Upon collision, appropriate events are triggered in the game.

    a. For example, collectables may be stored in the player's inventory and heroes may be added to the player's group, while drakes cause the player to lose an inventory item.

4. The MapGenerator enables heroes and drakes to be spawned in each level. Custom functions may be used to determine how and when these objects are spawned.

a. For instance, a random hero might be spawned every few levels, while the number of drakes spawned gradually increases with each level.

Intriguingly, the system that you have developed over the course of this book is capable of making many different types of games. The hints and example solution will describe a game similar to what is listed in the requirements. However, if you have plans for a different game, you should not feel constrained by these parameters. Feel free to explore beyond the requirements and code your own game from the available components. There are many different pieces to work on, so remember to organize your thoughts before diving into the code.

Hint: Obstacles and Artificial Intelligence

Obstacles are a key component in video games. They force players to use their skills to overcome meaningful challenges. Obstacles can come in many forms, including puzzles, enemies, and terrain. Thus far, there are no obstacles in our game. It is time to change that. In games, artificial intelligence (AI) refers to the behaviors defined for computer-controlled entities, such as characters and obstacles. Almost all games have some degree of AI in them. For instance, any time your character talks to a store clerk, dodges moving laser beams, or battles against a boss, AI is involved.

In our game world, drakes will be pesky obstacles that make it difficult for Luna to get from the starting point to the exit (stairs) in each level. To make them work, we will create a custom script that defines their AI behavior. We certainly want the drakes to move around the map, since that will make it more challenging for the player to navigate. How, exactly, they move is up to you to define in your code. Here is an example suggestion for the AI behavior of drakes. Feel free to come up with a different system that reflects how you think the drakes should behave.

- From a random spawn point, a drake will move toward the farthest edge of the map in a straight line at a random speed.

- Once a drake reaches the edge of the map, it will reverse direction and return to its spawn point.

- A drake will continue moving back and forth between its spawn point and the edge of the map unless interrupted, such as through a collision with the player.

With your drake AI behavior defined, it's time to code. This time, you will create your own script from scratch and apply it to your game. Inside the *Assets > Scripts* folder, right-click and select *Create > C# Script* (Figure 13.5). Give it a name of *AIMove*.

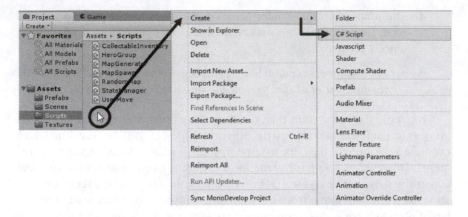

Figure 13.5 To create a new script, right-click inside the *Assets > Scripts* folder and select *Create > C# Script*.

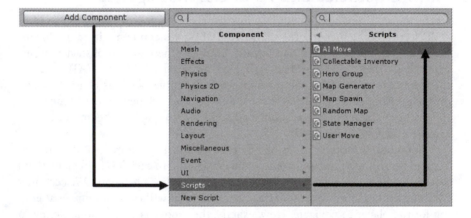

Figure 13.6 Add your AIMove script to each drake prefab in the *Assets > Prefabs* folder by clicking on the *Add Component* button, followed by *Scripts > AI Move*.

Then, add the AIMove script component to each of the drake prefabs in the *Assets > Prefabs* folder (Figure 13.6).

You now have an empty script in which you can write the AI behavior for your drakes. Open the AIMove script in your code editor and begin working on this, the first challenge requirement.

By the way, for testing purposes, it would be helpful to drag a drake prefab directly into your Unity scene. This allows you to witness the AI behavior of your drake without worrying about the player, spawning, or scenes. Every time you test the scene, the drake will automatically move according to what you have coded so far. Thus, you can rapidly test and revise its behavior. Once you have the drake working how you want it to, you can simply delete the testing prefab from the scene.

■ Hint: Game State and Score

With obstacles and AI behavior in place, you can turn your focus toward expanding the game state manager. In the previous challenge, you coded a state manager to switch between levels. The other major responsibility of the state manager is to keep track of the game state. That is, it needs to know whether the player has won or lost the game and act accordingly in real time. These features are noted in the second requirement for this challenge.

To begin expanding your state manager, determine the win and loss conditions for your game. For instance, one suggestion is to imagine that Luna is on a quest through the dungeon to save the other heroes. She has to explore the levels to find her friends and add them to the party. Once she has saved all of the heroes, the game is won.

On the other hand, recall that the drakes are Luna's obstacles in the dungeon. Meanwhile, Luna collects objects in her inventory throughout her journey. In order to lose the game, we might subtract an object from the inventory every time Luna collides with a drake. Thus, the game is over when Luna collides with a drake, but has no collectables remaining.

Another item to consider is how you will score the game. How will you know if the player performed well? Generally, it is a good idea to keep track of the player's overall performance. This is a way to provide feedback and motivate the player to improve over multiple sessions. One example might be to keep track of how many dungeon levels have been explored. Another could be to tally up the total number of collectables gained. Yet another option would be to track the number of times the player collided with a drake. Of course, a lower number would be desirable in that case. Think of how you want to keep track of the player's score and what you need to do to incorporate it into your state manager.

Regardless of the exact win, loss, and scoring conditions you have designed, the state manager will require variables to keep track of them. Therefore, you need to declare and initialize the necessary variables in your StateManager script. These variables will be modified in other areas of your game, such as when the player collides with objects.

■ Hint: More Collisions

You can use collisions as a method to update your state manager on the current status of the game. As detailed in the third requirement, you want to incorporate collectables, heroes, and drakes into your UserMove script's collision checks. To do this, you should practice using Unity's 2D physics engine, which was introduced in the previous challenge. Recall that your prefabs already have BoxCollider2D components and tags added to them. Thus, inside the UserMove script's OnTriggerEnter2D() function, you can add tag checks to detect collisions for these objects.

Not only do you need to check for collisions with collectables, heroes, and drakes, but you also want to update the status of your game when they are triggered. Therefore, you will need to reference other scripts and send commands accordingly. Here are some ideas for how you can handle collisions with collectables, drakes, and heroes. As always, feel free to adjust these systems to your liking. The important thing is that you can execute your game's design through code.

- When the player collides with a collectable, add it to the inventory by referencing the CollectableInventory script.

- When the player collides with a hero, add it to the group by calling to the HeroGroup script.

- When the player collides with a drake, remove an item from the inventory via the CollectableInventory script.

▮ Hint: More Spawns

It's time to revisit the MapGenerator script. As noted in the fourth requirement, you need to incorporate the heroes and drakes into your level. Each hero and drake prefab has been given a tag. In the Dungeon scene, all of the drakes and heroes have been set up inside the Middleground with MapSpawn scripts. Therefore, similar to how you spawned collectables and stairs, you need to incorporate heroes and drakes into your MapGenerator script. However, rather than simply calling all these objects by tag in your SpawnObjectsWithTag() function, it is recommended that you write custom functions to handle them. This is because you may want to add special conditions on how these objects spawn in your levels. For example, if your game is won based on whether Luna finds and saves all of the other heroes, it wouldn't make sense to spawn them all at once in the first level. Instead, you could spawn a random hero every few levels. Furthermore, there are five colors of drakes, and they all do not need to be spawned every level. It might be nice to randomly choose the drake prefabs to spawn. In addition, you could vary the number of drakes spawned per level. One way to increase the challenge of the game over time would be to spawn more drakes as Luna explores more levels. If you tracked such information in your StateManager script, you could reference it in the MapGenerator to determine how many drakes to spawn each level. For instance, level 3 could have 3 drakes, level 4 could have 4 drakes, and so on.

Regardless of how you choose to spawn your heroes and drakes, take the time to test and refine your design. Get the initial system working in your MapGenerator script. Then, play through your game, note any less than ideal points, refine your code, and play again. This iterative cycle will help you to improve your game's design and code.

▮ Hint: Reset the Game

With your state tracking variables, collision triggers, and spawns established, there is another important feature to incorporate into your state manager. Win or lose, once the game ends, you need to be able to reset it and allow the player to start all over again. To reset the game, you must ensure that all variables are returned to their initial state. In addition, you have to delete any objects that were previously marked with `DontDestroyOnLoad()`. That way, when you reload your Map scene to restart the game, said objects will not be duplicated. You should write a custom function in your StateManager script to handle resetting the game. This will allow you to call the reset function whenever the win or loss state is triggered during play. Where should you call the reset function? In our current game, it would be best to trigger a reset when the player has won or lost. For instance, you could use the following conditions to determine when the reset function is called. Alternatively, you could come up with your own definitions and incorporate them into the appropriate areas of your code.

- In the UserMove script, the player collides with the final hero needed to complete the group. The player has won and the game can be reset via the StateManager.

- In the UserMove script, the player collides with a drake, but doesn't have any collectables remaining in the inventory. The player has lost and the game can be reset via the StateManager.

It may take some practice and testing to ensure that you reset everything you needed to. You will need to play through the game several times to make sure your reset function is bug-free. Try adding console log messages to your code to print variable values. Also, pay attention to the Hierarchy window to see which objects are present during play. Lastly, watch for any unexpected occurrences that appear during subsequent rounds of play. These measures will help you verify that your reset function is working. Once it is, you will be able to endlessly play your game over and over again!

Example Solution: Bringing the Gameplay Together

The example solution demonstrates one way to pull together the different components into a working game. Your solution may vary from what is presented here, especially if you chose to customize the game's design in any way. Here are the basic challenge requirements again:

1. The AIMove script defines how drakes move around the screen.

2. The StateManager script keeps track of the game's score and win–loss state. It includes a function to reset the game once it ends.

3. The UserMove script uses Unity's 2D physics engine to detect collisions between the collectables, heroes, and drakes. Upon collision, appropriate events are triggered in the game.

4. The MapGenerator enables heroes and drakes to be spawned in each level. Custom functions may be used to determine how and when these objects are spawned.

The specific implementation of each requirement in the example solution will be noted as each is discussed. Let's begin with the first requirement and the AIMove script. No matter where a drake is spawned on the tile map, the AIMove script will find the farthest edge of the screen. The drake will move toward the edge position until it is reached. Afterwards, it will turn back and return to the starting point. This process continues indefinitely. In the code of the AIMove script, variables are declared to handle the drake's speed and position.

```
//excerpt from AIMove script

public class AIMove : MonoBehaviour {

    //speed boundaries
    public float minSpeed;
    public float maxSpeed;

    //speed object is moving
    private float _speed;

    //origin position of the object
    private Vector3 _originPos;

    //destination position of the object
    private Vector3 _destPos;
```

The minSpeed and maxSpeed variables, which are set in the Unity Inspector, allow us to randomize the _speed of each drake. This makes the game a bit more interesting, since the drakes will be moving at different speeds, rather than one fixed speed. We also set up variables to store the origin and destination positions for the drake's movement. The private variables are initialized in the Start() function.

```
//excerpt from AIMove script

//init
void Start() {

    //generate random speed
    _speed = Random.Range(minSpeed, maxSpeed);

    //set origin
    _originPos = gameObject.transform.position;

    //calculate destination
    _destPos = FindEdgeFor(gameObject);

} //end function
```

The Random.Range() function is used to generate a random movement _speed between minSpeed and maxSpeed. The _originPos is set to the drake's current position, which is its initial spawn point on the map. The _destPos is set to the farthest edge from the drake, which is returned by the custom FindEdgeFor() function.

```
//excerpt from AIMove script

//calculate farthest screen edge given object
private Vector3 FindEdgeFor(GameObject theObject) {

    //get object properties
    Vector3 currentPos = theObject.transform.position;
    float objWidth = theObject.GetComponent<SpriteRenderer>().
       bounds.size.x;
    float objHeight = theObject.GetComponent<SpriteRenderer>().
       bounds.size.y;

    //store distance to edges of screen
    float distUp = Mathf.Abs(0.5f * Screen.height / 100.0f - 0.5f
       * objHeight - currentPos.y);
    float distDown = Mathf.Abs(-0.5f * Screen.height / 100.0f
       + 0.5f * objHeight - currentPos.y);
    float distLeft = Mathf.Abs(-0.5f * Screen.width / 100.0f + 0.5f
       * objWidth - currentPos.x);
    float distRight = Mathf.Abs(0.5f * Screen.width / 100.0f - 0.5f
       * objWidth - currentPos.x);

    //find the maximum distance
    float maxDist = Mathf.Max(distUp, distDown, distLeft,
       distRight);

    //store position variables
    float edgeX = currentPos.x;
    float edgeY = currentPos.y;
    float edgeZ = currentPos.z;

    //update position based on direction
    //up
    if (maxDist == distUp) {

        //update y
        edgeY += distUp;

    } //end if

    //down
    else if (maxDist == distDown) {

        //update y
        edgeY -= distDown;

    } //end if

    //left
    else if (maxDist == distLeft) {

        //update x
        edgeX -= distLeft;

    } //end if
```

```
    //right
    else if (maxDist == distRight) {

        //update x
        edgeX += distRight;

    } //end if

    //create destination
    Vector3 edgePos = new Vector3(edgeX, edgeY, edgeZ);

    //return
    return edgePos;

} //end function
```

Let's break down the FindEdgeFor() function. A drake GameObject is passed into the FindEdgeFor() function. The position, width, and height of the drake are stored in local variables.

```
//excerpt from AIMove script
//from FindEdgeFor() function

//calculate farthest screen edge given object
private Vector3 FindEdgeFor(GameObject theObject) {

    //get object properties
    Vector3 currentPos = theObject.transform.position;
    float objWidth = theObject.GetComponent<SpriteRenderer>().
        bounds.size.x;
    float objHeight = theObject.GetComponent<SpriteRenderer>().
        bounds.size.y;
```

Next, the distance to each edge of the screen—up, down, left, and right—is calculated. Each distance is fed into the Mathf.Max() function, which returns the maximum value to be stored in a variable named maxDist.

```
//excerpt from AIMove script
//from FindEdgeFor() function

    //store distance to edges of screen
    float distUp = Mathf.Abs(0.5f * Screen.height / 100.0f - 0.5f
        * objHeight - currentPos.y);
    float distDown = Mathf.Abs(-0.5f * Screen.height / 100.0f
        + 0.5f * objHeight - currentPos.y);
    float distLeft = Mathf.Abs(-0.5f * Screen.width / 100.0f + 0.5f
        * objWidth - currentPos.x);
    float distRight = Mathf.Abs(0.5f * Screen.width / 100.0f - 0.5f
        * objWidth - currentPos.x);

    //find the maximum distance
    float maxDist = Mathf.Max(distUp, distDown, distLeft,
        distRight);
```

The edgeX, edgeY, and edgeZ variables are set up to store the location of the farthest edge relative to the drake's current position. If conditions are used to determine whether the farthest edge is up, down, left, or right of the drake. Depending on which edge is farthest, the edgeX or edgeY variable is updated.

```
//excerpt from AIMove script
//from FindEdgeFor() function

    //store position variables
    float edgeX = currentPos.x;
    float edgeY = currentPos.y;
    float edgeZ = currentPos.z;

    //update position based on direction
    //up
    if (maxDist == distUp) {

        //update y
        edgeY += distUp;

    } //end if

    //down
    else if (maxDist == distDown) {

        //update y
        edgeY -= distDown;

    } //end if

    //left
    else if (maxDist == distLeft) {

        //update x
        edgeX -= distLeft;

    } //end if

    //right
    else if (maxDist == distRight) {

        //update x
        edgeX += distRight;

    } //end if
```

A new Vector3 named edgePos is then created using edgeX, edgeY, and edgeZ. This represents the position of the farthest edge from the drake. Lastly, the edge position is returned.

```
//excerpt from AIMove script
//from FindEdgeFor() function

    //create destination
    Vector3 edgePos = new Vector3(edgeX, edgeY, edgeZ);

    //return
    return edgePos;

} //end function
```

At this point, the AIMove script has randomized the drake's speed, noted its origin point, and calculated its destination at the farthest edge of the screen. Subsequently, the actual movement of the drake is handled in the `Update()` function by calling to two custom functions.

```
//excerpt from AIMove script

//update
void Update() {

    //move object
    MoveObjectTo(gameObject, _destPos);

    //check destination
    CheckPosFor(gameObject, _destPos);

} //end function
```

The `MoveObjectTo()` function accepts two arguments. One is the `GameObject` to be moved, and the other is a `Vector3` representing its destination position. Thus, the drake and its calculated destination position are passed into this function.

```
//excerpt from AIMove script

//move the object towards destination
private void MoveObjectTo(GameObject theObject, Vector3 theDestPos) {

    //retrieve current world position
    Vector3 currentPos = theObject.transform.position;

    //store new coordinates
    float newX = currentPos.x;
    float newY = currentPos.y;
    float newZ = currentPos.z;

    //update movement based on speed and direction
    //up
    if (currentPos.y < theDestPos.y - _speed) {

        //update y
        newY += _speed;

    } //end if

    //down
    else if (currentPos.y > theDestPos.y + _speed) {

        //update y
        newY -= _speed;

    } //end if

    //at destination
    else {

        //update y
        newY = theDestPos.y;
```

```
    } //end if

    //left
    if (currentPos.x > theDestPos.x + _speed) {

        //update x
        newX -= _speed;

    } //end if

    //right
    else if (currentPos.x < theDestPos.x - _speed) {

        //update x
        newX += _speed;

    } //end if

    //at destination
    else {

        //update x
        newX = theDestPos.x;

    } //end if

    //store the movement position
    Vector3 movePos = new Vector3(newX, newY, newZ);

    //update object position
    theObject.transform.position = movePos;

} //end function
```

To start, the MoveObjectTo() function retrieves the drake's current position. It stores the drake's initial x, y, and z position variables, so they can be utilized later.

```
//excerpt from AIMove script
//from MoveObjectTo() function

//move the object towards destination
private void MoveObjectTo(GameObject theObject, Vector3
theDestPos) {

    //retrieve current world position
    Vector3 currentPos = theObject.transform.position;

    //store new coordinates
    float newX = currentPos.x;
    float newY = currentPos.y;
    float newZ = currentPos.z;
```

With each frame, the MoveObjectTo() function compares the drake's current position to its destination using if statements. It then updates the drake's x and y coordinates according to the movement speed and direction.

```
//excerpt from AIMove script
//from MoveObjectTo() function

    //update movement based on speed and direction
    //up
    if (currentPos.y < theDestPos.y - _speed) {

        //update y
        newY += _speed;

    } //end if

    //down
    else if (currentPos.y > theDestPos.y + _speed) {

        //update y
        newY -= _speed;

    } //end if

    //at destination
    else {

        //update y
        newY = theDestPos.y;

    } //end if

    //left
    if (currentPos.x > theDestPos.x + _speed) {

        //update x
        newX -= _speed;

    } //end if

    //right
    else if (currentPos.x < theDestPos.x - _speed) {

        //update x
        newX += _speed;

    } //end if

    //at destination
    else {

        //update x
        newX = theDestPos.x;

    } //end if
```

Note that the if statements factor in the drake's speed as part of the distance to the destination. That's because we don't want the drake to overshoot its target once it gets very close. If the drake comes so close to its destination that it would pass it in the next frame at its current speed, we instead set the drake's position to equal the destination. That way, the drake always exactly reaches its destination position without error. To complete the function, a Vector3 named movePos is created with the updated coordinates and the drake's position is set equal to it.

```
//excerpt from AIMove script
//from MoveObjectTo() function

    //store the movement position
    Vector3 movePos = new Vector3(newX, newY, newZ);

    //update object position
    theObject.transform.position = movePos;

} //end function
```

Thus, each frame, the drake is moved a little closer to its destination at a rate equal to its speed. Meanwhile, the other custom function called in Update() every frame is CheckPosFor().

```
//excerpt from AIMove script

//check whether object reached destination
private void CheckPosFor(GameObject theObject, Vector3
  theDestPos) {

    //if object has reached destination
    if (theObject.transform.position == theDestPos) {

        //update destination position
        _destPos = _originPos;

        //update origin position
        _originPos = gameObject.transform.position;

    } //end if

} //end function
```

The CheckPosFor() function also accepts the drake and its destination position as arguments. It makes a single check to determine whether the drake's current position is equal to its destination. That is, it checks whether the drake has already arrived at its destination. If not, the drake's movement continues as before. However, if the drake has reached its destination, the destination position is set equal to the origin point, whereas the origin point is updated to the drake's current position. Effectively, this swaps the drake's starting and finishing positions. Hence, the drake will turn around and go back to where it started. Without this swap, the drake would only move from its origin to its destination a single time. However, thanks to the CheckPosFor() function, every time the drake reaches its destination, it will turn around and head back. This cycle continues endlessly, so long as the object is not destroyed or otherwise altered somewhere else in our code. With that, the AIMove script is complete. With a plan for the drake's movement behavior and a few custom functions, we were able to introduce relatively interesting AI into our game.

The second requirement is all about expanding the capacity of our StateManager script. Much of this script is identical to the one that was created for the previous challenge. Therefore, only the changes will be highlighted in this discussion. To keep track of the game state, two variables are declared. The `levelsCompleted` variable tracks how many total maps the player has completed. It is a way to score the player's performance, as well as scale the difficulty of the game over time. The `heroesSaved` variable counts the number of heroes Luna has saved on her journey. In this version of the game, she must find each of her friends in the dungeon. Once all three are rescued and added to the group, the game is won. Note the loss state will be triggered when Luna collides with a drake, but has no collectables remaining in her inventory. Since the CollectableInventory script already keeps track of how many objects are in Luna's inventory, it is not necessary to duplicate that information inside the StateManager. Thus, the `levelsCompleted` and `heroesSaved` variables are declared in the StateManager script.

```
//excerpt from StateManager script

//keep track of total number of levels completed
public int levelsCompleted;

//keep track of total number of heroes saved
public int heroesSaved;
```

These variables are initialized to 0 inside the `Awake()` function. At the beginning of the game, the player has neither completed any levels nor saved any heroes. Thus, 0 is the proper initialization value for these variables.

```
//excerpt from StateManager script

//awake
void Awake() {

    //prevent this script from being destroyed
    DontDestroyOnLoad(this);

    //start with no levels completed
    levelsCompleted = 0;

    //start with no heroes saved
    heroesSaved = 0;

} //end function
```

The `levelsCompleted` variable is incremented every time our `SwitchSceneTo()` function is called to load a new Dungeon map. Meanwhile, the `heroesSaved` variable will be incremented only when Luna collides with a hero, which occurs elsewhere in our code.

```
//excerpt from StateManager script

//switch scene by name
public void SwitchSceneTo(string theScene) {

    //check scene
    if (theScene == "Dungeon") {
```

```
        //increment levels completed
        levelsCompleted++;

    } //end if

    //load next scene
    Application.LoadLevel("theScene");

} //end function
```

The remaining addition to our StateManager is a reset function. When called, this function needs to reset everything, so the player can replay the game with a fresh start. The ResetGame() function handles this responsibility.

```
//excerpt from StateManager script

//reset game
public void ResetGame() {

    //reset levels completed
    levelsCompleted = 0;

    //reset heroes saved
    heroesSaved = 0;

    //destroy old player
    Destroy(GameObject.FindWithTag("Player"));

    //destroy old inventory
    Destroy(GameObject.FindWithTag("Inventory"));

    //load map scene
    SwitchSceneTo("Map");

} //end function
```

As you can see, the ResetGame() function returns our StateManager's variables to their initial values of 0. It also destroys the Player GameObject and Inventory GameObject. Previously, we prevented these objects from being destroyed when switching scenes. Therefore, we have to manually destroy them ourselves, so they do not get duplicated when the game is restarted. Lastly, the Map scene is loaded, since it is the first scene in our game. Thus, whenever the ResetGame() function is triggered in our code, Luna will begin her journey over again.

For the third requirement, we need to incorporate collectables, heroes, and drakes into the collision checks made by our UserMove script. In addition, we need to trigger any events that modify the game's status in the StateManager as part of handling these collisions. The entire OnTriggerEnter2D() function is provided and will be discussed piece by piece.

```
//excerpt from UserMove script

//check collisions
void OnTriggerEnter2D(Collider2D theCollider) {
```

```
//disable collisions
theCollider.enabled = false;

//retrieve the tag for the collider's game object
string tag = theCollider.gameObject.tag;

//retrieve collectable inventory
//used for collectable and drake collisions

CollectableInventory collectInventory = GameObject.
    FindWithTag("Inventory").
    GetComponent<CollectableInventory>();

//check the tag
switch (tag) {

    //stairs down
    case "StairsDown":

        //check heroes saved
        //if all heroes saved
        if (StateManager.Instance.heroesSaved >= 3) {

            //reset game
            StateManager.Instance.ResetGame();

        } //end if

        //if heroes remain
        else {

            //continue to next dungeon level
            StateManager.Instance.SwitchSceneTo("Dungeon");

        } //end else

        break;

    //collectable
    case "Collectable":

        //inventory has space remaining
        if (collectInventory.inventory.Count <
            collectInventory.maxObjects) {

            //add collectable to inventory
            collectInventory.AddItem(theCollider.gameObject);

        } //end else if

        //otherwise, reenable collisions
        //item may be collected again later
        else {

            //enable collisions
            theCollider.enabled = true;

        } //end else

        break;
```

```
        //hero
        case "Hero":

            //increment counter in state manager
            StateManager.Instance.heroesSaved++;

            //retrieve hero sprite from collision
            Sprite heroSprite = theCollider.
                GetComponent<SpriteRenderer>().sprite;

            //add to the hero group
            gameObject.GetComponent<HeroGroup>().memberSprites.
                Add(heroSprite);

            //destroy
            Destroy(theCollider.gameObject);

            break;

        //drake
        case "Drake":

            //check inventory
            //if inventory is empty
            if (collectInventory.inventory.Count <= 0) {

                //reset game
                StateManager.Instance.ResetGame();

            } //end if

            //inventory has items remaining
            else if (collectInventory.inventory.Count > 0) {

                //remove collectable from inventory
                collectInventory.RemoveItem();

                //destroy
                Destroy(theCollider.gameObject);

            } //end else if

            break;

        //default
        default:
            break;

    } //end switch

} //end function
```

Recall that the `OnTriggerEnter2D()` function automatically receives the collider of the object our player collided with as an argument from the Unity physics engine. Immediately, the collider is disabled to prevent multiple collisions from being detected on the same object. Following, the tag of the colliding object is stored in a local variable, so it can be handled appropriately. In addition, the CollectableInventory script from the Inventory GameObject in our scene is stored. This script will be needed by certain collision checks, so it is useful to store it in a local variable.

```
//excerpt from UserMove script
//from OnTriggerEnter2D() function

//check collisions
void OnTriggerEnter2D(Collider2D theCollider) {

    //disable collisions
    theCollider.enabled = false;

    //retrieve the tag for the collider's game object
    string tag = theCollider.gameObject.tag;

    //retrieve collectable inventory
    //used for collectable and drake collisions
    CollectableInventory collectInventory = GameObject.
        FindWithTag("Inventory").GetComponent<CollectableInventory>();
```

Afterwards, a switch statement is used to differentiate between potential collision objects by tag and handle them accordingly. We begin with the "StairsDown" tag.

```
//excerpt from UserMove script
//from OnTriggerEnter2D() function

    //check the tag
    switch (tag) {

        //stairs down
        case "StairsDown":

            //check heroes saved
            //if all heroes saved
            if (StateManager.Instance.heroesSaved >= 3) {

                //reset game
                StateManager.Instance.ResetGame();

            } //end if

            //if heroes remain
            else {

                //continue to next dungeon level
                StateManager.Instance.SwitchSceneTo("Dungeon");

            } //end else

        break;
```

The StairsDown collision has been updated to account for our win state. In this implementation, the player wins the game once Luna has added all 3 heroes to her party. Therefore, the StateManager's heroesSaved variable is checked.

If it is greater than or equal to 3, the game has been won and the `ResetGame()` function is called. However, if there are still heroes remaining to be found, the StairsDown collision triggers a new Dungeon map to be loaded. Next, our `switch` statement checks for the `"Collectable"` tag.

```
//excerpt from UserMove script
//from OnTriggerEnter2D() function

    //collectable
    case "Collectable":

        //inventory has space remaining
        if (collectInventory.inventory.Count < collectInventory.
            maxObjects) {

            //add collectable to inventory
            collectInventory.AddItem(theCollider.gameObject);

        } //end else if

        //otherwise, reenable collisions
        //item may be collected again later
        else {

            //enable collisions
            theCollider.enabled = true;

        } //end else

        break;
```

A check is made to determine whether empty space remains in the player's inventory. Thus, the CollectableInventory script's count of total objects is compared against its maximum allowable objects. If there is room, the collectable object is passed into the CollectableInventory's `AddItem()` function. Otherwise, if the inventory is full, the collectable's collider is enabled once again. Thus, the player may choose to collect it again at a later time if space frees up in her inventory. Following collectables, the `"Hero"` tag is checked for collisions in our `switch` statement.

```
//excerpt from UserMove script
//from OnTriggerEnter2D() function

    //hero
    case "Hero":

        //increment counter in state manager
        StateManager.Instance.heroesSaved++;

        //retrieve hero sprite from collision
        Sprite heroSprite = theCollider.
            GetComponent<SpriteRenderer>().sprite;
```

```
//add to the hero group
gameObject.GetComponent<HeroGroup>().memberSprites.
   Add(heroSprite);

//destroy
Destroy(theCollider.gameObject);

break;
```

When Luna collides with a hero character, the StateManager script's
heroesSaved counter is incremented. The hero's sprite is saved locally
as heroSprite. Next, the HeroGroup script is accessed from the Player
GameObject. The heroSprite is then added to the memberSprites
List managed by the HeroGroup script. Subsequently, the original Heroes
GameObject is destroyed and removed from the scene. After at least one hero
has been added to the group in this manner, the player can switch between the
group members by pressing the spacebar key. Lastly, our collision switch statement checks for the "Drake" tag.

```
//excerpt from UserMove script
//from OnTriggerEnter2D() function

        //drake
        case "Drake":

            //check inventory
            //if inventory is empty
            if (collectInventory.inventory.Count <= 0) {

                //reset game
                StateManager.Instance.ResetGame();

            } //end if

            //inventory has items remaining
            else if (collectInventory.inventory.Count > 0) {

                //remove collectable from inventory
                collectInventory.RemoveItem();

                //destroy
                Destroy(theCollider.gameObject);

            } //end else if

            break;

        //default
        default:
            break;

    } //end switch

} //end function
```

Recall that colliding with a sneaky drake will cause Luna to lose one of
her collectables. Therefore, the drake collision check first examines whether

the player's inventory is empty by accessing the `inventory.Count` property from the CollectableInventory script. If empty, the game is lost and the StateManager is told to reset the game. On the other hand, if Luna has collectables remaining in her inventory, the CollectableInventory's `RemoveItem()` function is called to take one item away. In addition, the drake is destroyed to remove it from the scene. This gives the player a chance to recover and adjust her strategy after colliding with a drake. With collectables, heroes, drakes, and state changes incorporated, our `OnTriggerEnter2D()` function is complete.

The fourth, and final, requirement for this challenge requires us to spawn heroes and drakes in our levels by updating the MapGenerator script. To do this, two custom functions will be used. To spawn heroes, the `SpawnHeroes()` function accepts two integers. One represents the number of heroes saved thus far, while the other represents the number of levels completed. Both of these are stored in the StateManager. Hence, `SpawnHeroes()` can be called from inside the MapGenerator's `Start()` function, like so:

```
//excerpt from MapGenerator script
//from Start() function

//spawn heroes
SpawnHeroes(StateManager.Instance.heroesSaved, StateManager.
  Instance.levelsCompleted);
```

The example `SpawnHeroes()` function communicates a specific design for how the heroes should be spawned in the game. It is assumed that the game is won once all three of the unique heroes, including Lily (the Dryad), Pink Beard (the Dwarf), and Larg (the Orc), are saved by Luna. Thus, the function will only spawn Lily until she joins Luna's group, followed by Pink Beard, and then by Larg. If the player misses a hero for whatever reason, it will reappear in a later level. Meanwhile, the function randomizes how often any hero is spawned, thus making it less predicable and more challenging for the player. The complete function is provided:

```
//excerpt from MapGenerator script

//spawn heroes
private void SpawnHeroes(int theNumHeroesSaved, int
  theNumLevelsCompleted) {

    //determine whether this level should have a hero spawned
    //25% chance that the check value will = 0
    int spawnCheck = Random.Range(0, 4);

    //the check value will equal zero every few levels
    //skip the first few levels
    if (spawnCheck == 0 && theNumLevelsCompleted > 3) {

        //check which heroes have been saved
        switch (theNumHeroesSaved) {

            //none
            case 0:
```

```
                    //spawn dryad
                    SpawnObjectsWithTag("Dryad");

                    break;

            //dryad only
            case 1:

                    //spawn dwarf
                    SpawnObjectsWithTag("Dwarf");

                    break;

            //dryad and dwarf
            case 2:

                    //spawn orc
                    SpawnObjectsWithTag("Orc");

                    break;

            //default
            default:
                    break;

        } //end switch

    } //end if

} //end function
```

Inside `SpawnHeroes()`, a random integer value named `spawnCheck` is generated using `Random.Range(0, 4)`. If at least three levels have already been completed and if the `spawnCheck` value comes out to 0 (a 25% chance), a hero will be spawned in the map. A `switch` statement checks for how many heroes have been saved thus far. We know that the StateManager's `heroesSaved` counter gets incremented each time Luna collides with a hero on the map. Thus, if Luna is all alone early in the game, the value passed into `SpawnHeroes()` will be 0 and Lily (the Dryad) will be spawned. Once Lily is saved, the value will equal 1 and Pink Beard (the Dwarf) will spawn. Further, with Lily and Pink Beard in the party, the value will equal 2 and only Larg (the Orc) remains to be spawned. In this manner, our `SpawnHeroes()` function randomizes when a hero is spawned and ensures the opportunity for Luna to find each one based on the status variables stored in the StateManager.

To spawn our drakes, we use the custom `SpawnDrakes()` function. It accepts a single integer as an argument. From the MapGenerator script's `Start()` function, we can see that the number of levels completed thus far is passed in.

```
//excerpt from MapGenerator script
//from Start() function

//spawn drakes
SpawnDrakes(StateManager.Instance.levelsCompleted);
```

As with `SpawnHeroes()`, the `SpawnDrakes()` function implements a game-specific design. Since there are five different drake prefabs in our game, each of them with the same abilities, the function will randomly choose which colors to spawn in a given level. This adds some variety to our levels. Furthermore, the number of levels completed thus far determines how many drakes are spawned in a given level. That is, 3 drakes are spawned in the 3rd level, 4 in the 4th, 5 in the 5th, and so on. This helps to scale the difficulty of the game over time and make it a challenging experience for the player. The complete function is provided.

```
//excerpt from MapGenerator script

//spawn a specified number of drakes
private void SpawnDrakes(int theNumDrakes) {

    //store all of the drake tags in an array
    string[] tags = {
                "BlueDrake",
                "GreenDrake",
                "GreyDrake",
                "OrangeDrake",
                "PinkDrake"
                };

    //set up counter to keep track of spawns
    int numSpawned = 0;

    //while there are still spawns remaining
    while (numSpawned < theNumDrakes) {

        //randomly select an object tag
        string randTag = tags[Random.Range(0, tags.Length)];

        //spawn the object with the associated tag
        SpawnObjectsWithTag(randTag);

        //increment counter
        numSpawned++;

    } //end while

} //end function
```

An array of strings named `tags` stores the tag for each of our drake prefabs. Afterwards, a counter variable and `while` loop are set up to spawn a number of drakes equal to the number of levels completed thus far. Inside the `while` loop, a random tag is selected from the `tags` array using `Random.Range()`. The tag is then passed into our existing `SpawnObjectsWithTag()` function. Remember that our Dungeon scene already has a `GameObject` and MapSpawn script prepared for each drake. Calling to the `SpawnObjectsWithTag()` function with a specific tag allows our MapGenerator to actually place the selected drake into our scene. Lastly, the counter is incremented to ensure our `while` loop exits. With that, we have randomly colored drakes spawning in gradually increasing quantities throughout our dungeon levels.

With the gameplay components fully assembled, take some time to play your game. Feel free to refine any features to your liking. Add more features to the game if you're craving even more challenge. Also make sure to enjoy what you have worked so hard to create.

Summary

Congratulations on coding a complete, playable game. Luna, the heroes, the drakes, and the world you created are ready to be enjoyed. You should be proud of what you have accomplished thus far. Now that you're a coder, you should be capable of applying these techniques:

- Create autonomous moving objects using artificial intelligence (AI)

- Manage win and loss states in real time

- Track data, such as scoring, throughout the game

- Compile several features, including characters, collectables, and obstacles, into a playable game

When you started reading this book, you embarked on a journey to become a better coder. While you have completed all of the challenges written here, the challenges you will face in the future have only just begun. You are encouraged to begin a new coding journey. On this quest, you will continue to learn and improve your skills day by day. You may want to go beyond the scope of this book to further expand Luna's world and make it your own. Perhaps you are even ready to code your first game from scratch. You have come a long way on your coding journey. If you are committed to code and gradual self-improvement, you will be making bigger and better games in no time at all.

Appendix A: Pseudocode Reference

This listing contains some commonly used pseudocode keywords. Usage examples are provided.

Status

These words describe the present state of things:

- Is
- On
- In
- Has
- Set
- Reset
- Update
- Load
- Reload

- New

- Destroy

- Win

- Lose

```
//example: a player wins a level
Player WINS level 1
LOAD level 2
```

Conditional

These words qualify the circumstances in which events can occur:

- If

- Then

- Else

- Otherwise

- Therefore

- Whether

- For

- But

- Instead

- So

```
//example: determining whether the player should walk or swim
IF player IS IN water, THEN swim
ELSE IF player IS ON land, THEN walk
```

Boolean

These words alter conditions using Boolean logic:

- And

- Or

- Not

- True

- False

```
//example: a player encounters a locked door

//this version is more like human language
IF player encounters door AND has key, SET door to open
ELSE IF player does NOT encounter door OR does NOT have key,
SET door to locked

//this version is more like computer language
IF player encounters door IS TRUE AND player has key IS TRUE,
THEN SET door locked IS FALSE
ELSE IF player encounters door IS FALSE OR player has key IS FALSE,
THEN SET door locked IS TRUE
```

Math

These words make value comparisons and perform mathematical operations:

- Equal

- Greater than

- Less than

- Add

- Subtract

- Multiply

- Divide

- Modulus

```
//example: a player runs into the edge of the screen and cannot
  proceed further
IF player's right edge x value IS GREATER THAN screen's right edge
  x value, THEN:
SET player speed EQUAL TO zero
SET player's x position EQUAL TO right edge of screen
```

Process

These words describe the flow of information in a system:

- Start

- Stop

- Pause

- Continue

- Begin

- End

- Finish

- Loop

- While

- Do

- Check

- Try

```
//example: checking the game state
CHECK win condition
IF win IS TRUE, THEN LOAD victory screen
ELSE IF loss IS TRUE, THEN LOAD game over screen
ELSE continue playing
```

Timing

These words describe when and how often events occur:

- After

- Before

- When

- Again

- Except

- Until

- First

- Next

- Last

```
//example: a player collects a temporary invincibility powerup
START invincibility timer
WHILE invincibility timer IS GREATER THAN zero:
Player IS invincible
DO NOT CHECK player for enemy AND obstacle collisions
SUBTRACT from invincibility timer
IF invincibility timer IS LESS THAN OR EQUAL TO zero, THEN:
STOP invincibility timer
CHECK player for enemy AND obstacle collisions
```

Permission

These words introduce limits on what can or cannot be done:

- Can

- Cannot

- Should

- Must

- Allow

- Prohibit

- Only

```
//example: the player collects a powerup that grants the flight
  ability
IF player has flight powerup, player CAN run OR fly
IF player does NOT have flight powerup, player MUST run AND
  CANNOT fly
```

Appendix B: Process Mapping Reference

Table B.1 explains some of the most common symbols used to create process maps. Usage examples are provided in Figures B.1 through B.7.

Table B.1 Common Process Mapping Symbols

Symbol	Shape	Description
☐	Rectangle	Defines a single state, action, activity, or step in the overall process
→	Arrow	Connects one object to another, indicating the direction of information flow
◇	Diamond	Indicates a decision point at which the process can branch into multiple paths (from the different edges of the shape)
▭	Rounded rectangle or oval	Designates a start or end point for the process

(Continued)

Table B.1 (Continued) Common Process Mapping Symbols

Symbol	Shape	Description
(parallelogram)	Parallelogram	Represents information entering or exiting the process (e.g., user input, a call to an external process, or data passed to another process)
(circle)	Circle	Used to connect different sections of a process map together (e.g., when a diagram spans across multiple pages)

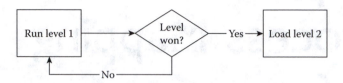

Figure B.1 Example process map: a player wins a level.

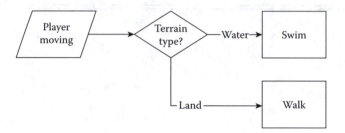

Figure B.2 Example process map: determining whether the player should walk or swim.

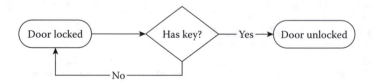

Figure B.3 Example process map: a player encounters a locked door.

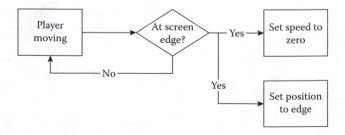

Figure B.4 Example process map: a player runs into the edge of the screen and cannot proceed further.

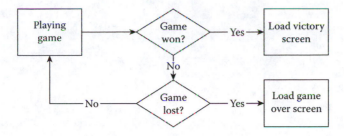

Figure B.5 Example process map: checking the game state.

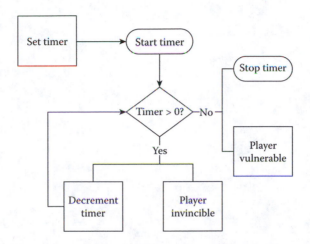

Figure B.6 Example process map: a player collects a temporary invincibility powerup.

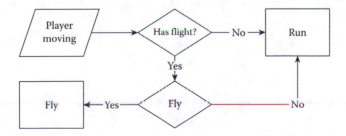

Figure B.7 Example process map: the player collects a powerup that grants the flight ability.

Index

D

"Dark Elf," 22
Data type descriptions, 18–22
Data types
  Boolean, 19
  challenge extension, 23–24
  character string, 21–22
  composite, 91–92
  descriptions, 18–25
  double precision, 21
  example solution, 24–25
  floating point, 20–21
  integer, 19–20
  overview, 18–19
  primitive, 91–92
dataType variable, 69
Debug.Log() command, 66
decimal data type, 21
Decimal numbers, *see* floating point
  (float) data type
Decrement (−−) operator, 68–69, 112
deltaMoveX variable, 33
Demo files
  Collectable, 60
  CollectableInventory, 120
  CollectableSpawn, 104
  HeroGroup, 136
  MapManager, 192
  MapSpawn, 172
  PlayerBounds, 40
  PlayerInvis, 60
  PlayerMove, 2, 60
  PlayerSprint, 60
  RandomMap, 152
  StateManager, 212, 234
Design pattern, singleton, 214–218
_destPos variable, 244
Destroy() function, 97, 132, 178, 180
Disabling *vs.* destroy functions, 97
DisplayMap() function
  functions, 173
  map scene generation, 201–202
  nested loops, multidimensional
    arrays, 162
  tile map generation, 152, 153, 163,
    165–168
Division math operator, 42
DontDestroyOnLoad() function, 218–219,
    228, 234, 243
Dot notation, 70–71

Double ampersand (&&), 78
double data type, 21
Double equal sign (==), 43
Double precision (double) data type,
    18, 21, 23, 180
Double slash (//), 32; *see also* forward
    slash (/)
Drake GameObject, 246
Drake prefab, 235–239, 240, 241
"Drake" tag, 258
Dropboxes, *see specific dropbox*
Dryads, 136, 235, 259–260;
    see also Lily character
dSpeed variable, 21
Dungeon scene, 235, 242, 261
Dungeon.unity file, 212, 234
Duplication, 217
_duration variable, 82, 84, 86
Dwarves, 136, 235, 259–260;
    see also Lily character

E

edgeX function, 246–247
edgeY function, 246–247
edgeZ function, 246–247
else and else if keywords, 63–66, 73, 87;
    see also if statements
enabled property, 83, 226
energy variable, 24
_energy variable, 18, 69
Equality operators, 43–44
Equal sign (=), 43
Events, 264, 266–267
Example solutions
  accounting for the character, 54–56
  background, 10
  boundary collisions, 47–50
  bounds of world, 47–50, 54–56
  collectables, tracking, 129–132
  collecting objects, 98–101
  data types, 24–25
  defining variables, 29–31
  gameplay, 243–262
  game state management, 227–231
  generating tile maps, 163–168
  initializing variables, 34–36
  make Luna move, 10–14
  making Luna invisible, 83–87
  making Luna sprint, 72–76
  managing a group, 142–148

N

O

P